Childhood in Medieval Poland (1050–1300)

East Central and Eastern Europe in the Middle Ages, 450–1450

General Editors

Florin Curta and Dušan Zupka

VOLUME 73

The titles published in this series are listed at *brill.com/ecee*

Childhood in Medieval Poland (1050–1300)

Constructions and Realities in a European Context

By

Matthew Koval

BRILL

LEIDEN | BOSTON

Cover illustration: Young Bolesław Wrymouth Fighting a Bear, Ksawery Pillati, Czesław Borys Jankowski, in Wizerunki Książąt i Królów Polskich, Józef Ignacy Kraszewski, Gebethner i Wolff, Warsaw, 1888.

Library of Congress Cataloging-in-Publication Data
Names: Koval, Matthew B., author.
Title: Childhood in medieval Poland (1050–1300) : constructions and realities in a European context / by Matthew B. Koval.
Description: Leiden ; Boston : Brill, [2021] | Series: East Central and Eastern Europe in the middle ages, 450–1450, 1872–8103 ; volume 73 | Includes bibliographical references and index. | Summary: "This volume analyses the constructions and realities of childhood in Poland, c. 1050–1300 CE, by examining a range of texts and considering the ways in which children fit within textual frameworks and genres. These texts include two major chronicles, monastic sources, and hagiography related to five major saints. The textual sources are put into conversation with findings from archaeology. The author argues that certain common themes, such as assumed care for children, the need for education, and the puer senex trope do feature through most texts of any genre, and the book also explores how Poland was similar to and different from the situation in western Europe"—Provided by publisher.
Identifiers: LCCN 2021002172 (print) | LCCN 2021002173 (ebook) | ISBN 9789004460997 (hardback) | ISBN 9789004461062 (ebook)
Subjects: LCSH: Children—Poland—History—To 1500. | Children—Poland—Social conditions.
Classification: LCC HQ792.P7 K67 2021 (print) | LCC HQ792.P7 (ebook) | DDC 305.2309438/0902—dc23
LC record available at https://lccn.loc.gov/2021002172
LC ebook record available at https://lccn.loc.gov/2021002173

Typeface for the Latin, Greek, and Cyrillic scripts: "Brill." See and download: brill.com/brill-typeface.

ISSN 1872-8103
ISBN 978-90-04-46099-7 (hardback)
ISBN 978-90-04-46106-2 (e-book)

Copyright 2021 by Koninklijke Brill NV, Leiden, The Netherlands.
Koninklijke Brill NV incorporates the imprints Brill, Brill Hes & De Graaf, Brill Nijhoff, Brill Rodopi, Brill Sense, Hotei Publishing, mentis Verlag, Verlag Ferdinand Schöningh and Wilhelm Fink Verlag.
All rights reserved. No part of this publication may be reproduced, translated, stored in a retrieval system, or transmitted in any form or by any means, electronic, mechanical, photocopying, recording or otherwise, without prior written permission from the publisher. Requests for re-use and/or translations must be addressed to Koninklijke Brill NV via brill.com or copyright.com.

This book is printed on acid-free paper and produced in a sustainable manner.

Contents

Acknowledgements VII
List of Figures and Tables VIII

1 **Introduction** 1
   1   Historiographical Context 3
   2   Description of Contents 14

2 **Child and Hero: The Use of Childhood in the Narrative of Gallus Anonymus** 17
   1   Who Was Gallus? New Approaches to the Deeds of the Princes of the Poles 18
   2   Childhood as a Time of Development and Prophecy 21
   3   Age Terminology and Dynastic Status: When Is a Man a Man? 34
   4   Vulnerability and Care: From Parents and the Community 37
   5   Motherly Care and Female Children 42
   6   Comparisons: Cosmas of Prague 43
   7   Conclusions 45

3 **Vincent Kadłubek and Thinking with Children** 48
   1   Vincent's Overlap with Gallus 51
   2   Parental Love of Children ... and the Virtue of Violating It 57
   3   Filial and Familial Piety 59
   4   Childishness, a Negative Stereotype Applied to Rulers 63
   5   Prophecy and Children 67
   6   Child(hood) as a Rhetorical Device 69
   7   Conclusions 71

4 **The Henryków Book: The Weight of Future Children and the Threat of Youth** 73
   1   The Text and Its Purpose 74
   2   Youth as Part of Dynasty and Potential Threat 80
   3   How Many Roads Must a Man Walk Down: What Is a Responsible Age? 85
   4   "Kids These Days": Disappointment in the Next Generation 89
   5   Memory and Youth, a New Kind of Remembrance in Poland 94
   6   The Care for Children 98
   7   Conclusions 100

5 Children and Childhood in Hagiography 102
1. Are Good Children Serious Children? 104
2. Education Issues: Nature vs. Nurture, God as Teacher, Male vs. Female 112
3. Precious or Burdensome? Children Three Years and Younger 119
4. Children, Childhood, and Descendants in the Canonization Story of St. Stanisław 127
5. The Miracles 130
6. Latin Words Relating to Children in the *Miracula*: Exceptions and Rules 135
7. Conclusions 137

6 The Child in the Community of the Dead 139
1. Incidence of Child Burials 141
2. The Problem of Grave Goods in Child Burials 149
3. Multiple Burials 153
4. Spatial Features of Child Burials 158
5. In Search of Pattern: Micro vs. Macro Comparisons 166
6. Age, Sex, and Grave Goods 168
7. Final Thoughts 173

7 Conclusions and Comparisons 176
1. The Child as Symbol of the Future, Prophecy 176
2. Born Great or Achieving Greatness? 178
3. Age and Social Categories 181
4. Special Care for Children 185
5. Children and Emotion 189
6. Good Kid, Bad Kid 192
7. Thinking with Children 195
8. Children in a Wider Context 198

Appendix 203
Bibliography 210
Index of Modern Authors 221
Index of Subjects 222

Acknowledgements

Writing a book on childhood, development, and beginnings makes one conscious of all the people and influences that went into its composition. Parents and family are important in the story of every childhood development and mine laid the foundations for this book by infusing me with passion, curiosity, the love of learning, and a solid education on which to build. Numerous professors added to this foundation, teaching me historical thinking and analytical skills. At the beginning of this path was Mark Graham, my undergraduate adviser who ignited my love of the medieval world. At the core of this book is Florin Curta, who transformed me from a naive undergraduate who loved history into a professional historian. This was no easy feat and took years of his tireless effort. I must also thank my students at Valencia College and University of Florida for always helping me to see the beauty of the past for the first time again and again. Finally, I thank my wife Aurelia, who has kept me going step by step to the finish line through it all.

Research for this project required help from numerous scholars in Poland, who bear no responsibility for any errors and issues with my work. Much of my research for the archaeological section of the work, as well as the hagiographical, stems from my time on a Fulbright grant from 2016–2017 with the Institute of Archaeology and Ethnology Polish Academy of Sciences in Wrocław, under the unparalleled Sławomir Moździoch. Both the Fulbright, and the opportunities it provided for cultural and professional exchange, as well my time at the Institute, provided me with inspiration, ideas, and sources that would help this book take shape. Also at the Institute, I received the help of many world-class scholars, including Aleks Paron and Błażej Stanisławski. These contacts in Wrocław led me to so many others, including Dorota Żołądź-Strzelczyk and Małgorzata Delimata in Poznań. All my contacts, colleagues, and friends from Poland constantly have proved the truth of the legend of superb Polish hospitality.

Figures and Tables

Figures

1   CA analysis of Kałdus   170
2   CA analysis of Radom   171
3   CA analysis of Masłowice   171
4   CA analysis of Cedynia   172
5   CA analysis of Czersk   172

Tables

1   Multiple burials in selected Polish cemeteries   203
2   Graves and incidences at Kałdus   207
3   Graves and incidences at Radom   208
4   Graves and incidences at Masłowice   208
5   Graves and incidences at Cedynia   209
6   Graves and incidences at Czersk   209

CHAPTER 1

Introduction

When early chronicler of medieval Poland, Gallus Anonymus, compared Polish duke Bolesław Chrobry's treatment of recalcitrant nobles to a kind father correcting his misbehaving children while washing them in a bath,[1] there was no known conscious intention to provide later scholars with information about the treatment and perception of childhood and children in medieval Poland. Indeed, writing about social categories and age groups generally is an interest of contemporary historians, and certainly not a goal of those of the pre-modern past. As the historiographical discussion below will illustrate, the explosion of interest in the topic of childhood specifically stands in contrast to the seeming lack of medieval interest in the topic as such. It would be deceiving, however, to conclude that the next generation was not on the minds of medieval people. Inheritance, education, lineage, naming, and much else besides of importance was intimately connected to young age. Even when children as embodied beings were not themselves of interest, the whole concept of the life cycle and age was and remains a fundamental guiding concept in human societies.[2] Therefore, children and childhood are a fundamental building block of human society and a necessary part in understanding it.

This book will focus on perceptions of childhood in medieval Polish history from a period when Poland was transitioning from a pre-Christian collection of disparate peoples into a Christian kingdom, namely from 1000 to 1300. This places it alongside the Czech lands, Hungary, and Scandinavia as a sort of borderland of Europe, all in the same processes of Europeanization, and scholars have produced much literature comparing phenomena in these borderlands of Europe to each other, as well as to the "core" countries of France, England, Italy the Low Countries, and western Germany.[3] This makes Poland of this

---

1 Gallus Anonymus, *The Deeds of the Princes of the Poles*, ed. Karol Maleczyński, trans. Paul W. Knoll and Frank Schaer (Budapest/New York: Central University Press, 2003), 63.
2 For an excellent description of the nuance in discussions of medieval life cycle, see the essays in Isabelle Cochelin and Karen Elaine Smyth, *Medieval Life Cycles: Continuity and Change* (Turnhout: Brepols), 2013.
3 Paradigms for how to theorize these relationships and the literature on this topic is extensive. Produced here are a few suggestions for further reading. For a general discussion see: Robert Bartlett, *The Making of Europe: Conquest, Colonization and Cultural Change 950–1350* (Princeton: Princeton University Press), 1993 and Nora Berend, Felipe Fernandez-Armesto, and James Muldoon *The Expansion of Central Europe in the Middle Ages* (Florence: Taylor and Francis), 2013. For a discussion focused on the region covered in this book, see: Gerhard Jaritz

time period an excellent candidate for the kinds of discoveries that come from comparison. As an additional motivation, the Polish sources of this time, while few, are in a number of ways highly unique. Not only are there unusual sources such as Gallus Anonymus' twelfth century *Gesta* or the twelfth through early fourteenth century Henryków Book, produced by Cistercians monastics in Silesia, but there are also a series of saints' lives written about elite women from this era. Sources like these need to be brought into the general discussion of childhood in Europe.

The downsides of focusing on this time and region are, of course, the general lack of sources in number. This might lead one to conclude that scholars can only reconstruct an incomplete image of the meaning childhood for this region. The reality is, however, that, as we will see in later chapters, even sources that are very close together in time often betray strikingly different purposes for and illustrations of children. In other words, there is not necessarily one monolithic "childhood" to reconstruct, anyway, but many different childhoods.[4]

In fact, this is the real purpose of my book, namely to show the value not of trying to reconstruct some whole societal vision of an age category, but to show how images of children and childhood are best understood within the context of the purposes of texts themselves. Children are not simply narrative chaff, a disposable note at the margins of larger stories, but are often right at the heart of the themes and goals of the writers. We cannot just read stories of children as "unwitting evidence," having no real place in the minds and imaginations of past peoples, as has been argued, as we will see below, from Philippe Ariès in the past to James Schultz more recently, but instead we must first carefully analyze their place within their contexts, and then we can begin to evaluate whether we can detect more general themes and mindsets about children. This is precisely the method this book will employ. Each chapter will examine children within a broader context of a source, and within that context show how

---

and Katalin Szende, *Medieval East Central Europe in a Comparative Perspective From Frontier Zones to Lands in Focus* (London: Routledge), 2016 and Florin Curta, *East Central & Eastern Europe in the Early Middle Ages* (Ann Arbor: Univ. of Michigan Press), 2007 and Jean Sedlar *East Central Europe in the Middle Ages, 1000–1500* (Seattle: University of Washington Press), 1994.

4 The literature and the state of the field on childhood as a "construction" is best summarized, theorized, and explained in Phyllis Gaffney, *Constructions of Childhood and Youth in Old French Narrative* (Burlington: Ashgate, 2011), especially in Chapter 2, pages 23–56. This chapter in Gaffney establishes the wide range of associations and concepts associated with children of different ages throughout the medieval period. What swiftly emerges from this discussion as that age categories were extremely fluid and differed in their meanings not just across time and cultures, but also across genres.

children functioned within its argument and purpose, and then consider what impression this leaves of children and childhood. In the conclusion, I make broader conclusions across texts and sources about any common themes that emerge, and then put these in conversation with the situation in other parts of Europe. Through this whole process, I will argue that children and childhood, far from being unimportant or tangential, are often highly relevant even to sources that seem to have nothing to do with childhood.

1   Historiographical Context

It is obligatory in all historiographical discussions of medieval childhood to begin with the 1960 publication of Philippe Ariès *L'Enfant et la vie familiale sous l'ancien regime*. In this seminal work, Ariès challenged the traditional narrative that "the family constituted the ancient basis of our society, and that, starting in the eighteenth century, the progress of liberal individualism had shaken and weakened it."[5] Ariès was concerned that his contemporaries were imposing modern "common sense" categories on the past and assuming that the family-life prized by bourgeois culture was constant throughout time. Central to this traditional narrative was a phase of life called "childhood," in which younger members of society were conceived of and treated as different from adults. Ariès questioned this notion by pointing out that "in the tenth century, artists were unable to depict a child except as a man on a smaller scale. How did we come from that ignorance of childhood to the centering of the family around the child in the nineteenth century?"[6] From an examination of mostly art historical sources, Ariès concluded in a chapter tellingly named "The discovery of childhood," that "medieval art until about the twelfth century did not know about childhood or did not attempt to portray it. It is hard to believe that this neglect was due to incompetence or incapacity … it seems more probable that there was no place for childhood in the medieval world."[7] Along these lines, Ariès suggested that the origins of a more realistic and sensitive depiction of children appeared in medieval art only in the thirteenth century. This "type" of the child, according to him, slowly became more similar to the modern artistic representation of children, though the modern type of childhood did not

---

5   Philippe Ariès, *Centuries of Childhood: A Social History of Family Life* (New York: Vintage Books, 1965), 10.
6   Ariès, *Centuries*, 10.
7   Ibid., 33.

completely develop until well into the seventeenth century.⁸ Ariès went as far as to suggest that only by the thirteenth century did Christian societies really begin to realize that "that the child's soul too was immortal" and begin to treat children as anything more than weaker, less valuable adults.⁹

Ariès' idea that there was no place for children (as a separate social category) in medieval society has been thoroughly dismantled in recent decades. Nicholas Orme's work collates and summarizes this transition in thought in his 2001 book, *Medieval Children*.¹⁰ Orme argued that Ariès' evidence was insufficient to explore fully the issue of childhood as a social category, for he drew only from "paintings, sculpture, and a few (mainly literary) records of the fifteenth century."¹¹ In contrast, Orme points to a slew of scholars writing during the last two decades of the twentieth century in a number of disciplines (from archaeology, to sociology, to art history, to literary theory, etc.), all of whom successfully chipped away at Ariès' thesis. From this work, Orme heralds a new consensus that medieval "adults regarded childhood as a distinct phase or phases of life, that parents treated children like children as well as like adults, and that they did so with care and sympathy, and that children had cultural activities and possessions of their own."¹² Drawing mainly on literary and art historical evidence (without ignoring archaeology), Orme draws on a wide variety of sources—philosophical, religious, and medical texts, childhood songs, paintings, and toys—to show that there indeed existed a unique social role for children.

How did we get from Ariès to Orme? In literary studies, Shahar Shalmuth, is recognized as one of the first scholars to question old paradigms about the role of children. One of her most famous examples concerns St. Ida of Louvain's 13th century vision (as recorded in 14th century hagiography), where Ida helps St. Elisabeth bathe a rambunctious and playful young Jesus who liked to splash around in the tub. The Vision, as reproduced by Shahar reads, "he [Christ] made noise in the water by clapping his hands, and as children do, splashed in the water until it spilled out and wet all those around him."¹³ For Shahar, this text, and many other similar texts, show that childhood indeed existed as a unique category for medieval people, and that there were certain behaviors associated with this state by adults. Nevertheless, Shahar can be accused of

---

8   Ibid., 34.
9   Ibid., 43.
10 Nicholas Orme, *Medieval Children* (New Haven: Yale University Press, 2001).
11 Ibid., 5.
12 Ibid.
13 Shulamith Shahar, *Childhood in the Middle Ages* (London and New York: Routledge, 1990), 96.

collapsing time and trying to reconstruct one late medieval version of "childhood" where in fact many "childhoods" existed during the long span of the Middle Ages and its various regions. An alternative the Shahar's overly broad analysis over time and space is Barbara Hanawalt's discussion of the meaning of the transition from childhood to adolescence in mostly late medieval London, which adds much of the age and gender nuance that Shahar lacks.[14] Benefiting from a fortunate well of textual sources which this author can only behold with jealousy from the vantage point of medieval Poland (including her use of wills, apprenticeship contracts, manuals on child-rearing), Hanawalt tries to distinguish different stages of life for children (identifying apprenticeship as a key turning point in society's view of a child) and examines to what extent wealth and gender altered conceptions of a child. Hanawalt's work shows the benefit of focusing on one region and time period.

A more recent treatment of views of medieval childhood, and one to which this book is indebted in terms of method, is Phyllis Gaffney's *Constructions of Childhood and Youth in Old French Narrative*, which mines Old French poetry, and especially such new forms as the *chanson de geste* and the romance, from 1100 to 1220 for tropes and images of children.[15] Gaffney shows how different genres of French secular literature exhibit strikingly different portrayals of childhood. While the creation of a new genre may reflect a new conception of social categories in society, this is not necessarily the case. Significantly for this book, Gaffney examines how images of children work within the purposes of the text and within the context of age and gender paradigms and expectations.

Despite the new enthusiasm for childhood, some scholars have urged caution, questioning whether references to the behavior of children actually allow us to access a coherent medieval view of childhood as a positive category, while others have suggested the evidence actually suggests a general devaluing of children and childhood. The most noted example of this concern is found in James Schultz's *The Knowledge of Childhood* in the German Middle Ages 1100–1350, in which courtly and chivalric poetry is combed for references to childhood. Schultz concludes from his study that children "knew that they were members of lineages but knew nothing of families in the modern sense ... they knew that though their parents loved their offspring according to a law of nature, [but] as children per se they had little status."[16] In other words, children

---

14   Barbara Hanawalt, *Growing Up in Medieval London: The Experience of Childhood in History* (Oxford: Oxford University Press, 1993).
15   Phyllis Gaffney, *Constructions of Childhood and Youth in Old French Narrative* (Burlington: Ashgate, 2011).
16   James Schultz, *The Knowledge of Childhood in the German Middle Ages, 1100–1350* (Philadelphia: University of Pennsylvania Press, 1995), 265.

only had relevance to medieval Germans in relation to adult behavior, acts, concerns, and goals. Childhood, if it existed at all in people's minds as a positive concept, was simply an expression of alterity and difference from adults. A more recent study by Patrick Joseph Ryan investigates how words and concepts related to children and childhood function within the social hierarchies, as expressed in medieval language, law, and literature.[17] Ryan tries to reconstruct the discursive structures, metaphors, and connections of the medieval English worldview, while focusing especially on the evidence of linguistics, and concludes that the best parallel of the relationship between children and parents is that of the slave to the master. This conclusion does not negate emotional feelings towards children, nor does it imply that children were actually treated like slaves, but simply posits that young age had a particular place structurally within the wider hierarchies and expectations of the medieval worldview. While Ryan's short study can be challenged for its oversimplification of an enormous body of evidence and for its adherence to dictionary definitions of words rather than examination of words in dynamic context, my research in this book suggests that the function of children within hierarchical dynasties as a conceptual theme does have some resonance with certain texts in Poland.

While the question of accessing childhood(s) remains a topic of debate, the past decade has shown the discussion is moving away from a critique of Ariès and has taken on a life of its own, as seen in a proliferation of collected editions of articles which bring new dimensions and topics to the conversation, from medieval emotions to regional customs and habits, as well as treating the methodological problems facing scholars interested in childhood, from the issue of sources to the problem of imposing modern social categories on the past. Most notably, various authors in Albrecht Classen's *Childhood in the Middle Age and the Renaissance* betray a steady optimism about the potential of using a variety of sources to access childhood from legal records, hagiography, family manuals, inscriptions, art, and letters.[18] Classen is convinced that this new wave of research has produced a "paradigm shift" in the way scholars understand past children. A few years later, a prominent student of Anglo-Saxon childhood, Sally Crawford, published *Children, Childhood, and Society*, a collection of studies in which archaeological analysis was used in conjunction with textual evidence to discuss childhood from the Bronze Age in the Near East to the High Middle Ages in Europe, presenting childhood as

---

17   Patrick Joseph Ryan, *Master-Servant Childhood: A History of the Idea of Childhood in Medieval English Culture* (New York: Palgrave Macmillan, 2013).

18   Albrecht Classen, *Childhood in the Middle Ages and the Renaissance: The Results of a Paradigm Shift in the History of Mentality* (Berlin: Walter de Gruyter, 2005).

a shifting social category that can be usefully compared across time.[19] More relevant to my own research is Shannon Lewis-Simpson's *Youth and Old Age in the Medieval North*, which contains a series of essays that, among other things, are concerned with establishing different stages of childhood in the medieval north, as well as exploring what social markers (such as initiation rituals and legal customs) marked off these stages.[20] Last but not least is the magisterial *Kindheit und Jugend, Ausbildung und Freizeit*, the proceedings of a colloquium, which includes a series of short studies on childhood in the medieval north from Ireland to Russia, including five articles from Poland. These compare across regions a similar range of topics and provide an excellent foundation for comparative studies and conclusions.[21]

Jane Baxter describes an interesting archaeological parallel to the shifts in the discussion of children from Ariès to Orme.[22] Initially, archaeologists regarded children as either insignificant to understanding a culture or labored under an uncritical acceptance of the modern constructions of childhood. This situation changed in 1989 when Grete Lillehammer published the first archaeological study of childhood.[23] This seminal article "underscored the lack of consideration that children had received previously in archaeological interpretations despite ample evidence of children in the material record of the past."[24] Nevertheless, childhood has proved difficult to study archaeologically for two major reasons. First, as with discussions of children in texts, archaeologists have struggled with the realization that "childhood is a socio-cultural construct that is shaped and formed," which implies that archaeologists cannot assume too much about age categories and their characteristics in other cultures.[25] The second challenge is the "perceived invisibility in the archaeological record" of child activity and children's bodies.[26] The archaeology of children has been influenced by approaches introduced for the study of gender, since traditional societies may have attempted to create gender roles for children through practice and ritual. However, children often appear to be

---

19 Sally Crawford and Gillian Shepherd, eds., *Children, Childhood and Society* (Oxford: Archaeopress, 2007).
20 Shannon Lewis-Simpson, *Youth and Age in the Medieval North* (Leiden: Brill, 2008).
21 Manfred Glaser, ed., *Lübecker Kolloquium zur Stadtarchäologie im Hanseraum VIII: Kindheit und Jugend, Ausbildung und Freizeit* (Lübeck: Schmidt-Römhild, 2012).
22 Jane Eva Baxter, "The Archaeology of Childhood," *Annual Review of Anthropology*, Vol. 37 (2008): 159–175.
23 Grete Lillehammer, "A Child is Born: the Child's World in an Archaeological Perspective," *Norwegian Archaeological Review* 22 (1989): 89–105.
24 Baxter, "The Archaeology of childhood," 160.
25 Ibid., 161.
26 Ibid., 162.

treated (especially in mortuary contexts) in ways radically different from both male and female adults (though somewhat more similar to females), in other words, almost like a separate gender category.[27] It is through this connection with gender that the archaeology of childhood has come to partake in "more sophisticated theoretical levels through associations with more general trends and emphases on identity and agency as important ways of understanding the archaeological record."[28] This has resulted in a new research paradigm where "identity in general and the overlapping constructions of age and gender specifically have been central in attempts to expand understandings of what childhood meant in different times and places."[29]

The challenge for this book is to bring text and archaeology, two radically kinds of sources of information, in conversation with each other. John Moreland has noted a long history of skepticism and hesitation surrounding this endeavor, beginning with the 1950s and Christopher Hawkes famous "ladder," which was interpreted as implying that archaeology was mostly useful for understanding technology and production, and not particularly adept at illuminating ideas and mentalities, which makes archaeology unsuitable for comparison with texts.[30] Lewis Binford, on the other hand, with his processualist approach suggested that ideological elements could indeed be deciphered in archaeology, as they were encoded in the systems that archaeology studied, and indeed archaeology for Binford provided a more complete image of ideology than texts ever could.[31] These assumptions were, in turn, challenged by those who critiqued the treatment of human action and intention as mindless processes endemic in the New Archaeology.[32] Responses to this controversy ranged from attempts to decipher meaning in archaeology, including looking at the "biographies" of objects to determine how they expressed meaning in different contexts, to considering archaeology itself to be a "text" which can be "read" by the careful and informed scholar. These approaches are, of course, problematic because they assume that 21st-century researchers can truly understand and reconstruct past meanings, while also assuming that any object in the past bore only a singular meaning. Moreland concludes that while the search for one definitive meaning from archaeology may elude us, multiple perspectives, voices, and meanings of modern scholars will nevertheless create

---

27 This is, of course, a highly speculative endeavor, as the sex of children cannot be determined from anthropological methods used by archaeologists.
28 Baxter, "The Archaeology of childhood," 162.
29 Ibid., 163.
30 John Moreland, *Archaeology and Text* (London: Duckworth, 2007), 13–16.
31 Ibid., 21–24.
32 Ibid., 24–26.

a useful and enriching conversation about the past.[33] One of the methods by which patterns across modes of human expression, including archaeology, can be put into conversation is through the concept of metaphors, as expressed in Scott Ortman's classic article, in which he argues that the human propensity to relate experience through metaphor allows for comparison and analysis of patterns, even when exact meaning cannot be reconstructed.[34] In this book, metaphors and higher level relationships between concepts in archaeology and text will be related in that fashion.

Before discussing the Polish historiography related to childhood, it is important to look at the Polish historiography of the Middle Ages, in general. The state of research in the field, its major research centers, and its topics of concern are described in detail in Ryszard Grzesik's survey published in English in the yearbook of the Central European University.[35] According to Grzesik, the major turning point in Polish medieval historiography was 1956, with the death of Stalin and the emergence of relative Polish independence within the Soviet sphere, rather than in 1989 with the fall of communism generally. Since the 1960s Polish medievalists have generally kept abreast of developments within western medieval studies, whether or not their own contributions were recognized outside their country.[36] Instead, Polish historiography had been driven by cultural, political, and religious interests. The year 1966 was a momentous year in the evolution of Polish historiography and archaeology, as both state and church competed to further their narratives on the 1000 year anniversary of the conversion of Mieszko I and the entrance of Poland into the European Christian community of the Middle Ages. This year did not simply have ramifications for the church celebrating religious history, but also was the traditional date for the founding of the Polish state, and thus the anniversary sparked a renewed interesting in explaining the emergence of the Polish nation.[37] Discussions of ethnicity, and the ethnogenesis of the Slavs, as well as their relationship to Germanic peoples both in pre-historic times and in the period of colonization in the High Middle Ages were also significant, as well as the recent attempts to critically analyze the major primary sources, especially their origins, transmission, and influences.[38] More recently Polish medieval

---

33   Ibid., 28–30, 111–119.
34   Scott Ortman, "Conceptual Metaphor in the Archaeological Record: Methods and an Example from the American Southwest," *American Antiquity* 65 (2000): 613–645.
35   Ryszard Grzesik, "The study of the Middle Ages in Poland," *Annual of Medieval Studies at CEU* 15 (2009): 265–277.
36   Grzesik, "The study," 265.
37   Ibid., 270–273.
38   Ibid., 273–276.

history has experienced its own "literary turn" with a significant proportion of these studies focused on the 12th century *gesta* of Gallus Anonymus. For example, Jarosław Nikodem writes about how Gallus portrays the weak and defective rulership (and fatherhood) of Władysław Herman compared to his glorious son Bolesław.[39] Other Polish scholarship involved in this literary turn was translated into English and now informs a wider audience. For example, Przemysław Wiszewski analyzes Gallus in terms of his role in the construction of the Piast dynasty, its attempts at legitimizing itself, and its efforts to shape its image.[40] Most significant for this book, Zbigniew Dalewski showed how Gallus Anonymus labored to turn a victim into a villain when he crafted his narrative so that Zbigniew appeared a grasping, dishonorable, untrustworthy character and thus almost deserved his horrific fate at the hands of his half-brother Bolesław III, which had shocked Polish popular opinion.[41] In this book, Dalewksi revealed for all to see how Gallus was not a passive recorder of events, but instead a masterful shaper and weaver of stories for his own ends, and it is with just this in mind that this book will approach Gallus.

In terms of childhood specifically, scholarship on medieval childhood in Poland has taken off in the 1990s at the same time as in western Europe. One of the first forays into the topic was Beata Wojciechowska's article on childhood in medieval culture.[42] This pioneering work noted a number of trends that this book will expand upon and develop, such as the *puer senex* trope, the importance of education for children, and the special concern and care for children that appears in the *miracula* of the saints. On this foundation the study of childhood in Poland began to grow, until the year 2004, when, as signaled by two seminal publications, one might say, with only a hint of humor, that the field of childhood came of age in that country. First, Małgorzata Delimata published her book on childhood in medieval Poland, which remains a standard within the field.[43] Delimata's work takes a bird's eye perspective to childhood in Poland, and tries to outline the reality of childhood from birth to youth in law, health, education and care. The legal status of children in various contexts

---

39 Jarosław Nikodem, "Parens tanti pueri: Władysław Herman w Gallowej wizji dziejów dynastii," *Kwartalnik historyczny* 117 (2010): 5–22.
40 Przemysław Wiszewski, *Domus Bolezlai. Values and Social Identity in Dynastic Traditions of Medieval Poland (c. 966–1138)* (Leiden/Boston: Brill, 2010).
41 Zbigniew Dalewski, *Ritual and Politics. Writing the History of a Dynastic Conflict in Medieval Poland* (Leiden/Boston: Brill, 2008).
42 Beata Wojciechowska, "Dziecko w kulturze ś redniowiecznej," *Kieleckie Studia Historyczne* 9 (1991): 5–21.
43 Małgorzata Delimata, *Dziecko w Polsce średniowiecznej* (Poznań: Wydawnictwo Poznańskie, 2004).

INTRODUCTION   11

is a special focus of this masterfully researched book. Also in 2004 a major collection of essays on childhood was published by Wojciich Dzieduszycki and Jacek Wrzesiński, which covered a number of issues regarding medieval and early modern times.[44] These essays cover a wide range of mortuary topics across time, but in the medieval context discuss the anthropology of child bones, the description of child deaths in texts, the presence of various kinds of grave goods (such as painted eggs) within child graves and the placement of children within cemeteries. In 2013, a similar, yet smaller, collection appeared, edited by Paulina Romanowicz, focusing on a wide range of topics, with toys being the major topic of a number of chapters.[45] It would be out of place not to mention here the work of Dorota Żoładź-Strzelczyk, particularly her book on childhood in "old Poland," which, covers everything from childrens' diets to the nature of their education and play to their depiction in art.[46] Unfortunately, her work focuses on early modern Poland, from the fifteenth century onward, and therefore can only aid this book indirectly, namely by proving a perspective on how things "turn out" in the centuries after those covered in the following pages.

With all of this excellent historiography already published on childhood in Poland, what use is this project at hand? There are three essential, yet interrelated, justifications, which will be discussed in turn. First, due to the general paucity of sources for the time period covered by this book, namely 1000–1300, Polish scholars have tended to note this informational drought and, perhaps more wisely than the author of this book, have focused their efforts on the greener pastures of later centuries. No book exists solely for childhood in these three centuries as multiple books do for the later period. Nevertheless, there are sources from the early Piast period that are highly pertinent to any conversation about medieval childhood, and they merit fuller treatment than they have garnered. This is related to the second justification, namely that this book approaches the problem of childhood from the opposite angle from previous attempts on the problem in Poland. Instead of selecting sundry topics related to childhood and then mining the sources for information about these topics, this book takes each source as its own starting point, and winnows them to find what patterns and topics emerge. In this process, the sources themselves help to guide what themes will receive treatment. This is not some naive

---

44   Wojciech Dzieduszycki and Jacek Wrzesiński, eds., *Dusza maluczka, a strata ogromna*, Funeralia Lednickie spotkanie 6 (Poznań: Stowarzyszenie Naukowe Archeologów Polskich, Oddział w Poznaniu, 2004).
45   Paulina Romanowicz, *Child and Childhood in the Light of Archaeology: Studies* (Wrocław: Wydawnictwo "Chronicon," 2013).
46   Dorota Żoładź-Strzelczyk, *Dziecko w dawnej Polsce* (Poznań: Wydawnictwo Poznańskie, 2002).

attempt to take sources at face value or to pretend that the bias of modern researchers will somehow magically not affect the nature of the discussion, but simply an attempt to find what medieval authors themselves have to say about children, and how they say it, and from this foundation make our analysis and conclusions. This method of approaching childhood in the Middle Ages is itself rather innovative, and the closest parallel is in Phyllis Gaffney's work mentioned above, for Gaffney also tries to tease out childhood and its construction from the context of each source, though the scope of my work and the nature of the sources examined covers a wider range of kinds of sources (such as archaeology) and topics (such as saintly children) than Gaffney's. This book will enumerate a number of reasons why Poland has sources that are put in useful dialogue with Gaffney and with so many of the other scholars writing on this topic, and this leads to the final justification for it. The vast majority of the material written on childhood in Poland is in Polish, which, unfortunately, seems to remain impenetrable to most scholars outside that country. The introduction of the goldmine of the Polish material to the rest of the field will be a contribution in and of itself.

Before continuing, two issues of content and scope must receive attention. First, the scope of years covered in this study might raise questions. After all, the Piast dynasty ruled Poland from the mythical days of before Mieszko I's conversion in 966 to the death of Kazimierz the Great in 1370. This book, on the other hand, ends its investigation around the year 1300. Scholars will probably suspect, given this date range, an underlying chronological scheme relating to the concept of the "High Middle Ages," often dated from 1000–1300,[47] as well as a commitment to the concept of "Medieval Transformations" taking place in the twelfth and thirteenth centuries.[48] The time span of 1000–1300, and especially the latter end of it, is thus associated with changes such as population growth, the spread of new agriculture, Christianization, colonization, the rise of new religious orders, the appearance of new architectural styles, and a whole array of other phenomena that shaped both eastern and western

---

47   It would be difficult to provide even an overview of the literature surrounding the concept of the High Middle Ages, as it seems to have universal appeal and status. For a general introduction to the concept and what it entails, please see William Chester Jordan, *Europe in the High Middle Ages* (New York: Viking, 2003).

48   The concept of a major transformation in European civilization beginning in the twelfth century was originally popularized in the early 20th century by the ground-breaking work: Charles Homer Haskins, *The Renaissance of the Twelfth Century* (Cambridge, Mass: Harvard Univ. Press, 2011). The concept has been extended as a form for cultural comparison between eastern and western Europe, as is most clearly represented by a series of essays in Thomas Noble and John Van Engen, *European Transformations: The Long Twelfth Century* (Notre Dame, Ind: University of Notre Dame Press, 2012).

Europe, and as this book tries to compare eastern and western Europe, it will adopt this widely accepted framework within which to do this. This could still leave the question of if and to what extent this framework, often applied to other parts of Europe, is useful for Poland, though many scholars appear to answer in the affirmative.[49] In terms of strictly political history, the early fourteenth century marks the end of the division of Poland into various regions by the Piast dynasty, and the creation of a more unified and organized society and state, which in itself suggests a natural stopping point for our study.

The second important issue to address is the choice of texts for inclusion into this study. Scholars will note that I chose to include all the major texts from the early Piast period in terms of chronicles and have done likewise with hagiography. Some notable texts have been excluded from this study due to questionable dating. For example, *Kronika Wielkopolska* (The Chronicle of Greater Poland), records Polish history up to 1273 from the perspective of this province and contains the first mention of a number of famous Polish legends, such as that of Lech, Czech, and Rus'. The problem with this text is that it was compiled through multiple editions, and this creates the situation where authorship for parts or all of the text is dated through the late thirteenth through late fourteenth centuries, with the latter dating far beyond the scope of this book.[50] Another reason for a text's exclusion is related to size of the text in question. This criterion stems from the aims and methodology of this work, which is to see how childhood functions within a narrative framework. This method requires, of course, a large enough of a narrative to produce significant results. It is for this reason that a few minor works, especially chronicles, composed near the end of the thirteenth century and beyond have been excluded from this study. The most notable example of this is *Chronicon Polono-Silesiacum* (The Polish-Silesian Chronicle), which, by most accounts, was written at the

---

49 Nora Berend, Przemysław Urbańczyk, and Przemysław Wiszewski, *Central Europe in the High Middle Ages: Bohemia, Hungary and Poland c.900–c.1300* (Cambridge: Cambridge University Press, 2013).

50 My goal here is not to take a side in this debate, but simply to strike out a source that happens to be of contested date. Foreign scholars writing about a history not their own prefer to keep to their point, not needlessly enter debates not related to their purpose. For more discussion of this debate, one might consult: Roman Pollak, *Piśmiennictwo staropolski* (Warsaw: Państwowy Instytut Wydawniczy, 1963), 246. Henryk Łowmiański, "Kiedy powstała Kronika Wielkopolska?" *Przegląd Historyczny* 51/2 (1960): 398–410. Edward Skibiński, *Vademecum historyka mediewisty*, eds. Jarosław Nikodem, et al. (Warsaw: Wydawnictwo Naukowe PWN, 2012), 260–265. Brygida Kürbis, ed., *Kronika wielkopolska* (Kraków: Towarzystwo Autorów i Wydawców Prac Naukowych Universitas, 2010), 7–33. As Pollak notes, the text itself is heavily reliant on other works for its source material, such as Master Vincent.

end of the thirteenth century, and thus could technically qualify for inclusion in this book.[51] Unfortunately, much of this text is not original and relies heavily on borrowings from Vincent Kadłubek for much of its early material. To make matters worse, the size of the text itself does not make it particularly useful for comparison to Gallus or Vincent. In the Monumenta Germaniae Historica, the Latin text of this chronicle extends only 15 pages, with the majority of these pages closely following Vincent.[52] Texts such as this simply cannot receive the same sort of literary analysis to make it comparable to the rest of the material in this study.

2 Description of Contents

The book will begin with a chapter on the early twelfth century *gesta* attributed to Gallus Anonymus, which is perhaps the most famous text from Poland during the early Piast dynasty. This text, one of battles and warriors, while seemingly an unlikely place to find children, nevertheless turns out not only to be riddled with passages and references to children, but even uses youth and coming of age as a major metaphor and structuring principle for the text itself. At the beginning of the book a series of initiation rituals are used to mark the coming of age of Poland itself into a Christian society. Furthermore, the greatest hero of this work, namely Bolesław III Wrymouth, is described and praised extensively through stories of his childhood and youth, and readers are both drawn to his courage and heroism, but also often driven to sympathize with his tender years and the threats he faced as a boy in a chaotic and badly ruled kingdom. Parents and people are presented as sympathetic and caring towards children, and especially towards the noble young Bolesław III.

The second chapter is dedicated to another chronicle, much less famous, at least in Anglo-Saxon scholarship, the chronicle of Vincent Kadłubek, who composed his work about a century after Gallus, but with some overlapping material. Vincent does not use childhood to such an extent as Gallus as a structuring principle for his work, but he nevertheless uses youth and age as a powerful rhetorical tool to lampoon the wicked leaders, nobles, and peasants of Poland, while at the same time using it to enshrine the virtues that he

---

51 For more on this text, please consult: Roman Pollak, *Piśmiennictwo staropolski* (Warsaw: Państwowy Instytut Wydawniczy, 1963), 244. Wojciech Mrozowicz, "Śląska Kronika polska. Wstęp do studium źródłoznawczego," in *Acta Universitatis Wratislaviensis 2512, Historia 163*, 2003): 119–128.

52 "Chronicon Polono-Silesiacum," in *Monumenta Germaniae historica digital* (München: Monumenta Germaniae historica: Bayerische Staatsbibliothek). 553–570.

INTRODUCTION   15

champions. In doing this he makes great use of the *puer senex* trope, in which a virtuous child is presented as having the behavior of a mature person, to highlight the worthiness of his youngest heroes. At the same time, the associations he imputes to youth, namely foolishness, intemperate behavior, impatience, wasting time on worthless games, and general stupidity, are attached to those Vincent finds unworthy.

The third chapter covers the Henryków Book, one of the most intriguing and singular sources to survive from the medieval period. It has no one identifiable genre, but draws elements from many, and tells of the foundation and expansion of a Cistercian monastery in Silesia from the 13th through early 14th centuries. This book, which has the primary purpose of confirming the landholdings of the monastery, is nevertheless filled with considerable detail about the nature of rural relationships in this part of the Piast lands, and even includes many in-depth, fascinating, and often scandalous stories about the colorful characters that inhabited these lands. The primary focus of children in this book is their potential to challenge the status quo of the holdings of the monastery. Old Polish patrimonial customs clashed with the purchases, assumed to be final by the monks, of valuable resources and assets. The Henryków book is, in essence, written entirely with the younger generation in mind, which will need to be reminded through the written word of the deeds of their ancestors. In this sense, the Henryków Book is all about the shaping of memory and the education of generations in the works of older days. There is a deep consciousness in the terminology used in the increasingly precise language of the charters issued for donations that the children, grandchildren, or other descendants of contemporaries will return and be instructed by these documents. In this sense, the Henryków Books is a sort of child for childless Cistercians, who can stand face-to-face with their enemies' offspring and defend the monastery against future challengers and threats. At the very least, the Henryków Book provides brief glimpses into the lives and behaviors of children from the less exalted rungs of society.

The hagiography discussed in the fourth chapter is extremely illuminating for several reasons. First, the flurry of female saints in the thirteenth century Poland such as Hedwig, Kinga, and Salomea provide the only extensive descriptions of female children from the early Piast era. While these holy girls are by no means portrayed as typical, and the descriptions of their lives fall within the conventions of hagiography from all of Europe during this period, they nonetheless can be compared with the images of saintly and heroic male children like Stanislaus and Adalbert. The hagiography raises a number of issues, such as whether saintly virtue is inborn or learned, and whether all forms of play and childlike behavior are always unbecoming to a saint to not.

In the canonization process of St. Stanislaus in particular, children also play an important rhetorical role in pre-figuring and bringing about his elevation. From another angle, the *miracula*, or lists of miracles attached to the *vitae* for the purpose of proving a saint's sanctity, we can also draw a number of conclusions about the incidence of children in these miracles, what kinds of miracles children experience, and even about the treatment and the events in the lives of non-elite children.

Standing somewhat apart from the other the other chapters is the fifth, about the archaeology of childhood in mortuary contexts in medieval Poland. The purpose of this chapter is simply to see what, if any, conclusions can be drawn about children and their place in society from archaeology. This is no simplistic attempt to test for elements already found in the textual portions of the book, but instead to observe the major issues and patterns in the archaeology of childhood in Poland and see if, broadly speaking, there can be any conversation between text and archaeology. This chapter addresses a number of pertinent issues including: the incidence of child burials, the presence/absence of grave goods and their nature, children in multiple burials, and the placement of children together in different segments of the cemetery. To conclude the chapter, correspondence analysis, a mathematical tool, will allow us to explore patterns in relation to children, gender, and sex, to see how children appear on this spectrum.

The final chapter also serves as the conclusion of this book. In this chapter, all the material covered from the very different sources surveyed up to this point will be finally compared and larger themes emerging from all the chapters will receive treatment. These themes include: the prophetic nature of childhood, growth/age categories, emotions toward children, care towards children, and negative vs. positive examples of children. Once the similarities among chapters have been teased out, these similarities will be compared to relevant examples across medieval Europe, so as to situate the nature of conceptions of childhood in Poland within a larger conversation, and to assess how similar or different Poland was from its contemporaries.

CHAPTER 2

Child and Hero: The Use of Childhood in the Narrative of Gallus Anonymus

In terms of textual remains from early and high medieval Poland, the earliest of any great length is the "chronicle" of Gallus Anonymus. This text is focused on the glorification of the Piast dynasty of Poland, and primarily argues for the right of the Piasts to rule through proof of their victory in a series of intense and bloody military encounters. One might not expect to find much about childhood in a work like that. Indeed, while Gallus has inspired generations of Polish scholars to discuss the minutiae of ancient Polish customs, territorial extent, Christianity, and, especially, state formation, discussions of the role of childhood are relatively rare. Nevertheless, childhood and children appear several times in the text, for a few different purposes and reasons. These appearances have not, of course, escaped the attention of so many scholars, and some have noted that certain scenes relating to children are important to the immediate argument of the text. However, no one has yet done a complete analysis of the role of children and childhood in the overall purpose of Gallus Anonymus.[1] In fact, I will argue that the surprisingly frequent references to children are not mere cultural vignettes or throwaway passages, but are essential elements in the overall economy of the work. Yet while children and childhood appear frequently in Gallus, not all children are equally visible. Most of the narrative concerns male ducal heirs and their youthful, elite entourage. Female children are scarcely visible, and lower-class children only appear in the very beginning of the text, when the Piast family itself had low status. With this in mind, I will show that for Gallus elite childhood was: first, a time of development and prophecy, second a tool to define rank and worth within the dynastic system, and third, a time of vulnerability when people expected fathers and society in general to protect and provide.

---

1 For children in Gallus, see Jacek Banaszkiewicz, "Młodzieńcze gesta Bolesława Krzywoustego czyli jak zostaje się prawdziwym rycerzem i władcą," in *Theatrum ceremoniale na dworze królów i książąt polskich. Materiały konferencji naukowe zorganizowanej przez Zamek Królewski na Wawelu i Instytut Historii Uniwersytetu Jagiellońskiego w dniach 23–25 marca 1998*, edited by Mariusz Markiewicz and Ryszard Skowron (Kraków: Zamek Królewski na Wawelu, 1999), 15–16; Małgorzata Delimata, *Dziecko w Polsce średniowiecznej* (Poznań: Wydawnictwo Poznańskie, 2004), 36–37; Przemysław Wiszewski, *Domus Bolezlai, Values and Social Identity in Dynastic Traditions of Medieval Poland (c. 966–1138)* (Leiden/Boston: Brill, 2010), 130–180.

1   Who Was Gallus? New Approaches to the Deeds of the Princes of the Poles

To understand the role of childhood in the *Deeds of the Princes of the Poles*, it is important to briefly unpack the context, background, and purpose of the text. Most scholars agree that the text was composed at the court, or at least in the midst of the military and ecclesiastical elite, of Duke Bolesław III Wrymouth (1097–1138),[2] at some point between 1112 and 1117.[3] Practically nothing is known about the author. Though the term "Gallus" brings to mind someone from the region of modern day France, that name was given to the unknown author by the sixteenth-century Polish historian Martin Kromer, who inscribed it on a manuscript copy.[4] Using a biblical citation (e.g., Genesis 23:4), the so-called "Gallus" referred to himself as "an exile and sojourner among you."[5] He was very likely a monk, possibly from the Benedictine abbey of Somogyvár in Hungary. Gallus may have come to Poland with Bolesław upon his return from the penitential pilgrimage to Hungary. The Somogyvár abbey was dedicated to St. Giles, and had been established in the 1090s by monks from the Abbey of St. Giles in Provence.[6] It is therefore commonly assumed that Gallus came from the mother house in Provence, where he must have been educated.[7] However, Tomasz Jasiński has found compelling similarities in

---

2   The exact date of the beginning Wrymouth's reign is contested, as his earliest years consisted various power-sharing schemes with his brother and father.

3   Marian Plezia, *Kronika Galla na tle historiografii XII w.* (Kraków: Nakład Polskiej Akademii Umiejętnośći, 1947), 190–93; Wiszewski, *Domus Boleszlai*, 124. Increasing consensus narrows this range to 1113 to 1116.

4   Zbigniew Dalewski, "A new chosen people? Gallus Anonymus' narrative about Poland and its rulers," in *Historical Narratives and Christian Identity on a European Periphery. Early History Writing in Northern, East-Central, and Eastern Europe (c. 1070–1200)*, edited by Ildar H. Garipzanov (Turnhout: Brepols, 2011), 145.

5   Gallus Anonymus, *The Deeds of the Princes of the Poles* III, Letter, ed. Karol Maleczyński and trans. Paul W. Knoll and Frank Schaer (Budapest/New York: Central University Press, 2003), 211.

6   For the Somogyvár abbey, see Gergely Kiss, "La fondation de l'abbaye bénédictine de Somogyvár," in *Les Hongrois et l'Europe. Conquête et intégration*, edited by Sándor Csernus and Klára Korompay (Paris/Szeged: Université de Szeged (JATE)/Paris III-Sorbonne Nouvelle (CIEH)/Institut Hongrois de Paris, 1999), 327–39. For Gallus and the Hungarian background of his work, see Dániel Bagi, *Gallus Anonymus és Magyarország. A Geszta magyar adatai, forrásai, mintái, valamint a szerző történetszemlélete a latin Kelet-Közép-Európa 12. század eleji latin nyelvű történetírásának tükrében* (Budapest: Argumentum, 2005).

7   Plezia, *Kronika*, 135–61 and 178–80 Wiszewski, Domus Boleszlai, 140. For the identity of Gallus, see now Jarosław Wenta, *Kronika tzw. Galla Anonima. Historyczne (monastyczne i genealogiczne) oraz geograficzne konteksty powastania* (Toruń: Wydawnictwo Naukowe Uniwersytetu Mikołaja Kopernika, 2011); Adrien Quéret-Podesta, "Travaux philologiques,

vocabulary and style between the *Deeds of the Princes of the Poles* and the *History of the Translation of St. Nicholas the Great*, written by an equally anonymous monk from the monastery on the Venice Lido.[8] Other regions of France, Flanders, as well as Dalmatia have also been considered as possible starting points for the author, but for the purposes for this book he will remain Gallus.[9] More important in that respect is the question of Gallus' sources and collaborators. In his introductory letters, which are before each of the three books, he mentions the help of the archbishop and bishops of Poland, as well as the royal chancellor Michael, at different places. A number of other stories refer to the knowledge of "venerable old men," but exactly who these were is unknown.[10] If the text of Gallus can be believed at all, then, it seems that his sources, helpers, and, presumably, editors, were those of the highest ecclesiastical and political officials of the realm, who had a serious stake in the success and stability of the Piast dynasty, and this was most likely the purpose behind the text itself.

No one doubts that Gallus' most important purpose in writing was to argue for dynastic legitimacy. Thomas Bisson puts Gallus squarely in the tradition of twelfth-century chronicles written throughout which strive to bolster the

---

recherches textuelles et identifications des auteurs anonymes dans la médiévistique du XIXe siècle: l'exemple du Gallus Anonymus," in *La naissance de la médiévistique. Les historiens et leurs sources en Europe (XIXe–début du XXe siècle). Actes du colloque de Nancy, 8–10 novembre 2012*, edited by Isabelle Guyot-Bachy and Jean-Marie Moeglin (Geneva: Droz, 2015), 269–84.

8   Tomasz Jasiński, "Czy Gall Anonim to Monachus Littorensis?," *Kwartalnik historyczny* 112 (2005), no. 3, 69–89. See also Tomasz Jasiński, "Rozwój średniowiecznej prozy rytmicznej a pochodzenie i wykształcenie Galla Anonima," in *Cognitioni gestorum. Studia z dziejów średniowiecza dedykowane Profesorowi Jerzemu Strzelczykowi*, edited by Dariusz Adam Sikorski and Andrzej Marek Wyrwa (Poznań/Warsaw: DiG, 2006), 185–93; Tomasz Jasiński, "*Cursus velox cum consillabicatione* w Kronice polskiej Galla Anonima i w Translacji św. Mikołaja Mnicha z Lido," in *Memoria viva. Studia historyczne poświęcone pamięci Izabeli Skierskiej (1967–2014)*, edited by Grażyna Rutkowska and Antoni Gąsiorowski (Warsaw/Poznań: Instytut Historii Polskiej Akademii Nauk, 2015), 114–31.

9   Dalewski, "A new chosen people?," 147.

10 Wiszewski, Domus Bolezlai, 146. For example, Gallus claims that the story of the unfortunate demise of Popiel was told (to him) by "venerable persons of old" (*seniores antiqui*; Gallus Anonymus, *The Deeds* I 3, 22–23). There is very little understanding of Gallus' oral sources, for which see Piotr Dymmel, "Traces of oral tradition in the oldest Polish historiography: Gallus Anonymus and Wincenty Kadłubek," in *The Development of Literate Mentalities in East Central Europe*, edited by Anna Adamska and Marco Mostert (Turnhout: Brepols, 2004), 343–63; Wojciech Polak, "'Gesta' Gallowe a kultura oralna," in *Tekst źródła. Krytyka, interpretacja*, edited by Barbara Trelińska (Warsaw: DiG, 2005), 65–76.

claims of lordship in an increasingly unstable time.[11] Polish scholars have generally agreed with this assessment, though they have highlighted a number of distinctions and local contexts that prompted Gallus' writing. Premysław Wiszewski, for example, has pointed out that Gallus does not simply give Piast monarchs a blank check to rule by divine will, but emphasizes that they must attain a certain level of virtue and valor to retain their favored position—or risk subjugation by a more worthy Piast. While God blessed Poland through the Piast dynasty, that by no means implied that the current Piast was assured of keeping God appeased—Bolesław II was deposed of because of their inadequacies. Furthermore, the semi-legendary chieftain of Poland before the Piasts, Popiel, failed to live in his duties and he and his dynasty lost their power to the Piasts, a sure to the audience reminder that God could replace while dynasties if they risked his displeasure.[12]

Zbigniew Dalewski, on the other hand, points out that Gallus probably had a very immediate political crisis on his mind when writing.[13] This occurred when his hero Bolesław III invited his exiled half-brother Zbigniew, with whom he had previously won a succession struggle, back into the country and gave him a small territory to govern. However, to the shock of the Polish realm, Bolesław III treacherously had Zbigniew captured and blinded, with Zbigniew dying soon after this humiliation. Popular fury was so intense at this event, that Bolesław was forced to take a pilgrimage to Hungary as penance. Gallus was, perhaps, added to the Piast court during that pilgrimage, and set to work to repair the damage to his patron's reputation.

Despite the enormity of research written about Gallus to this point, much of it has been focused on a limited range of questions. As Eduard Mühle pointed out in a recent survey of Gallus research, most recent material has been published on these questions: the origin of Gallus; his sources and literary models; the political function of the text.[14] What has been generally lacking is a discussion of the literary qualities (as opposed to models) of the Deeds, and there has been little notice of the links between the rhetorical qualities of the text

---

11 Thomas N. Bisson, *The Crisis of the Twelfth Century: Power, Lordship, and the Origins of European Government* (Princeton: Princeton University Press, 2009), 183–91. As well as: "Deeds of the Princes of Poland (1109–1113)," *Viator* 29 (1998): 275–89.

12 Wiszewski, *Domus Boleszlai*, 270–300.

13 Dalewski, "A new chosen people," 145–147; Zbigniew Dalewski, *Ritual and Politics. Writing the History of a Dynastic Conflict in Medieval Poland* (Leiden/Boston: Brill, 2008).

14 Eduard Mühle, "Cronicae et gesta ducum sive principum Polonorum. Neue Forschungen zum so genannten Gallus Anonymus," *Deutsches Archiv für Erforschung des Mittelalters* 66 (2009): 459–96.

and the social expectations of its audience.[15] In other words, new approaches are only beginning to apply the "linguistic turn" to Gallus, in the terms theorized and summarized in the seminal collected volume edited by medievalist Gabrielle Spiegel, in which issues of textuality and discourse displace attempts at more "objective" history.[16] It is precisely into this gap that I place my own scholarship, focusing particularly on constructions of and social reaction to children and childhood.

Gallus' work does not solely focus on Bolesław III. The first of the three books his work comprises is about the origins of the Piast dynasty in the non-Christian past. Only the third book discusses the life of Bolesław Wrymouth as an adult ruler, while the second book describes the miraculous conditions of his birth, his excellence in boyhood and adolescence, and finally his knighting and accession to the throne. It is therefore in the first two books that we draw much of this discussion of childhood.

2 Childhood as a Time of Development and Prophecy

The first item for discussion is how childhood and children, and their lives and actions, serve constantly as harbingers for things to come in Gallus. Some, such as James Schulz, might argue that this represents an "impoverished" image of childhood, where the lives of children are colonized by the concerns of adults.[17] But instead, I will argue that Gallus' use of children is a literary device, and one that places an important, almost prophetic emphasis on childhood, and while perhaps different from modern understanding of the value of a child, still suggests the child's importance in the minds of medieval people. Furthermore, at the same time I argue that childhood events and actions are prophetic in the long term, that these events and actions were presented as having significance in and of themselves for the growth and development of Piast kings and dukes.

---

15   Recent exceptions are Przemysław Wiszewski's *Domus Boleszlai*, which traces the rise of a dynastic tradition for the Piasts through communication of stories embodying tradition and values and Zbigniew Dalewski's *Ritual and Politics. Writing the History of a Dynastic Conflict in Medieval Poland*, which argues that Gallus plays in the expectations of readers to portray Zbigniew not as the victim of a vengeful brother, but a disreputable and untrustworthy character.

16   Gabrielle Spiegel, *New Directions in Historical Writing After the Linguistic Turn* (New York, NY: Routledge, 2005).

17   James Schulz, *The Knowledge of Childhood in the German Middle Ages, 1100–1350* (Philadelphia: University of Pennsylvania Press, 1995), 249.

The book's opening chapters, which deal with the period when Poland was still not Christian, include the descriptions of no less than three coming of age ceremonies for a series of young Polish boys. This ceremony, the cutting of hair in the seventh year of life,[18] is described as a pagan, or at least an "ethnic" custom (*qui more gentilitatis*), and was celebrated in the midst of a large gathering partaking in a feast.[19] The first was being held in Gniezno for the son of the non-Piast duke at the time, Popiel. Gallus tells of two mysterious strangers who came to visit the town, but were not invited to the ceremony, and were instead "injuriously" sent away.[20] The two strangers then came upon another coming of age ceremony, this time hosted by the peasant Pazt. The latter's name is commonly interpreted as a form of Piast, the name of the dynasty. Pazt, though poor, invited the strangers to his meager ceremony, and offered them the little food and drink he had available. Gallus then recounts what he considers to be a miracle, as everything was multiplied, and the insufficient meal became a great feast. It was then that the boy's parents realized that "something of great significance was being foretold for the boy."[21] Afterwards the duke Popiel and his party were invited to Pazt's feast, as the food had multiplied so much that is could feed many people. More importantly, the strangers are said to have cut the hair of Pazt's son and to have given him the name Siemovit (*Semouith*).[22]

Gallus' purpose behind including and interpreting these two ceremonies, which, if they occurred at all, must have happened over 200 years before he wrote his own chronicle, is relatively clear. Zbigniew explains that "the Piasts, though they still were pagans, had special relations with the sacred, and through them their subjects were able to gain divine favor."[23] This was the beginning of the long relationship between the Piasts and God. Stanisław Rosik argues that, as the Old Testament prefigured the coming plan of salvation, in a similar way the pre-Christian times of Poland were part of a larger plan of salvation for the country and this plan was marked by a number signs.[24] Most interesting

---

18 For early medieval comparisons, see: Yitzhak Hen, "The Early Medieval Barbaratoria," in M. Rubin, *Medieval Christianity in Practice* (Princeton 2009).
19 Gallus Anonymus, *The Deeds*, 16.
20 Ibid., 16 and 18.
21 Ibid., 21.
22 The name appears as Samouithay in the section title, and as Semouith in the text. Its etymology and meaning are debated. The first Piast in history with that name lived more than a century after Gallus—Siemowit I of Mazovia (1248–1262), See Kazimierz Jasiński, *Rodowód pierwszych Piastów* (Warsaw/Wrocław: Volumen, 1992), 46–47.
23 Dalewski, "A new chosen people," 158.
24 Stanisław Rosik, "The World of Paganism in Gallus' Narrative," in *Gallus Anonymous and His Chronicle in the Context of Twelfth-Century Historiography From the Perspective of the Latest Research*, ed. by Sztopka, Krzysztof (Kraków: Polish Academy of Arts and Sciences, 2010), 96.

for my purpose, however, is that a childhood rite of passage, of all things, was chosen to bear that weight of meaning. In many ways, the opening chapters detail what is, in a sense, the childhood of Poland and of the Piast dynasty. This is a time of the development and display of virtue by the Piasts and their children, a time when their connection with God grows closer, even though not yet realizing Christianity, and a time where brief glimpses of a glorious future are provided through prophecy and miraculous events.

These themes are continued in the brief descriptions of the coming of age of Siemovit, who "increased in age and strength, and his excellence grew ever day by day."[25] While his virtue led him to glory, the misdeeds of Popiel's dynasty led them to ruin, with the old duke eventually eaten by mice on a deserted island. Siemovit seized ducal power. Hospitality towards guests and personal virtue paid off for the Piasts. But was Siemovit's virtue something he acquired after the hair cutting ceremony, or something he had to develop in youth and adulthood? This is a question that is raised by a discrepancy in the textual tradition of Gallus. The more recent editions of the text say that Siemovit "did not waste his youth (*iuventutum*) foolishly in pleasure (*voluptuose vel inepte*), but by his steady efforts (*usu laboris*) won both fame for martial prowess and the glory of honor."[26] However, some scholars argue that this represents a sixteenth century alteration of the text, which had originally stated that Siemovit had indeed wasted his youth, but through steady effort had acquired virtue.[27] In either case, youth is considered a time when boys usually carouse, and virtue must be attained through years of effort. But in the earlier textual tradition, we see that in the youth of Poland, even the dukes themselves had to grow into their role as champions of God and virtue.

The final rite of passage is connected with the famous scene of the miraculous healing of the blindness of the young Mieszko, who later in his life would be the first Piast duke to convert to Christianity (966). Gallus tells us that Mieszko was born blind and remained so for the first seven years of his life. Nevertheless, on his son's seventh birthday, duke Siemomysł hosted the ostentatious banquet to celebrate, and the guests enjoyed themselves and applauded, despite the duke' own deep sorrow for his son. But miraculously, the boy regained his sight to the joy of the duke and his retinue. Siemomsyl's seers saw this event as a portent of things to come—namely that Mieszko would illuminate Poland and subjugate its neighbors. But Gallus, with the benefit of hindsight, suggested another interpretation, in which Mieszko's blindness represented the blindness of his (and Poland's) paganism. Mieszko would

---

25   Gallus Anonymus, *The Deeds*, 23.
26   Ibid., 24–25.
27   Wiszewski, *Domus Boleszlai*, 174–175.

later have his eyes opened to the truth of Christianity, and would spread it to his people.[28] In this passage, an event in childhood again changes the destiny of Poland, as well as predicts future change. Mieszko's healing transformed him from an object of pity, for whom at best a mediocre future could be hoped, given his disability, and now physically gave him the opportunity to develop into a mighty warlord who would have the ability to transform Poland. But at the same time, the restoration of his sight, while important in its own right, also had metaphorical implications, which would further cement the Piasts' devotion to the Christian God and to his objectives for Poland.

Poland grew out of its metaphorical childhood with the conversion of Mieszko I to Christianity, and especially with the reign of his son, Bolesław I, but the childhoods of dukes are still mentioned, however briefly, until the coming of Bolesław III Wrymouth, whose youthful activities received extensive treatment. Before moving to an extensive discussion of his childhood, I would like to point out a few pertinent passages relating to other elite children. Of Bolesław I (992–1025), the model of the great ruler in the text, Gallus wrote that "with God's favor [he] so grew in courage and strength that, if I may put is so, his virtues gilded the whole of Poland."[29] The development of ducal virtue from childhood into adulthood mirrors the country's developing greatness. In a similar vein, we hear about the monastic education of Kazimierz the Restorer (1034–1058) after he honored the church and supported monasteries following his military victory crushing pagan rebels and invaders.[30] Finally, when Ladislas of Hungary (1077–1091) achieved the throne with the help of Bolesław II (1058–1079), Gallus could not resist emphasizing his upbringing in Poland, "Ladislas had been raised from childhood in Poland and had almost become a Pole in his ways and life. Hungary had never had as great a king, so they report, and the land thereafter never that much splendid fruit."[31] In each of these passages, the upbringing of each ruler was noted to be in correspondence with his later achievements, and at least in part their cause.

The upbringing of the main character of the story, Bolesław III Wrymouth (1107–1138) also demonstrated the importance of his growth and development in its own right as well as these developments' prophetic significance. Indeed, he was enveloped in prophetic significance before his own birth, for his father, Duke Władysław Herman and his wife Judith of Bohemia, were concerned about their infertility. Of course, Władysław already had a son, Zbigniew, but he

---

28   Gallus Anonymus, *The Deeds*, 26 and 28.
29   Ibid., 31.
30   Ibid., 86.
31   Ibid., 97.

was considered illegitimate. Gallus describes Władysław's agony and constant prayer and fasting. Finally, on the advice of his bishop, the duke had a golden image fashioned of a boy, and sent it together with many precious gifts to the abbey of St. Giles in Provence. There, his envoys asked the saint, "in place of this child-form, please grant a living boy, a real one for its sponsors." The monks "had not yet completed their fast in Provence when the mother in Poland was rejoicing to conceive a son."[32] The purpose of this heir was clear, namely to be the one "who should fear God, exalt holy church, exercise justice, and hold the kingdom of Poland to the honor of God and the salvation of he people."[33] Bolesław's birth was, by itself, a miraculous event that overjoyed his parents and emphasized the dynasty's legitimacy, but it also was an important portent of the great things Bolesław would achieve in his boyhood, adolescence, and adulthood.

One should also not miss the significance of the name of the boy itself. As Adam Krawiec notes, "Bolesław" was the name of two giants within the Piast family.[34] Bolesław Chrobry serves as Gallus' ideal ruler, the measurement by which later rulers could be compared, and the choice of this name, while not a rhetorical choice of Gallus, suggests the extent to which naming and reference to previous rulers was important to the Piast dynasty itself.

However, immediately before describing Bolesław's youth, Gallus introduced his audience to the rebellion of his (Bolesław's) illegitimate half-brother, Zbigniew. The latter's youthful mistakes and violence against his father and country serve as a foil against which the younger Bolesław's heroic deeds could shine. Gallus does not even pretend to hide his strategy, for immediately before going into a discussion of Zbigniew's shameful acts, he adds: "and let no thoughtful person think it inappropriate at all if we introduce [him] into our history, besides the legitimate son the son of the concubine as well … both sprang from the patriarch's seed, but they were not both equal in their birthright."[35] As I will show later, Gallus does not imply that Władysław was always the best parent, but nevertheless still finds ways to cast serious suspicion on Zbigniew. Because of his status, Zbigniew was shuffled into a clerical education track, with training first at the cathedral in Kraków, and was later sent to a monastery in Saxony. He then was captured in Silesia and used by count Magnus of Wrocław, at the instigation of the Bohemians, as a bargaining

---

32 Ibid., 109.
33 Ibid., 105.
34 Adam Krawiec, *Król bez korony: Władysław I Herman, książę polski* (Warsaw: Wydawnictwo Naukowe PWN, 2014), 114.
35 Ibid., 123.

chip against Władysław and his hated adviser Sieciech. Zbigniew, approaching his twentieth year, quickly went from bargaining chip to rebel leader, according to Gallus' account. Despite a brief reconciliation with his father, in which it was the "first time the father called him his son," and in which he was granted a share in the inheritance of the kingdom,[36] Zbigniew continued to fight after the overall conflict had ceased elsewhere in Silesia by sneaking away from Wrocław, and was forced to make a final, bloody stand near Kruszwica. Using a citation from Lucan's *Pharsalia*, Gallus rages: "this was more than a civil war, with son in arms against father and brother against brother in a cursed contest. There, I trust, the wretched Zbigniew earned by his father's curse what was later to happen."[37] In other words, Gallus implies Zbiegniew, though later a victim of Bolesław III's cruelty, was by no means undeserving of his fate. A final peace was reached and Zbigniew's life and newly won birthright were spared, because "his father was prepared to overlook his youthful stupidity."[38] Nevertheless, Gallus claims that Władysław still suspected treachery from his son, specifically in aiding unnamed pagans threatening the realm, and so he had him temporarily imprisoned. These stories show the youthful Zbigniew as the antithesis of all of the other, successful Piast ducal youths. He not only lacked martial virtue and honor, but he also showed tendencies towards treachery, lies, and deceit. Instead of expanding and defending Poland, he had divided it and sided with its enemies. Gallus notes that God Himself had turned against Zbigniew in his defeat and humiliation.

The valiant boyhood of the young Bolesław contrasts sharply with that of his half-brother:

> let no one in any way be surprised if we write something about matters memorable in Bolesław's boyhood, For he did not indulge in silly games, the way children usually like to play, but he did his best as much as a boy could to imitate vigorous and martial deeds. And although sons of nobles commonly take delight in hounds and hunting-birds, Bolesław, even as a young lad, always had more pleasure and things martial.[39]

This passage is significant for a number of reasons. Małgorzata Delimata regarded it as indirect evidence for what childhood entailed for normal

---

36 Ibid., 127.
37 Ibid., 129.
38 Ibid.
39 Gallus Anonymus, *The Deeds*, 135.

children in medieval Poland.⁴⁰ Przemysław Wiszewski and others have noted the *puer senex* (the "boy as old man") trope, where the young future notable engages in activity which is presented as utterly uncharacteristic of his age to presage his future deeds.⁴¹ In other words, we can assume that while Bolesław did not partake in "silly games" or "hounds and hunting birds," other noble boys filled their time with such pursuits, and that this was a trope of play associated with this time of life. This is, of course, an interesting insight, but not particularly important for my purpose, which is to understand what childhood meant to Gallus' overall argument. What we should notice is that Bolesław's deeds only imitate (*imitare*) the martial deeds of adults, but, at least early in his life, he is not actually participating in any of them. Judging from the following passages, this does not necessarily mean that such deeds were unimportant, or somehow representative of a childhood collapsed into adulthood. Instead, some are uniquely, childlike (but not childish) deeds of importance in proving Bolesław's character in relation to his half-brother, and in prophesying the future triumphs and vulnerabilities of the future king. Jacek Banaszkiewicz has pointed out the resemblance between the childhood deeds of Bolesław, and those of other great heroes in medieval literature, stressing how violent hunting and martial activities were part of a hero's upbringing and progression into the role of knight and ruler.⁴²

It is important to note that where Bolesław most clearly falls into the stereotype of disobedient and rebellious child, it is often to his credit:

> Even before he was able to mount or get off a horse by himself, he would march against the enemy at the head knights, against the wishes of his father or at times without his knowledge.⁴³

The boy Bolesław, instead of sneaking off and causing mischief, only chose to disobey his father when it came to participating in military matters and protecting the country. This contrasts to the "youthful stupidity" of Zbigniew mentioned above. In disobedience Zbigniew worked treacherously against the interests both of the family and of Poland, while Bolesław's only misbehavior is to escape his father's watch to defend his homeland. This is further reinforced

---

40   Delimata, *Dziecko*, 37.
41   Wiszewski, Domus Boleszlai, 269.
42   Banaszkiewicz, "Młodzieńcze gesta."
43   Gallus Anonymus, *The Deeds*, 135.

in the next chapter, where Bolesław joins palatine Sieciech in a campaign against the Moravians, who had instigated of the rebellion of Zbigniew.[44]

Among Bolesław's boyhood acts, the most famous are the two encounters with ferocious, wild animals, told in consecutive chapters. These should not be taken at face value, for, as Jacek Banaskiewicz suggests, they are full of symbolic meaning—and a bit like a modern action film.[45] Unlike other boys of his age, who hunted defenseless deer or small game, Bolesław successfully defended himself against surprise attacks in potentially life threatening situations. In the first encounter, Bolesław sees a boar while eating breakfast, and chases after it alone deeply into the forest, while armed only with a spear. But when, right before he could strike the boar, one of his warriors suddenly blocked his blow and wanted to take the spear from him,

> On one occasion, the son of Mars was in the forest, sitting down to breakfast, when he saw a huge boar crossing his path and disappearing into the dense woods ... Bolesław in fury, or rather in boldness, won single-handed an amazing double duel, against both against the man and against the beast. For he managed both to wrench back the spear and kill the boar. Afterwards, when asked why he did this, the man maintained that he had not known what he was doing; all the same, for a long time he was out of favor with the prince. The boy returned exhausted and only after much fanning did he finally recover his strength.[46]

Apart from demonstrating Bolesław's bravery and courage, even as a child, this passage also notes his vulnerability and how his impetuous temperament, while such a critical element in his heroics, can also lead him to near disaster.[47] Indeed, despite his strong performance, the boy could barely move in exhaustion after the event. But there is also a much darker element to vulnerability. What exactly was the objective of the disrupting warrior? A number of scholars have suggested that Gallus' story is about a failed attempt on the boy's life.[48] This perhaps explains the disgrace the solder apparently suffered for a long time afterwards, though Banaskiewicz rightly notes that that seems to be

---

44   Ibid., 134 and 136.
45   Banaszkiewicz, "Młodzieńcze gesta," 14 and 17.
46   Gallus Anonymus, *The Deeds*, 137.
47   To Banaszkiewicz, "Młodzieńcze gesta," 18, the event is little more than a literary construction to show a twofold victory of the young Bolesław—over both beast and knight.
48   Karol Maleczyński, *Bolesław III Krzywousty* (Wrocław: Zakład Narodowy im. Ossolińskich, 1975). Plezia, *Kronika*, 72.

a rather light penalty for an attempt at assassination.[49] If the implication was treachery, however, who would have been behind such a treacherous deed? The conniving palatine Siechiech, or Bolesław's older brother Zbigniew, who did not wish to share a divided kingdom? If the latter, one is led to believe that Bolesław may not have overreacted with the blinding of his brother later in life, for he had been the victim of treachery from his earliest years.

Despite his near death at the hands, or rather tusks, of the boar, Bolesław showed no signs of being daunted, humiliated, or afraid. Gallus writes that "another of his boyhood exploits was not dissimilar, and I will not keep silent about it, though I know that there are jealous persons whom I will not in all respects please."[50] This is a significant, if surprising opening to a boyhood story. The fact that even the rash deeds of child could prompt jealousy and merited recollection even decades later bespeak the importance that boyhood has to Gallus, and presumably his readers, in proving the virtue of elite sons. Strolling in the woods with his companions, Bolesław came upon a male and female bear in the midst of "play," and:

> at the sight he rushed to the level, waving his friends back, and along upon his horse and without fear he approached the bloodthirsty beasts. The male bear turned upon him and with its arms raised, but Bolesław ran him through with a spear. Those at hand found this deed quite astounding, and a tale to tell to those who had not seen it, as an example of the boy's enormous courage.[51]

Bolesław had again amazed everybody with his actions. Even with friends nearby to aid him, he chose to engage enemies by himself. Later in life, this tendency would lead to a horrific military tragedy, in a battle where his companions were forced to sacrifice their lives in order to extricate Bolesław from a battle into which he had brazenly jumped without much consideration for consequences.[52]

---

49 Banaszkiewicz, "Młodzieńcze gesta," 17.
50 Gallus Anonymus, *The Deeds*, 139.
51 Ibid.
52 Gallus Anonymus, *The Deeds*, 176 and 178. It is worth noting that when jumping in that battle, the warlike Bolesław, now almost an adult, was "like a lion driven to fury with the beating of its tail (*sicut leo caude stimulis iracundia concitatus*)." While this is clearly a citation from Lucan's *Pharsalia* (1 205–12), the fury in question is the same one that Bolesław manifested when his warrior wanted to wrest the spear with which he (Bolesław) was about to kill the boar.

Bolesław later participated in a successful mini-campaign against the Pomeranians, the perennial enemy of the Poles.[53] This campaign was the capstone of a longer trajectory, beginning with the defeat of the boar, then the defeat of the bears, then the sneaking into combat, then participation in raids, then finally full military conflict. By starting with boyish, yet nonetheless heroic, actions, Bolesław had grown into a man of heroic proportions, capable of leading successful ventures against Poland's bitterest foes. Not surprisingly, Bolesław's "campaign" was compared with the inactivity of his much older brother, who refused to leave his section of the divided kingdom to attack Poland's enemies, while the boy Bolesław marched forth despite having only a small war band at his disposal.

It is very important here to note an attribute ascribed to young Bolesław III by Gallus in Book II, namely language linking Bolesław to the ancient god Mars. This phrase is first seen prophetically in Chapter III, in which after the failed siege of Nakło castle in Pomerania by Władysław Herman, Gallus notes that through the son of Mars (*per puerum Martis*) the Pomeranians would eventually face defeat.[54] This reference is immediately following a description of the birth of the boy and before any of his childhood heroics, and contrasts him with the failure of his own actual human parentage, namely Władyław. The phrase appears again in the aforementioned story of Bolesław's encounter with a boar, which begins with a reference to the boy as a son of Mars.[55] By Chapter 13, when Bolesław shifts from attacking animals to people, he is referred to as a "boy-Mars" (*Martialis puer*) and Gallus expands on this theme, mixing it with the *puer senex* trope:

> A boy by age, an old man in capability, he already held the duchy of Wrocław, yet he had still not attained the rank of knighthood. So there was great hope in a boy of such good qualities, and clear signs of martial glory were already apparent in him, so that all the magnates held him in great affection, for they sensed there was something great in store for him.[56]

This passage, while connecting to the premonition of the defeat of Pomeranians in Chapter 3, also connects Bolesław's military skill with the respect and affection of the elite—something he earned before he was even a knight. Martial

---

53   Ibid., 150 and 152.
54   Ibid., 120.
55   Ibid., 137.
56   Ibid., 139.

references multiplied in his later boyhood military activity. He is called the "young scion of the offspring of Mars" (puerulus, Martis prole progenitus) in reference to his capture of the Pomeranian fortress at Miedzyrzecz.[57] The aforementioned story of Bolesław defending the country while Zbigniew hesitated in Book 17 features two similar references, one praising the "boy devoted to Mars" (de puero Marti dedito) and another "the boy Bolesław, son of Mars" (*puer Bolezlauus, Martis filius*).[58] This phrase "boy-Mars" is used once again in reference to Bolesław's defeat of the Pomeranians after their surprise attack during the arrangements for his knighting ceremony.[59]

The literary and classical connection of Bolesław as a boy to Mars is important, as no other figure in Gallus' text, or any other child from contemporary literature, received this description. To be sure, references to Mars (all with hints at authors using Roman mythology) are not rare in the eleventh and twelfth centuries, but Gallus is unique because of his use of "puer Martis." The fact that Gallus matches reference to Mars with a boy is truly unique, and one must ask for what purpose Gallus chooses to employ this trope and connect it with youth. It is evident that references not only serve as a prophecy for Bolesław's adult military triumph, but also serve to elevate him far above his failed brother and father even while he himself is still a boy, and also connect him to the favor of the nobility and people of the realm who admire his remarkable courage and skill. The highly unusual nature of and repeated usage of this trope strongly suggests that Gallus is working and thinking with categories related to children to make his points.

Of any moment in Bolesław's youth and childhood, the knighting ceremony has attracted the greatest amount of attention from scholars. Dariusz Piwowarczyk notes that in the time of Wrymouth, knighthood was the culmination of the education of the young warrior and the act confirming his acceptance among adults. Around the age of seven, boys of members of the *drużyna* (military retinue) and of warriors passed into the care of men, and in the following years, learned from them martial skills, such as riding horses, combat practice, and physical fitness, as well as conditioning in courage, discipline, and swift decision making.[60] While the age for becoming a knight varied in this

---

57   Ibid., 140 Latin text, 141 English text.
58   Ibid., 150 Latin text, 151 English text.
59   Ibid., 153.
60   Dariusz Piwowarczyk, "Funkcje i ceremoniał rycerskiego pasowania na ziemiach polskich (XI–XVIII wiek)," in *Od narodzin do wieku dojrzałego: dzieci i młodzież w Polsce, V/1. Od średniowiecza do wieku XVIII*, ed. Maria Dąbrowska and Andrzej Klonder (Warsaw: Instytut Archeologii i Etnologii Polskiej Akademii Nauk, 2002), 194.

period, in the case of Bolesław, his knighting probably took place between his 14th and 16h year of age.[61]

I shall return to the implications of Bolesław's knighthood for his role in the kingdom. For the moment, it is worth noting Gallus' approving comment on the event:

> Władysław, seeing that the boy was in the prime of his life and had a special gift for soldiering, and that he had won the approval of all the wise men of the the kingdom, decided he should be girded with the sword on the feast of the Assumption of Saint Mary, and prepared a great celebration in the city of Płock.[62]

This story appears immediately after Bolesław's raid against the Pomeranians, and is placed in sharp contrast to Zbigniew's inactivity. According to Zbigniew Dalewski, in the *Deeds of the Princes of the Poles*, the knighting of the young prince is not so much a clear-cut right of passage, as a culmination of a process of martial development in the boy Bolesław. Through eight chapters of Book II (10 to 17), the audience had the opportunity to see the child Bolesław progress from impetuous animal fighter to a successful leader of men, who has earned the respect of all in the land.[63] As mentioned above, in the midst of the preparations for the knighting ceremony, the Pomeranians invaded and laid siege to the castle of Santok. Bolesław again showed his prowess and "against his father's wishes and in spite of protests from many others the boy Mars sped to that place, and there he triumphed over the Pomeranians. Returning as a victorious esquire, he was girded with the sword by his father and celebrated the festivity with great joy."[64] Again, Bolesław shows his youthful willingness to disobey authority, even that of his father, to oppose an enemy that no other leader in Poland would face. And his initiative is rewarded with the joy of his father and the kingdom. In many ways, knighthood is honored to be associated with Bolesław, and not the other way around. To cap off this magnificent achievement, immediately after receiving his sword-belt, Bolesław marches out to fight the Cumans, and wins an important victory, which supposedly cowed the Cumans so much that they did not attack Poland again during his subsequent reign.[65] Interestingly, the story of the campaign against the Cumans is placed

---

61 Maleczyński, *Bolesław III*, 47.
62 Gallus Anonymus, *The Deeds*, 153.
63 Zbigniew Dalewski, "The knighting of Polish dukes in the Early Middle Ages: ideological and political significance," *Acta Poloniae Historica* 80 (1999): 26.
64 Gallus Anonymus, *The Deeds*, 153.
65 Ibid., 155.

between two episodes concerning the knighting ceremony—the one involving Bolesław and his companions, and the prophecy uttered at the "council of the knightly girding" by a "certain person."⁶⁶ Knighthood is thus the framework against which Gallus projects Bolesław's accomplishments in the past, as well as the future. This is in contrast to Zbigniew, whose past, present, and future (in the narrative) are marked by military disgrace, despite having been knighted, like Bolesław, and even given a part of the realm to rule.

It is important to note at this point that Bolesław's repeated disobedience towards his father is not depicted as a negative attribute. As Jarosław Nikodem has recently noted, Gallus does not present Władysław as a particularly adept duke, warrior, ruler, or father.⁶⁷ Bolesław's disobedience may therefore be seen in contrast not just to the poor behavior of his brother, but also to the inactivity and incompetence of his father.

During the ceremony, an important, and apparently controversial prophecy was uttered about Bolesław by an unnamed character. The mysterious man proclaimed that "today the good Lord has visited the Kingdom of Poland," and through Bolesław's knighting has exalted Władysław's old age and the entire country. "Blessed is the mother who raised such a son (*puer*). Until now Poland was trodden by her enemies, but this young lad (*puerulum*) will restore as she was in times of old."⁶⁸ Zbigniew Dalewski has noted similarities between this prophecy and the Magnificat in the Gospel of Luke (1:46–55). The implication is that Gallus presents Bolesław as a Christ figure.⁶⁹ While this interpretation is, perhaps, a rather more than the text itself explicitly says, Bolesław is no doubt exalted above his father, Władysław, who was a lesser king, under whose reign Poland had continued to decline from her former glory. Gallus, to be sure, is ready to endorse that interpretation. Citing the Book of Revelation (19:10), he understands the prophecy as announcing that the exploits the boy Bolesław (*puer*) boy, "Poland would one day be restored by him to her pristine state."⁷⁰ Poles who wanted to see a restoration in the fortunes of Poland had to put their hope fully in the one God had selected for the task, and not in any other members of the dynasty (specifically Zbigniew).

While the boyhood and youthful deeds of Bolesław have a prophetic function, they also show a clear progression and development. Virtue and greatness, at least those of a great hero, are not inborn traits. Elements of greatness

---

66 Ibid.
67 Jarosław Nikodem, "*Parens tanti pueri*: Władysław Herman w Gallowej wizji dziejów dynastii," *Kwartalnik historyczny* 117 (2010): 5–22.
68 Gallus Anonymus, *The Deeds*, 154–155.
69 Dalewski, "A new chosen people," 152–153.
70 Gallus Anonymus, *The Deeds*, 154 and 157.

are present even before Bolesław's birth, as he is a member of a dynasty blessed by God, but he still must develop these elements into something greater. So we see Bolesław begin by fighting wild animals (and fainting in the attempt), then later tagging along in raids against enemies, then leading a small foray himself against the Pomeranians, then defending the country against an enemy raid, and finally, after knighthood, defeating a mighty enemy—the Cumans. This progression of events raised Bolesław up from boyhood to full kingship in the eyes of Gallus, and presumably, his readers.

3 Age Terminology and Dynastic Status: When Is a Man a Man?

One thing one notes when carefully examining Gallus is the terminology associated with age. For example, when does he use the word *puer*, and when *iuvenis*? A close examination of Gallus' usage shows that such words related to age have less to do with a particular stage of life or with a rite of passage, and more with a particular position within the royal family. This is apparent when, *after* Bolesław III's knighting ceremony Gallus warns his audience: "for the moment let the boy, or son (*puer*) take some rest from his labors, while our pen brings Duke Władysław, that good and gentle man, to his grave in peace."[71] The word *puer* was until this point in his life consistently to refer to Bolesław as a child. Judging from the chronology of the narrative, he must have been at least 14 years old by this moment in time. Even knighthood could not erase the memory of him being a child not too long ago. The idea of a single, unified age category of "child" before adulthood has some resonance with many ancient and medieval models of childhood. Most notable, in the tradition of the Benedictine Rule, childhood ("infantum") ended at age 15, and with it the period when it was permissible to use corporal punishment on a child. Gallus may well have been a Benedictine monk, and therefore highly aware of that age category and terminology, but there is no sign of its use in the *Deeds of the Princes of the Poles*.[72]

In fact, terminology used by Gallus refers to a number of older individuals as children, which accords with no scheme of age development in the Middle Ages. One of the most egregious examples of an apparently erratic use of age terminology is the mention of Mieszko II as *puer* in the story about Bolesław Chrobry's campaign against Kiev. Scholars agree that Mieszko could

---

[71] Ibid., 157.
[72] There is in fact very little evidence that Gallus saw the world through the lens of the Benedictine Rule.

not have less than 25, and was almost certainly 28 years old at that time (i.e., in 1018). The use of *puerum* seems to have been intentional, for Gallus mentions Bolesław, the father, being "now lord of numerous realms and he had not seen the boy Mieszko, who was now old enough to rule."[73] In other words, Gallus was clearly aware that at the time of this particular episode, Mieszko was not a child any more. Puzzled by this usage, some have suggested that the Latin must have been garbled, with the correct translation reading "who was *not* old enough to rule." but that is by no means a superior explanation.[74] Another odd use of *puer* in relation to adults appears in a passage concerning the division of the kingdom following Zbigniew's rebellion mentioned above: "So the kingdom was divided, as had been told, and the father delivered this quite fine speech, and each of the boys (*puerorum quisque*) visited his own part of the realm."[75] While Bolesław may well have a "boy" at this point, Zbigniew was around twenty years of age. Unlike the example of Mieszko II, who died 78 years before the earliest date advanced for the *Deeds of the Princes of the Poles*, the episode of the realm's division under Władysław had taken place within the lifetime of too many of Gallus' informants to have gone unnoticed.

How can one explain such a usage? When a duke is still living, the sons in right standing with him are referred to as *pueri* in relation to him, for this word means "son" as much as "boy" in Latin, for they are his legitimate heirs. Indeed, as shown above, Bolesław III continued to be called a boy, or son, even after being knighted. The point is made after Gallus describes the funeral of Duke Władysław and the argument over succession:

> Now that he had his share of the patrimony and supported by his council and knights, the young Bolesław (*puer autem Bolezlauus*) set about developing his courage and his bodily strength, and in repute and years began to grow into a youth (*iuvenis*) of fine character.[76]

To judge from the evidence of this passage, Bolesław needed his share of the patrimony, a council, his knights, and, grimly speaking, the death of his father to turn from *puer* to *iuvenis*. From this point onward, *iuvenis*, and not *puer* is the consistent category under which his development is described in Book II. Yet, the memory of the traits developed during his childhood lingered for while, and and on a rare occasion, and usually for rhetorical effect, Gallus will

---

73   Gallus Anonymus, *The Deeds*, 43.
74   Knoll and Schaer, in Gallus Anonymus, *The Deeds*, 43 with note 5.
75   Gallus Anonymus, *The Deeds*, 135.
76   Ibid., 156–157 and 158–159.

return to it. This is particularly clear in the episode of how Bolesław lost a great number of men in the battle against the Pomeranians:

> It happened that a certain noble had built a church in the borderlands, and invited Duke Bolesław and his young companions to the consecration, though was still little more than a boy (*Bolezlauum ducem, adhuc satis puerum cum suis iuvenibus invitavit*) ... Bolesław, the warrior, who set soldiering and hunting above feasting and drinking, had left the older persons with the main crowd at the feast, and went with a few companions into the forest to hunt. But instead he ran into hunters: for the Pomeranians had been raiding through Poland ...[77]

This episode ends badly, as Bolesław and his band of young people are surrounded and outnumbered by thousands of Pomeranians, and only the self-sacrifice of his young companions allows Bolesław to escape. The military defeat, and the young duke's reckless and immature behavior, seems to have taken a toll on Bolesław's status of *iuvenis*, which had been bestowed upon him earlier in Book II. Because of his lack of maturity in the passage, Gallus in this story chooses to refer to his Bolesław as "little more than a boy." Reminding the audience of the hero's tender years and inexperience, and the fact that he was still only fresh in his new status as a youth, seems to be designed to exculpate Bolesław from at least some of the blame for his foolhardy and poorly thought out behavior. At the very least, this sort of foolish behavior diminishes Bolesław's masculinity.

The rhetorical usage of Bolesław's status, in Book II between *puer* and *iuvenis*, is mirrored in Book III, where he is both *iuvenis* and a mature man. When describing his wise deeds and character in a positive light, Gallus employs such words as *homo*, *dux*, or *princeps*. Whenever he deals with Bolesław (few) rash decisions, he is *iuvenis*. Although *vir* is the word that Gallus reserves for mature dukes, it is not applied consistently to Bolesław.[78] *Iuvenis* appears with great frequency at the end of Book III, where Bolesław takes the ill-fated decision to invite Zbigniew back into Poland and then treacherously inflicts punishment upon him (chapter 25), then later repents of his horrible deeds. It is important to note that only after that horrible crime has been committed, Bolesław appears to have reached the borderline of full masculinity. Only now Gallus begins to call him *vir*: "For we have seen such a man (*talem virum*), such a favored prince (*tantum principem*), such a favored youth (*tam*

---

77 Ibid., 176–177.
78 The emblematic *vir* of the *Deeds of the Princes of the Poles* is of course Bolesław Chrobry.

deliciosum iuvenem) fasting...."[79] He has reached manhood through understanding the consequences of his rash actions, and the steps of his evolution to manhood are projected backwards to describe him (*vir*, *princeps*, *iuvenis*) and evoke pity for actions of which he later deeply repented.[80]

This discussion leads to an inescapable conclusion: words related to age categories in the *Deeds of the Princes of the Poles* are associated with the holder's political and social status within the dynasty and his expected role and behavior. *Puer* is often used before the death of the parent to describe an age of growth and foreshadowing under the supervision and control of a parent. *Iuvenis* is often used to describe the intermediate period when one strives to achieve the height of power, but has not reached full wisdom and maturity. Language relating to adulthood is only activated when one achieves or enters the height of power or a period of glory. Bolesław III barely reaches this full manhood as the book concludes, and this is clearly intended to have a rhetorical effect, in which words related to age serve to define one's role in the dynastic chain. The use of words related to age to score rhetorical effects is of course not unique either to Poland or the early twelfth century. As Kathleen Cushing has demonstrated, the use of such words for rhetorical effect is a characteristic of the early Gregorian Reform movement, although in association more holiness and effectiveness than with the position in dynasty.[81]

4 Vulnerability and Care: From Parents and the Community

Parent-heir relationships are an important theme in the *Deeds of the Princes of the Poles*. First, obviously, sons are expected to be loyal to their fathers, and, for the most part, obey them. Zbigniew rebelled against his father to secure his birthright and was condemned for it harshly. The second obvious point is that succession is a constant thought on the mind of the parent, and fathers are constantly making reference to this essential dynastic function. However, responsibilities were not in one direction only. Fathers were expected to care for their children practically and provide honorable treatment in life and a just inheritance in death. Likewise, Gallus seem to assume that his audience

---

79 Gallus Anonymus, *The Deeds*, 275.
80 Another possibility is that Gallus uses *homo* and *vir* interchangeably, as he seems to do in chapters 19 and 21 of Book II, in which he describes the return of Kazimierz. But since Gallus does not employ those words for Bolesław III until after Zbigniew's death, it is more likely that his vocabulary choices for that case are not an accident.
81 Cushing, "'*Pueri,' iuvenes,* and *viri*: Age and utility in the Gregorian Reform," *Catholic Historical Review* 94 no. 3 (2008): 435–449.

expects care for children and feels sympathy when they are under threat. Such assumptions become crucial for Gallus' rhetorical construction, especially when he has to explain Bolesław III's decision to march against his father along with his treacherous half-brother in order for them to secure their rights. Before turning to that story, it is worth examining a few some passages outlining expected paternal duties.

One of the most surprising incidents, especially for scholars of the later Middle Ages, when fathers slowly receded from direct childcare, is a reference to Bolesław Chrobry, duke then later king of Poland from 992–1025 CE. In this story, Bolesław's wife would sneak rebellious nobles, whom her husband had condemned to death, out of prison. Once she had worked to secure their pardon from Bolesław, she would have them first brought before her and:

> She would rebuke them with both sharp and mild words, and them have them taken to the king's bath. There King Bolesław would bathe them as a father would with his children (*filios*), berating them and dwelling on the praises of their forebears. "It is unworthy of you, who are descended from such a distinguished family, to stoop to such things." The older ones (*provecciores*) he would merely rebuke, either personally or through others, while for the younger ones (*minoribus*) the words would be accompanied by the switch.[82]

This passage strongly suggests fatherly involvement in at least the lives of elite boys. The admonishments that Bolesław uses suggest that this may have even been things that children could expect to hear while receiving a bath. It is highly likely the switch was received by elite boys as well.

Physical care, as well as moral formation, was an expected fatherly occupation. Repeatedly, when Gallus is trying to describe Bolesław's love and good treatment of his nobles and people, he turns to familial imagery, such as when we are told that "he king loved his dukes, *comites*, and princes as if they were his brothers or his sons (*filios*)."[83] And again, in regards to those of lesser status we hear, "[Bolesław] did not treat peasants like a lord and exact forced labor from them, but cared for them as a kind-hearted father and left them to live in peace."[84] Language comparing rulers to parents is by no means uncommon in the Middle Ages, but the fact that Gallus repeats this imagery and imbues

---

82   Gallus Anonymus, *The Deeds*, 63. There is clear pun marked by alliteration in "minoribus vero verbera cum verbis adhibebat."
83   Ibid., 59.
84   Ibid.

it with unusual intimacy is suggestive. His audience must have assumed that that parental care was some of the most intimate and secure, and this made it a perfect metaphor for Bolesław's care for his recalcitrant subjects. Repeatedly tapping into these connotations showed a remarkable connection between parenthood and good uses of power, at least from rhetorical standpoint.

Bolesław III's troubles with his father began when he was still a boy, before his knighting, and after Zbigniew had seized a part of the inheritance from Władysław Herman. In this story, Gallus' bête noire, the count palatine Siechiech,[85] trusted adviser of Władysław Herman begins to formulate plans against the duke's children:

> [he] was weaving plots against the boys (*pueris*) and using all manner of wiles to turn the father's feelings from love of his sons (*ab afectu filiorum*). He even installed his *comites* or bailiffs, either from his own clan or an inferior, to take control of the castles in the boys' assigned areas, and by skillful cunning he encouraged them not to pay heed to the boys (*pueris*).[86]

The implication is that the father's love was expected to support the claims of his sons, so in order to split the dynasty effectively and build up his own power, Siechiech had to work against that natural relation. This implies that a successful and stable dynasty, one that could endure the plots of courtiers, required strong bonds between father and sons, and the most effective way to steal a succession was to infiltrate those bonds. To be sure, the passage may be regarded as an oblique critique of Władysław, who not only did not protect his sons from this treachery, but also failed to notice that Siechciech was scheming to seize Poland. In the face of such a looming disaster, Gallus tells us that Bolesław III and Zbigniew, who never before or after were on particularly good terms, took an oath for mutual protection against their father.

Władysław Herman, for reasons that remain unclear, decided to send Bolesław to Silesia, ostensibly to repel a rumored Czech invasion, although others suspected treachery. Whose treachery that really was is not mentioned, but Gallus seems to imply that Władysław's incompetence compounded the problem. Bolesław was ordered to meet up with the *comites* of the kingdom near Wrocław, but these men had all been appointed by Siecheich. Realizing that the young Bolesław was in danger, his companions explained to the boy (*puer Bolezlauus*) that he was walking into a trap. He was so impressed that,

---

85 For more discussion of the exact nature of Sieciech, see Krawiec, *Król bez korony*, 180–185.
86 Gallus Anonymus, *The Deeds*, 140 and 142, 141 and 143.

"tears flowed and his body ran with sweat."[87] Such words are meant to highlight Bolesław's vulnerability and the boy's weakness. Up to this moment, Gallus has been busy showing the martial masculinity of Bolesław at even the youngest age. Why did he suddenly switch to his boyish weakness? For weakness Bolesław showed again when going before the citizens of Wrocław to make his case and to ask for their aid:

> In tears, as a boy would be (*sicut puer cum lacrimis*), he told them point by point of the plot that Siechiech had set for him. They in turn wept out of affection for the boy (*pueri lacrimantibus*). Angry and indignant, they fired out against Siechiech, reviling him in his absence.[88]

This passage, particularly the rhetorical effect of the contrast between a boy crying and mature men crying for a boy, suggests that Gallus attempted to pull readers emotionally onto the side of young Bolesław. The reader's intended reaction is most likely mirrored by that of the townspeople of Wrocław, who upon witnessing the vulnerability and sadness of the boy, are instantly transformed into champions for his cause. Zbigniew, in a speech to townspeople, plays upon these very emotions for the purpose of channeling the popular fury: "Young and weak (*puerilis etatis inbecillitas*), we have been victims of terrible events, and find ourselves hard-pressed by enemies on all sides."[89] Interestingly, while the wily Zbigniew claims to be weak and young to elicit sympathy from others, it is the young Bolesław who fits these words more closely. He then directly accuses his father of having failed in his parental duties: "our father is old and infirm, and is less able to see his own needs and ours or the needs of the country. Thus we have no one but ourselves to protect us."[90] The reaction of the townspeople of Wrocław, after being "touched to the heart with grief," was that that Zbigniew and Bolesław expected, namely to provide military support to the two brothers confronting their father. In other words, they all thought that the two boys were right, when rebelling against their father, who had not lived up to his role as a dynastic parent.

The boys confronted their father, who, after some negotiation, agreed to dismiss Siechiech. They then pledge their allegiance to their father with "bowed necks and meek hearts."[91] That, unfortunately, did not end the matter, for when

---

87   Ibid., 143.
88   Ibid., 144–145.
89   Ibid.
90   Ibid., 145 and 147.
91   Ibid., 149.

the sons and father were marching to seize Siechiech, Władysław inexplicably left his party and went over to Siechiech. Gallus notes that the magnates were furious about that, for "it was not the action of a wise person ... it was the decision of a madman to forsake his sons (*deserere filios*) and all the nobles as well as his army."[92] Władysław's failure as a father and leader was now complete, so the nobles and the boys decided to seize power militarily and to force a confrontation with the duke. After difficult and unpleasant negotiations at Płock, for which Archbishop Martin of Gniezno served as mediator, Władysław agreed to expel Siechiech from Poland. After further betrayals, the duke was eventually pushed aside by his sons, and "he was no longer allowed to exercise any authority."[93]

This is an ugly story of fatherly incompetence, youthful rebellion, and violence ending in pointless negotiations and betrayals. These events, like the seizure and blinding of Zbigniew, leave of cloud of doubt on the actions of Bolesław. Was he really so innocent in this highly selective, glossed over, and unlikely chain of events? The constant justifications given by Gallus for the actions of the nobility in regards to the boys suggest that that was a still contentious and painful matter. But one of Gallus' main rhetorical strategies to exonerate Bolesław was to evoke the practical and emotional damage Siechiech and Władysław had inflicted upon Bolesław and Zbigniew *as children*, as well to incriminate Władysław as bad father, two points on which, according to him, the nobility, army, and the townspeople of Wrocław agreed.

While parental love and honor was expected for legitimate children, it was nevertheless not something that was automatically given at birth. This was the case for Zbigniew, a child born to Władysław from an illegitimate union. As a bastard, Zbigniew was not only initially barred from any sort of inheritance, but also, according to Gallus, bereft of filial love for the first years of his life. It was only after a stalemate was reached in war with his father that Zbigniew wrested a proper inheritance for himself. Gallus informs us "that the father made peace with his son; and it was then that for the first time the father called him his son."[94] Was Gallus trying to gather sympathy for Zbigniew? In my opinion, given his overall negative treatment of Władysław's illegitimate son, the answer must be negative.[95] It is more likely that the intention of the author

---

92   Ibid., 151.
93   Ibid., 127.
94   Ibid.
95   It is important to note that the subject of the sentence "pacem invitus cum filio pater fecit, eumque tunc primum suum fiilium appelavit" is Władysław. In other words, it is Władysław that makes peace with Zbigniew, not the other way around. Zbigniew was not on some quest to make up with his long estranged father, as in a Hollywood film.

was to shed a bad light on Władysław as a father, and the consequences of this bad parenting for the dynasty and for Poland. Once he was called "son" by his father, Zbigniew could now complain, as he did in front of the townspeople Wrocław, that, being "old and infirm," his father could not take care of his son's interests.

To be clear, this point about Władysław's failure in his role as a parent is not to sentimentalize medieval Piast fatherhood in a twenty-first century way. This is not a Disney film, where a distant and incompetent father tearfully apologizes to a wronged son. As this discussion of age terminology in the perviuos section makes clear, terms and roles related to age in the dynasty in Gallus was tightly connected to place and expected behavior within the dynasty. Władysław was not a bad father because he missed his son's baseball game or ignored his talents in theater, as one might expect in modern storytelling, but because he incompetently failed to rule his house well and organize succession and power-sharing in a functional manner. This negative portrayal can be connected with Gallus' larger aims to diminish Władysław to contrast his weak and passive nature with Bolesław III's dynamism.[96]

5   Motherly Care and Female Children

Along with the fatherly care and general care for children mentioned above, motherly care is mentioned on a few occasions in Gallus, albeit briefly. As opposed to fatherly care, which is "practical," and therefore stern, motherly care is often presented as lavish and sometimes excessive. For example, Bolesław Chrobry speaks to his men as his "brothers, whom I have fostered and spoilt as a mother her sons (*tanquam mater filios enutrivi*)."[97] Indeed, a mother's love is so potent a concept that Bolesław supposedly invokes it as a model for his ideal of rulership. A similar metaphor is used for the young death of Bolesław II's son Mieszko, which reportedly "threw the whole of Poland into mourning like a mother mourning for her only son."[98] Motherhood, alongside saintly acts of charity,[99] is one of the few roles adult women play in the *Deeds of the Princes of*

---

[96]   Krawiec, *Król bez korony*, 283. It should also be remembered the tightrope Gallus had to walk in this scene of childhood rebellion. He had to discredit Władysław without making him appear so bad as to discredit the while dynasty as collateral damage. See Krawiec, *Król bez korony*, 18.

[97]   Gallus Anonymus, *The Deeds*, 68–69.

[98]   Ibid., 103.

[99]   Such as the pious deeds of Judith of Bohemia, the mother of Bolesław III (Gallus Anonymus, *The Deeds*, 117).

the Poles. Whenever mentioned, motherhood is always charged with emotion and purpose—and often is used as a metaphor of intense or immoderate love. Such a rhetorical use of a mother's care for her children has also been noted in Polish hagiography. The emphasis of the care of mothers for children is also a prominent feature of the Polish hagiography in the twelfth and thirteenth centuries.[100]

In stark contrast to the numerous references to male children in Gallus, female children receive practically no attention. Perhaps this is not too surprising given Gallus' aforementioned objectives of demonstrating the legitimacy and divine sanction of the Piast dynasty through martial prowess and virile acts. In fact female elite children appear only when married or sent to monasteries. Even these did not attract much notice. For example, Gallus mentions that Władysław Herman "took to wife the sister of Emperor Henry III," but did not mention her name, perhaps because from her the duke "begot no sons, but three daughters." One of those daughters married in Rus', another became a nun, and the third married someone (most likely a member of the aristocracy) in Poland. Again, none of those women is named.[101] An unequally unnamed Rus' girl (*Ruthena puella*) married Mieszko III before he was poisoned.[102]

6   Comparisons: Cosmas of Prague

To understand the significance of Gallus' use of childhood, and to see how heavily childhood influences his work and its purposes, it is helpful to compare his to a similar work, namely that of Cosmas of Prague, who served as dean of the cathedral in that city and probably began writing in the same decade as Gallus about the history of the Bohemians. As the title of the work, *Chronica Boemorum*, suggests, Cosmas is not just concerned about the deeds of the rulers of the realm, but seems to presenting a kind of "national history," in which the origins and values of a people are the central concern.[103]

---

100 Małgorzata Chołodowska, "Matka—opiekunka małoletnich dzieci w Polsce wcesnośredniowiecznej na podstawie opisów cudów św. Jadwigi i św. Stanisława," in *Partnerka, matka, opiekunka: status kobiety w starożytności i średniowieczu*, ed. Julia Jundziłł (Bydgoszcz: Wydadnictwo Uczelniane Wyższej Szkoły Pedagogicznej, 1999), 260–69.

101 Gallus Anonymus, *The Deeds*, 117. Later historians have had to try to piece together the girls' names and fates through other sources. See Krawiec, *Król bez korony*, 137–138.

102 Ibid., 100–101.

103 For Cosmas' concerns in terms of group identity, he clearly had the Přemyslid dynasty in mind. On the other hand, his "Czechs" are not a nation in the modern sense of the word, but a *natio* in a medieval sense (the community of the nobility of the Czech lands). That explains Cosmas' negative attitude towards German knights, as well as his criticism of

Unlike in Gallus, Cosmas begins his history in the depths of time, specifically the Flood and the Tower of Babel, and places the Czechs into the geography of the ancient world. Instead of children being the symbols of the future, two adults served that purpose. First is the arrival of adult man Bohemus (a pagan) and his followers into Bohemia (named after him) and his proclamation that it was the land of Bohemian destiny. Second are the prophecies of Libuše, the adult seeress and judge of the Bohemian people, compared with Sybil of Cumae and Circe, who oversaw the appointment of the first duke of the land (but also warned against the tyranny a duke would bring).[104] Cosmas includes a story of how the young women of Bohemia (who previously supposedly lived like Amazons) were conquered by the young men through trickery, though the connection with childhood is tenuous here, and the story seems to have little relevance to the other themes of the text rhetorically.[105]

Nevertheless, childhood does have occasional importance for some themes of the texts in a number of other locations throughout the text. This certainly seems the case with the horrifying story of During the Sorbian. In this case, Duke Bořivoj I, after defeating and killing Vlastislav of Lučane, spared his young son "moved by compassion for him ... [and] had mercy on his young age and small size."[106] The duke left they boy in the care of During the Sorbian (technically a subject of the child), who treacherously killed the boy with an axe, in hopes of getting the duke's favor by doing the dirty work of removing a future rival. Instead of favor, During incurs Bořivoj's wrath and condemnation, and During committed suicide. Lisa Wolverton noted that much of Cosmas' message is against the violence and conniving of his last two decades, where kin fought against kin and pretenders rose to fight for title of duke in the Czech lands.[107] This story shows the pertinent contrasts, a duke's compassion for the child of a rival and the fitting reward for betrayers. Cosmas admits this story is of dubious truthfulness, but clearly thinks it worth including in his narrative as a warning for those who might rise up against their lords. An innocent child served the role of making this deed more horrifying a thus more effective. The child, in other words, is an instrument of ducal power, not a subject of ducal interest.

---

        dukes who became kings (particularly Vratislav II), thus altering the balance of power between kings and nobility).

104 Cosmas of Prague, *The Chronicle of the Czechs*, translated by Lisa Wolverton (Washington: Catholic University of America Press, 2012), 39–45. A boy does briefly feature in this story, but only tells Libuše's emissaries that they have arrived at the right town.

105 Cosmas, *The Chronicle of the Czechs*, 48–53.

106 Ibid., 60.

107 Wolverton, *The Chronicle of the Czechs*, 3–4.

Much like in Gallus, but to a lesser degree, the actions of parents for their young children could foretell and shape the future destinies of their children. This is clearly seen in the life of Strachkvas (whose name meant "terrifying feast), who was born during the fateful feast where his father, Boleslav, had Saint Wenceslaus killed. Fearing divine retribution on his son, Boleslav promised his son to God and the church if he should survive, so Strachkvas was educated in a monastery. Nevertheless, despite his parents' love and foresight, Strachkvas still reflected the ugliness of his father's action, and when he attempted to take advantage of St. Adalbert's flight from Prague and assume the bishopric, he was instead possessed (and presumably destroyed) by demons.[108] While Pazt's hospitality could bless Poland through his son Siemovit, the cold-blooded murder by a father in Bohemia could foreshadow the ignominious end of his son.

Despite such superficial similarities between Gallus and Cosmas, there were substantial differences. While Gallus downplays sexuality in the young, noting only lawful marriages, Cosmas Břetislav I kidnaps his beautiful German bride Judith against the wishes of father Otto. On hearing of Otto's initial rejection of his entreaties, Cosmas tells us "that yet the more difficult the path to love, the more robust a fire a of Venus, the mind of the youth rages, just as Etna roils with fire."[109] Not only is young lust discussed in Cosmas' *Chronicle*, but it is even celebrated, in contrast to Gallus' comparative stodginess. Břetislav is Cosmas' ideal duke in many ways, and the fact that he chooses to adorn his biography with an extended account of Judith's kidnapping says, among many other things, much about the rhetoric related to youthfulness that he wished to tap into, along with the violence endemic in medieval masculinity.

7 Conclusions

After examining the most salient comparisons to Gallus, we are able to see that, despite sharing similar tropes and themes with other authors, Gallus is unique in his treatment of children and childhood. Children and youth show up often in Gallus, despite the fact that this is a work primarily about and for adults, and was written at the court of an adult (Bolesław III), and was written at least partially with the purpose of exonerating one adult and casting shadows on another (Zbigniew). While there are a number of useful insights about children in medieval Poland that might be learned from Gallus, we have seen that often stories and references to childhood have their own purpose in

---

108 Cosmas, *The Chronicle of the Czechs*, 65–66, 81–83.
109 Ibid., 102.

the text. Prophetic actions of and including children bolster dynastic legitimacy and the growth of young Piasts in virtue and valor was an important component of demonstrating their right to rule and hinting at God's blessing of dynasty. Mieszko I's blindness and restoration cemented the Piasts' role in Christianizing Poland, while the boyhood deeds of Bolesław III both aided Poland in its need as well as illuminated the qualities that made him fit to rule. The failure of Zbigniew to embody these same qualities were further proof of his inadequacy. Similarly, we have seen how language referencing childhood strongly mirrored position and role within the dynasty. *Puer* was connected to dependent children of living dukes, *iuvenis* to young dukes with full control of their patrimony but still growing into their new role, while adult status was for dukes at the height of their achievement and power. Finally, Gallus clearly presents childhood as vulnerable phase, one that required emotional and material support from parents. Failure for a parent to live up to those expectations could justify even a child's rebellion against the parent.

Methodologically speaking, it is within the context of rhetoric that one finds a useful way to tease out concepts of childhood in Gallus, as it allows us to get glimpses of cultural expectations and assumptions that were presumably shared at the time. Instead of ripping passages about children out of context and trying to distill what they mean for "childhood," the method employed here may help us escape our own prejudices about the meaning of childhood, and aid us in seeing how children fit in with larger currents of meaning in a given situation. With that in mind, a few, partial conclusions may be drawn on which I will expand at the end of the book. First, the sheer number of references to childhood, and the the fact that it was deemed important enough to include in the rhetorical strategies of the *Deeds of the Princes of the Poles* suggests that children were on the minds of people in medieval Poland, and that their social potential and even actions were deemed important to both present and future. Second, children were often thought of in terms of their future potential. This is a theme that will appear in the next chapter on the Henryków Book. This does not mean that childhood actions were insignificant in and of themselves, but that child actions, and even childish actions, were considered significant even to the world of adults. Along these lines, we have seen that growth in behavior and character were expected of children, and that despite royal blood, fitness to rule was not a given. Gallus hints at a number of places that childhood education and upbringing was important connected with a child's later actions, and even implies that this is at least a partial aim of his writing:

As it is a holy task to preach in a church of the lives and passions of the saints, so it is a glorious one to recite in schools and in palaces the triumphs and victories of dukes and kings. And as the lives and passions of the saints when preached in churches instruct the minds of the faithful in religion, so the exploits and victories of the dukes and kings fire the hearts of soldiers to bravery when they are recited in schools and capitols.[110]

Children may be born blessed by God and have inborn virtue, but they still had to be educated to develop these traits to a usable degree. Another important point is related to the terminology connected with childhood. Scholars have spend much time discussing age categories of childhood connected with words like *puer*, but they had comparatively less interest in seeing how words connect with concrete roles of children and youths within their families. Piotr Górecki has suggested that social categories in early medieval Poland were less a rigid system of classification, but instead a network of social roles, and this way of thinking about social categories seems to have relevance to the discussion of the place of children in society.[111] Finally, Gallus strongly suggests that children were not thought of as slaves of their parents and communities, with no emotional attachments present, but instead were deserving of protection, care, and love. While none of this is explicitly stated, it emerges by following and understanding the rhetoric of the text. The townsmen of Wrocław were naturally expected to burn in anger against those who would threaten the crying young boy Bolesław III and thereby support his claims to be the rightful heir.

110 Gallus Anonymus, *The Deeds*, 213 and 215.
111 Piotr. Górecki, "Words, concepts, and phenomena: knighthood, lordship and the early Polish nobility (c. 1050–1150)," in *Nobles and Nobility in Medieval Europe. Concepts, Origins, Transformations*, ed. Anne J. Duggan (Woodbridge/Rochester: Boydell Press, 2000), 115–55.

CHAPTER 3

Vincent Kadłubek and Thinking with Children

While Gallus Anonymous was the first and, perhaps, the most famous chronicler in the Polish lands during the period under discussion, Vincent (or Vincentius) Kadłubek (1150–1223)[1] was by far the most sophisticated and erudite. However, little is known about his life. Born in Poland within the "landowning knighthood" and perhaps into a noble clan,[2] and educated in the west, perhaps in France or Italy, he returned to Poland sometime in the 1180s to serve in the Cathedral of Kraków as a canon. In the dynastic struggles that divided Poland at this time, Vincent came out on the side of Duke Kazimierz II the Just. It was Kazimierz II[3] who commissioned the *Chronicle of the Kings and the Princes of the Poles*, and it was completed sometime in the early thirteenth century before Vincent's elevation to the bishopric of Kraków in 1208.[4] He remained active in Polish, church, and international affairs, and attended the Fourth Lateran Council in 1215, in the company of a large delegation of Polish churchmen. Nevertheless, beyond this general outline of his life, very little is known about the origins of the man himself, including his real name, his family, their holdings, and his writings themselves provide minimal cues about their author.[5]

---

1 Dates on his life vary, these are taken from Darius Maria von Güttner-Sporzyński, "Bishop Vincentius of Cracow and his *Chronica Polonorum*," in *Writing History in Medieval Poland. Bishop Vincentius of Cracow and the Chronica Polonorum*, edited by Darius Maria von Güttner-Sporzyński (Turnhout: Brepols, 2017), 1–2. Güttner-Sporzyński acknowledges that these dates are debatable.
2 Jacek Maciejewski, "Vincentius's background and family origins: the evidence and hypotheses," in *Writing History in Medieval Poland. Bishop Vincentius of Cracow and the Chronica Polonorum*, edited by Darius Maria von Güttner-Sporzyński (Turnhout: Brepols, 2017), 21–23. Even this is primarily known through an examination of charters for Vincent's land donations to the Cistercians.
3 While most scholars agree that Kazimierz II was the patron, others disagree. See Józef Dobosz, "Motives and inspirations: an exploration of when and why the Chronica Polonorum was written," in *Writing History in Medieval Poland. Bishop Vincentius of Cracow and the Chronica Polonorum*, edited by Darius Maria von Güttner-Sporzyński (Leiden/Boston: Brill, 2017), 51–55.
4 Dobosz, "Motives and inspirations," 44–50. discusses at length different theories for the exact timeline of the writing the Chronicle. The issue is undoubtedly not settled.
5 Roman Grodecki, "Mistrz Wincenty Kadłubek, biskup krakowski," in *Rocznik Krakowski Vol. XIX*, edited by Jozef Muczkowski (Kraków: Wydawnictwo Towarzystwo Miłośników Historii i Zabytków Krakowa, 1923), 31–35.

Vincent's writings are complex, but a number of themes and objectives clearly permeate his writings. First, as Edward Skibiński points out, Vincent's discussion of all rulers and major characters takes the form of the medieval rhetorical genre of *de virtutibus et vitiis* (about virtues and vices), in which an evaluation of the morals of the actors, rather than a strict chronological timeline, guides the flow of the narrative.[6] That is in fact designed to serve as a larger example to those of present and future times. But to whom is this example directed? In contrast to Gallus' concentration on the Piasts, Vincent is far more concerned with the *regnum* ("realm") of Poland.[7] and in the general body politic, both prince and nobility, of the Polish realm, to which he refers as *res publica* ("Republic," or as later used in Poland, "Commonwealth").[8] Vincent was concerned with the moral quality of *res publica* and argued against ambition, pride, intemperance, immorality, or any attempt to destabilize the social order or move by one's own ambition outside one's prescribed role in society. Failure to live by virtue would cause disaster, as demonstrated by the vices of previous rulers of Poland. No dynasty or line of succession was safe, if tarnished by vice,[9] and even commoners, if endowed with virtue and divine favor, could be elevated to glory. Vincent "placed and defined his prince's legitimate authority, and to an extent justified it, in terms of the obligations and service the ruler provided to his subjects." In that respect, Vincent's is an approach different from that of Gallus, for whom "the right to rule was divinely sanctioned and its nature was perfect because the Piast dynasty was its custodian."[10] Vincent's message, however, was not for everyone, but for the elite. According to him,

---

6   Edward Skibiński, "The narrative in Vincentius's *Chronicle*," in *Writing History in Medieval Poland. Bishop Vincentius of Cracow and the Chronica Polonorum*, edited by Darius Maria von Güttner-Sporzyński (Turnhout: Brepols, 2017), 101–102.

7   Skibiński, "The narrative," 100.

8   Gallus only used the phrase *res publica* on a few occasions, most notably for the reign of Bolesław I, in relation to the rule over a large Christian empire and the duties of the ruler to the people. See Paweł Żmudzki, "Vincentius's construct of a nation: Poland as *res publica*," in *Writing History in Medieval Poland. Bishop Vincentius of Cracow and the Chronica Polonorum*, edited by Darius Maria von Güttner-Sporzyński (Turnhout: Brepols, 2017), 178. The notion of Poland as *res publica* persisted long after Vincent's death and is one of his greatest contributions to the Polish self-image (Güttner-Sporzyński, "Bishop Vincentius," 9–10).

9   Żmudzki, "Vincentius' construct," 193.

10   Przemysław Wiszewski, "The power of a prince: Vincentius on the dynasty's source of power," in *Writing History in Medieval Poland. Bishop Vincentius of Cracow and the Chronica Polonorum*, edited by Darius Maria von Güttner-Sporzyński (Turnhout: Brepols, 2017), 200.

only those with high minds, appropriately prepared could understand and appreciate his work.[11]

The *Chronicle*, in the first three of its four books, takes the form of a dialogue between John/Jan Gryfita, the Archbishop of Gniezno (1149–1167) and Matthew, the bishop of Kraków (1143–1166). Matthew usually introduces episodes from the history of Poland, to which John then replies with parallels from ancient history, as well as philosophical, moral or juridical reflections. John's philosophical reflections reveal a deep knowledge of a range of biblical and classical texts, including Plato's *Timaeus*, Cicero's *Cato Maior de senectute*, Seneca's *Epistulae Morales ad Lucilium*, and Boethius' *De consolatione philosophiae*.[12] Without a doubt, Vincent's worldview and work were shaped by the twelfth century Renaissance, and are best understood in that context.[13]

Vincent built upon the foundations laid by Gallus, but his work and its overall purpose are strikingly different. The first book is a much augmented mythical account of the origins of the Polish nation, which is projected far beyond the origins of the Piast dynasty as seen in Gallus. Vincent invents an ancient Polish state rival to the Roman Empire. He also introduces a host of fanciful characters, including Krak, a dragon-slayer and the founder of the Polish community in Kraków. Only at the end of Book I does one reach material that overlaps with that in Gallus, beginning with the story of Pompilius II (who is named Popiel in Gallus). Book II covers much the material discussed by Gallus and ends with a moralizing discourse on the reasons for the ugly end of Zbigniew at the hands of his brother, Duke Bolesław III. Book III and IV deal with the division of the kingdom between the sons of Bolesław III and their constant struggles, while the country is divided by each new generation, and reaches chronologically all the way to the thirteenth century, while covering the reign of Vincent's benefactor, and youngest son of Bolesław III, Kazimierz II.

Children and childhood (and age in general) are themes that, while not as overt as in Gallus, are nevertheless crucial in a number of respects, and often play a highly relevant, rhetorical role. Along with the common trope of childish incompetence used to berate under-performing, non-virtuous adults, Vincent employs childhood as a sign of the future, in a way similar to Gallus.

---

11   Skibiński, "The narrative," 101–102. On this topic see also Grodecki, "Mistrz Wincenty," 58–60.
12   Kałuza and Calma, 102.
13   For more on how Vincentius fits into the context of the twelfth-century Renaissance and how his use of the classics compares to western authors, see Zénon Kałuża, "Vincentius's *Chronicle* and intellectual culture of the twelfth century," in *Writing History in Medieval Poland. Bishop Vincentius of Cracow and the Chronica Polonorum*, edited by Darius Maria von Güttner-Sporzyński (Turnhout: Brepols, 2017), 139–73.

Love between parents and children, and the expectations created on the basis of that bond are a constant theme, as is the shadow of fear that both parents and the kingdom may suffer from incompetent, disobedient, and evil children. Filial piety is a particular obsession for Vincent, and bonds created in one's childhood to parents and siblings are regarded as highly significant. In sum, children play a distinct and important role in Vincent's wide project of encouraging virtuous behavior among members of the Polish elite.

1 Vincent's Overlap with Gallus

Because Vincent adapted and reworked much of the material found in Gallus for his own ends, it it is revealing to compare Vincent's treatment of childhood with that of Gallus. As noted, Vincent adds a completely new origins story for Poland, projecting Polish history far back into antiquity, while including famous Romans and barbarians from classical literature. Fantastic and completely fabricated tales fill the entire first book of Vincent's narrative, in which children are infrequently discussed. Instead, a heroic age of adults is posited for Poland, which connects it to Roman grandeur. A few young people do appear, but not as part of any larger strategy related to childhood comparable to Gallus' three initiation rituals. Furthermore, the "children" involved are not that young, for all appear to have reached puberty. This is the case of the tale of chieftain Wanda, the daughter of Krakus. Her *maiden* beauty impressed the invading Alamann barbarians so much that on seeing her, their chief committed suicide and the enemy army retreated. Vincent describes Wanda as *virguncula* ("young maiden") and she is praised for her elegant form, the abundance of grace, and the maturity of her council.[14] In a similar vein, older children appear in the story about Krak and his sons. Another youth, Leszko II, demonstrates his future capability as leader of the Poles through his prowess at horse race.

While children as such often fade into the background of these mythical beginnings, childhood is more frequently used as a rhetorical concept. The most extensive and most telling example is that of the story of Pompillius II. Popiel is not a particularly sympathetic character in Gallus, and for that reason he is replaced by the Piasts. In Vincent, Pompillius becomes a full-fledged villain of epic proportions, described as cruelly ambitious, tyrannical, disloyal,

---

14   Vincent Kadłubek, *Chronicle of the Poles*, edited by Marian Plezia and translated by Eduard Mühle (Darmstadt: Wissenschaftliche Buchgesellschaft, 2014), 100.

cowardly, faithless, and conniving.[15] Gallus' Popiel fails to practice hospitality before being devoured by mice, and to that story Vincent adds more detail. His Pompillius II kills his co-ruling uncles, who had ruled peacefully under the leadership of his father. Pretending to be sick, he invited them all to bid him farewell, and then passed around to all a cup into which he had poured poison. The divine retribution for that horrible crime comes in the form of mice growing out of the deceased uncles' bodies (which were left unburied) to devour Pompillius II and his family.

It is in the context of that story that Pompilius II's wife urges him to kill his uncles. Her argument hinges upon unfavorable comparison between Pompilius and children:

> After all, you are a boy (*puer es*) and you must do nothing but play. Those people [your uncles] keep you busy with such trivial things, as if they were important matters, but not in order to make you wiser through advice, but because they wait for the opportunity to make fun of you, or at least to put a stop to your youngish desires (*vota iuventutis*). Oh, you totally laughable old men, who in order to look younger, are looking for senile youths (*decrepitos adolescentes*). Choose whether you are slave or free, whether you are your own man or that of a stranger, whether you will be happy or unfortunate.[16]

Though a ruling adult, Pompilius appears here as a boy (*puer*) whose only concern is to play. His wife implies that his uncles are using him, merely giving him the appearance and feeling of ruling by distracting him with unimportant matters, and then mocking him once his gaze has turned. To her, his own designs appear as childish, giving at least some legitimacy to the actions of his uncles. It is interesting to note that once done eviscerating her own husband, she turns the sarcasm against the tottering uncles who reclaim their own youthful power by playing with a feeble fool, such as her husband. Vincent's use of Pompilius' wife to present childhood as effectively spurring murder when set in contrast with adult masculinity, speaks volumes about his audience's expectations.

By contrast, while borrowing from Gallus, Vincent minimizes the importance of the childhood in the story of the early Piasts. For example, while repeating the story of the initiation feast for Siemovit (*pro initianda paruuli*),[17] his comparatively shorter account, lays stress more on Pompilius' lack of hospitality,

---

15   See especially the description in Kadłubek, *Chronicle of the Poles*, 19:1.
16   Kadłubek, *Chronicle of the Poles*, 19:7–9. All translations in this chapter are mine.
17   Ibid., 132.

and the miracle that occurred at the feast. Moreover, Siemovit's initiation story appears in an extended parenthetical explanation, not as an independent component of a longer rhetorical sequence. Before being told of the miraculous feast, one reads that Siemovit "took up effort, grew up in zeal, and excelled in virtue"[18] for his future had long been foretold: "he, supported by his virtues not theirs, first was made commander of the soldiers and finally took on the majesty of rule, which they asserted because of a sense of foreboding about him almost since early childhood (*pene infantie crepundiis*)."[19] It is only then, as an explanation, that the initiation story is introduced.

A similar adaptation is visible in the case of the hair-cutting ceremony of the blind child Mieszko. Vincent interrupts the story to tell of Mieszko's immorality prior to his marriage to Dąbrowka.[20] Mieszko's blindness is reinterpreted as an allegory for the nation's error:

> For to what do you attribute these seven years of this boyhood (*pueritie*) other than the sum of our foolishness, our errors? For the number seven serves as [a symbol] of the whole in many instances.[21]

Vincent departs from Gallus at this point by inserting a list of Biblical passages pertaining to the meaning of the number seven: Jesus' injunction to forgive not seven, but seventy times seven (Mt. 18:22); Elisha's instructions to Naaman to wash seven times for healing (2 Kings 5:10); the seven deadly sins; and the seven angels mentioned by Raphael (Tobit 12:15). Gallus' story of prophecy has thus turned into an allegory for the sin(s) of the nation, a quite appropriate strategy for an author (Vincent) who he has already undermined the centrality of the early Piasts in order to replace them with a myth about the origin of the Polish people. Gallus' initiation rituals at the beginning of his chronicle, have now become a sideshow in a larger scheme of moralizing the beginnings of Poland. This may well be because Vincent (and his audience) regarded those initiation rites as barbarous. Bishop Matthew in fact asks whether the custom of hair-cutting descended from superstition. In his response, John connects the hair-cutting practice with the ancient Roman tradition of a father who either recognized officially his son at a certain age or adopted a boy as his son: "The recognition can happen to those who are of age (*qui sui iuris sunt*), while

---

18   Ibid.
19   Ibid.
20   Ibid., 140–141.
21   Ibid., 142–143.

adoption is for family sons who are still under the authority of their parents."[22] In other words, the latter are children under 7 years of age, an indication that Vincent applied the terms of the Roman law to his explanation of the "superstitious" meaning of the hair-cutting rituals in Poland. Such rhetorical use of legal texts reminds one of Paweł Żmudzki's observation, according to which Vincent's use of Gallus cannot be regarded as similar to that of a modern historian drawing on his primary sources. Instead of distilling external "facts" from their sources, medieval authors interacted with their sources and altered them according to the prestige of the author and in accordance with their own narrative goals. Vincent altered Gallus whenever and wherever he thought that he could tell the story better, or more according to his own narrative strategies. That is why he rarely changed the chronology of Gallus' stories, but reconfigured details, as well as the nature of events.[23]

A good example of Vincent's use of Gallus is the story of Kazimierz I's exile and return. In Gallus, traitors and malicious men rise up after Mieszko II's death. Kazimierz's mother is banished, but the boy is kept as a figurehead. When he grows up, they conspire against him as well, and and he is forced to take refuge in Hungary. There, however, King Stephen I throws him in jail, in order to satisfy the Bohemians, who take advantage of the ruler's absence to attack Poland. Before returning to Poland, young Kazimierz spends time being groomed at the court of the Holy Roman emperor.[24] Vincent introduces two versions of this story. In one of them, Kazimierz's father dies while his German mother rules as regent. She is a bad ruler surrounding herself with foreign Germans, which prompts the Poles to rise up and remove Kazimierz's mother from power. However, they are overzealous, and send him into exile as well. Furthermore, this version of the story furthermore contains no information about the young duke's reception and stay in the Holy Roman Empire. This is most likely because of its deep anti-German sentiment.[25]

A second version of the story appears in Chapter 14 of Book 2. Here Kazimierz's mother dies in childbirth, thus completely eliminating unwelcome connections to Germany. The threat now comes from an evil stepmother, who constantly conspires against the little boy. However, Mieszko II loves his son, as he sees his first wife in Kazimierz. The ruthless stepmother then hires a man to dispose of the boy, but the man leaves Kazimierz at a monastery:

---

22 Ibid., 138.
23 Żmudzki, "Vincentius' construct," 143–44.
24 Ibid., 150–51.
25 Ibid., 156–57.

> They say that the mother of his child [Mieszko II's first wife] died when giving birth to him [Kazimierz], but that he [was] ... a second Hercules ... The father, who at one moment kissed the baby's mouth, at another stroked the delicate little breast, often breathed heavily, sobbed silently, lost in tears, although he kept the ashes of his deceased wife in his heart forever. The face of the son was in fact a mirror of his mother. As the deceitful stepmother noticed that, she came up with new ways of deceit, put aside all restrictions, and tried to bring the little one to death, so that her dead rival could not shine through her child in the present, and so that in the end, her own children could succeed to the throne.[26]

In order to garner sympathy for young Kazimiez. Vincent opposes the evil stepmother to the innocent, youthful protagonist. Like Hercules, Kazimierz is whisked away from danger until the time when he would reemerge and lead his people. The parallel suggests that the audience familiar with Ovid's *Metamorphoses* was invited to see the evil stepmother as Juno and Mieszko II as Jupiter. However, the insertion of that mythological reference is far more than a show of classical education. Vincent was clearly concerned here with telling a better story than that of Gallus. He reduced the number of characters and adapted Gallus' story to a much simpler narrative, in which the child is saved by the goodness (virtue) of a commoner.[27] Childhood here is not simply a trope, but a narrative strategy designed to serve moralizing goals.

While comparing Kazimierz to Hercules, Vincent never compared Bolesław III Wrymouth to Mars in the way Gallus did, as "the child of Mars." Mars does appear in Vincent's chronicle, but in a different light, with no relation to childhood. Instead, of *puer Martis*, Vincent's Bolesław III is *Martis alumnus* (Mars' protégé).[28] He may have done so under the influence of other medieval authors in the twelfth and thirteenth centuries, who compared or associated Mars with adults, not with children. But he also had a different attitude towards Bolesław III whom he regarded not as a young prince, like Gallus, but as a mighty, older adult ruler of a unified Poland, and the father of Vincent's own patron.

---

26 Kadłubek, *Chronicle of the Poles*, 154–156.
27 Żmudzki, "Vincentius' construct," 156–57.
28 Kadłubek, *Chronicle of the Poles*, 26:1.

Vincent's Bolesław III is also rushed from the state of infancy directly into adulthood. When youth is mentioned, it is often in unfavorable terms. Duke Władysław Herman (1079–1102) and his son Bolesław III are unable to counteract the depredations of Sieciech, the former because he was too old, the latter because he was too young:

> indeed decrepit age is the nurse of nonsense and tender infancy is the nurse of all [kinds of] weaknesses. Thus, neither the king nor the child were competent [competere] for this burden, since they had neither the counsel nor the strength for it. Indeed, one does not set an old, rotten trunk as a pillar in a building, nor does one support a ruined wall through a mastic shrub.[29]

Following this brief mentions of his infancy, Bolesław III suddenly appears as a fully-formed, martial, vigorous young man. Vincent paid no attention to stories of boys fighting wild animals or sneaking out into the night to join raids against Poland's enemies. Instead, Bolesław III is directly contrasted to Zbigniew:

> Although still a young teenager, Bolesław surpassed him [Zbigniew] in his maternal virtues, and was above him in terms of the most honorable graciousness of his manners, so that the elders admit [that while] the grey hair was not in the teenager's chin (beard), it was in his spirit. You would think that the men of the council, whose heads are made white by the gray hair, were babbling infants [*respersos infantissimos*] when compared to his wise counsel.[30]

Not only has Bolesław III surpassed his much older brother in manly virtue, but is now superior in wisdom to old men. Vincent takes the *puer senex* trope to a natural conclusion: Bolesław III moves directly from an innocent, helpless infant, to a teenager who is already the venerable, wise old man that he was to become in the minds of subsequent generations in Poland. During Vincent's lifetime Bolesław III was already regarded as a mature, wise ruler of Poland's past, directly comparably to his namesake, Gallus' favorite hero. The emphasis on Bolesław III's many qualities as an adult left no room for his description as a prodigious child.

---

29   Ibid., 22:19.
30   Ibid., 24:1.

2   Parental Love of Children ... and the Virtue of Violating It

Like Gallus, Vincent highlights the joy that children bring to their parents. A poem inserted in his chronicle (which has otherwise far fewer verses than Gallus') is meant to convey the distress of Duke Władysław Herman and his wife Judith of Bohemia felt at not having children. Vincent introduces a letter that Judith and Władysław sent to the abbot of the Benedictine monastery of St. Giles in southern France. The letter mentions the "sting of sadness," and the "complete fruitlessness of sterility, which not only takes away paternal solace (*paternum solatium*), but also inflicts the grave disgrace of childlessness (*orbitatis obprobrium*)."[31] Not having children is not just a social disgrace, but also a deeply personal, emotional wound. A prayer on behalf of Judith and Władysław that the St. Giles monks recited after a three-day fast, concludes:

> Grant us [our desire], why do you hesitate? The spiked brambles are given an heir,
> The cherry tree is given a cherry, why are we without an heir?
> Grant us, that we not lack a shoot, that we not lack male offspring!
> Hear our vows and prayers, grant us, for you are able![32]

Personal grief at childlessness is combined here with fears of not having any male heir, a preoccupation of all dukes and noblemen mentioned in the Henryków Book as well. Without an heir, the realm would descend into chaos.

Vincent also discusses the value of children in episodes in which patriotic men are willing to sacrifice their children for the good of the fatherland. Virtue, Vincent's main theme, thus translates into the ability of brave and noble men to sacrifice what they held as their greatest values. In his efforts to destroy the dragon who was terrorizing the people living near the Vistula, Krak (to whom Vincent refers by the Latin name Gracchus) does not hesitate to put his own sons on the line: "Krak did not consider the calamity of this situation, so that the son was more loving towards the fatherland than a father towards his son, and with his sons gathered together secretly, he decided upon a plan. He said 'the enemy of laziness is strength, of old age is foolishness, of youth is sluggishness.'"[33] Krak's love for the country overcomes his parental love for his sons. He does not hesitate to put them in danger in order to get rid of the monster.

---

31   Ibid., 182.
32   Ibid.
33   Ibid., 98.

Similarly, at the siege of Głogów in 1109, Emperor Henry V uses child hostages taken from the town as human shields, in order to protect his siege machines:

> Oh, what truly manly, truly iron spirits. Oh, what steadfast men, who are not charmed by the splendor of gold, and are not bent by the spirit of imperial majesty! They are not terrified by the attack of the enemy, and neither does the severity of their labors, and neither are they softened by tender feelings towards their own children. For because the fathers furiously revolt without heed to their children, the children are now bound to machines and and exposed to the stones and arrows of their fathers; then, under the eyes of their fathers, they are tortured with all kinds of torments, but to no avail. But the decision of the fathers, made with unshakable force, is that the fathers should lose their children rather than that the fatherland should be despoiled, and that the honor of liberty is more honorable than the honor of freedom [for their children].[34]

When the stalwart defenders of Głogów make the terrible choice to fire upon their children, that was because their love for the country was greater than the love for their children. The underlying assumption is therefore that parents normally love their children the most. The defenders of Głogów could have been persuaded to lay down their weapons by many other ways—awe of the emperor, gold, the severity of their labors, and fear of death. Vincent elaborates rhetorically only the loss of children, no doubt because he knew that his audience would recognize that as what the defenders valued most, as it was the most valuable thing that Vincent could come up with to praise their heroism.

If parents' anguished attacks on their own children was a source of virtuous horror, in more ordinary circumstances Vincent stresses that kinsmen were expected to care for their younger kin. Bolesław IV kept the teenager Kazimierz II in his own house:

> But for a while he entertained Kazimierz as a teenager (*adolescentulum*), not by any means to begrudge him the grace of participating [in public life], but so as not to expose the tender vine to the wind of recklessness. For no supporting pillar of ignorance should be left to itself, and because freedom for the youth is what oil is to the flame. Therefore, as somebody has said "Nature has woven linen diapers for babes (*infantie*), and experience has cast golden chains for teenagers (*adolescentie*)."[35]

---

34   Ibid., 254.
35   Ibid., 288.

Vincent approves of the sheltering and care for orphaned youths like Kazimierz II, suggesting that leaving those of his age to themselves would lead to disaster through the recklessness of youth. Guidance, and not free reign, was necessary to direct youths towards productive lives. This passage suggests that Vincent did not see young people as bound by their lineage and inborn traits, but required nurture to evolve into mature individuals. One can hardly miss the other implication of the passage, namely that some could see such care as an attempt to keep the youth from getting rightful place in society.

3   Filial and Familial Piety

While parents were expected to love their children, the latter were also expected to be obedient, especially to their fathers. Such expectations applied not only to small children, but also to young adults. Vincent's Bolesław III is the paragon of filial piety, a son who literally lived with his father around his neck.

The context of such remarks is the 1099 rebellion of Sieciech against the the division of the kingdom between the Władysław's two sons, and the increasing marginalization of the palatine. The half-brothers Bolesław III and Zbigniew worked together to defeat him on the battlefield, and then to remove Sieciech from the position of Palatine. However, Vincent credited only young Bolesław III with this accomplishment (even though Bolesław at that time must have been in his mid-teens):

> And so he (Sieciech) brought together a rebellion, struck the spark of sedition, ignited the fires of hate, and promoted discord between father and sons. But Bolesław did not only restrain this revolt, but also eradicated it at its source. He united the dissenting parts of the kingdom and he occupied the provinces in act of sedition under the said Sieciech, and he restored them to his father, driven as much by piety towards his father as [by concern] with acting for the benefit of the fatherland. For he paid such great honor, such great devotion to his father, that he ordered the name of his father to be inscribed in a plate of gold, which he ordered to be placed on his chest suspended by a gold chain around his neck. This was so that, as if his father was present, it would serve as a yoke of sonship, a reminder of the reverence for the father, a custodian of virtue everywhere with him. So that the plate might suggest frequently: speak as if your father always heard it, act as if your father always saw it. For it is shameful to enact in the eyes of your father wicked deeds and shameful

words. And so greatly did he bind himself up with such veneration that you would think he was not venerating his father, but the divine spirit. And this love did not dissipate after his father died, but he was said to have worn black clothes for five years afterwards. Because virtue is a habit of a well-ordered mind, but a habit that is difficult to change, he transferred whatever he owed to his father even to his illegitimate brother [Zbigniew] and he guarded the secret of his brother's shame with no less earnest sincerity, despite the fact that he knew he was lurking at his heel.[36]

Sieciech may have planned to break down the bonds of fealty between father and sons, but his machinations led to nothing because the young Bolesław III was willing to do everything in the name of his father and to return the stolen territory to him at the end of the insurrection—even to the extent of allowing his conniving brother to receive his part of the inheritance back. His love of fatherland and his love of his father Władysław Herman is then illustrated by a detail which entirely concocted by Vincent (and has not even a remote parallel in Gallus). Wearing a chain with his father's image while the latter lived, working to uphold the dignity of his words and actions for the honor of his father, and mourning his father's passing with sincere and visible grief, Bolesław III was adorned with virtue by means of his self-less, pious actions, and thus brought peace and prosperity to his country.

Like Gallus, Vincent has no sympathy for Zbigniew, whom he often contrasts unfavorably to his younger brother. In the context of filial piety, Zbigniew is a disappointing child, who has repeatedly failed his father. The clearest example of that is his rebellion in order to seize his birthright from his father at the instigation of Břetislav II of Bohemia. Vincent accuses Zbigniew of taking advantage of his old father and his immature brother. As a faithless, rebellious son, Zbigniew was Władysław Herman the "sword of his own loins" which was drawn against himself.[37] In other words, Zbigniew was a self-inflicted wound because of Władysław's previous lust. Zbigniew's mother is called a prostitute and even his name supposedly means "maternal shame."[38]

Like Zbigniew, Duke Odon rebelled against his father Mieszko III in 1177. He supposedly felt threatened by his father's change of plans in matters of dynastic succession in favor of his sons from his second wife, Eudoxia. Odon therefore allied himself with his uncle Kazimierz II the Just, High Duke of Poland,

---

36   Ibid., 194.
37   Ibid., 184.
38   Ibid.

and with his cousin Bolesław I the Tall, the duke of Wrocław. Vincent portrays the rebellion as a violent, illegitimate grab for power, rooted in utter disrespect for familial bonds:

> But even as they had pledged themselves by holy law to die for him on any occasion, they forgot both their fidelity and their prince. But even the most dear to him forgot about the many benefits he has bestowed upon them and fell away from him. Among these was his first-born, Duke Odon, the most ruthless enemy, who strived to eradicate the root of his own tribe. He brought the flames down on his own head and presses for the downfall of his father with the greatest obstinacy, not to imitate a certain Bactrian, but to keep the sons of his stepmother, to whom his father has promised the succession, from rising to the throne. For the above-mentioned King of the Bactrians, Eucratides [II], having been made co-ruler with his father, killed him out of ambition, and as if he had cut down an enemy and not his father he drove his chariot through his blood and ordered to body to be left unburied, but not without retribution.[39]

Of all rebels, Odon is presented as the worst, because of pushing aside his own father's kindness towards him, and a desire to destroy his own family and its right to rule over Poland. The parallel to Eucratides II (who lived in the mid second century BC) betrays not only Vincent's knowledge of Justin's *Epitome*, a work that was very popular in the twelfth and thirteenth centuries, but also to draw a contrast between a parricide and an ungrateful son. The narrator John intervenes at this point to bring to the fore the question of filial piety by means of a comparison between adapted from a Eucratides II and his own son, terrified and appalled by what his father had done to his grandfather. Fleeing to the forest, the son soon got lost. On the point of starving, he ate a deadly root and was lying on the ground near death, when a snake, drawn to the poison, entered the boy's body, and inadvertently induced vomiting, thus causing the poison to exit the child's body. As the son was throwing up the lethal substance, Eucratides, his father, found him during a hunting trip. With tears flowing on his face, he rushed to kiss his mouth. But the same snake that had saved the boy, came from inside his body to bite Eucratides with deadly poison. While the pious boy survived, Eucratides II suffered a very painful death. Vincent concludes: "Can you recognize the divine justice here? For the serpent returned the piety of the youth [*adolescens*] by healing him, and the serpent avenged the sin of parricide on the offender by killing him. From one of them

---

39   Ibid., 326–329.

one can see how much the child's devotion deserved grace, and from the other how much punishment must be feared for the one who despises reverence for parents."[40]

Vincent viewed the violation of both filial piety and parental care of children as a symptom of broad social dysfunction. To him, the turmoil of the twelfth century started with Bolesław III's Act of Succession (1138), through which the kingdom was divided among his sons, with the oldest son, Władysław II, residing in Kraków as *princeps*, and his three brothers ruling their own domains under his leadership. Throughout the fourth book of his Chronicle, Vincent condemned the senseless violence that accompanied the struggle between brothers that erupted soon after that.[41] He describes the period of fratricidal strife as one in which "no son pays the father respect, no father pardons the son, no brother acknowledges brother."[42] In the absence of filial piety and brotherly love, Poland is brought to ruin.

But metaphors of filial piety may also be invoked in contexts that have nothing to do either with living or actual human parents or children. In a letter supposedly written to Magnus, the head of the province of Silesia, the local opposition party demanded the restoration of the exiled Zbigniew (Władysław Herman's son), in order to counteract the voracious palatine Sieciech. Magnus was the temporary guardian of Zbigniew, who lived at that time in Wrocław, and the opponents of Sieciech hoped the youth would become a rallying point. (The subsequent revolt, however, when it did erupt, was interpreted as a rebellion against Duke Władysław.) Like Gallus, Vincent presents Zbigniew as a quintessential rebel, but the Silesian opponents also applied the image of the disobedient child to Sieciech:

> Exceedingly cruel, exceedingly wretched, is the one who is not grieved by not only the suppression, but also the loss of liberty. And he is not a son, who hides the injustice of the maternal agonies without pain. Accordingly it escapes no one's notice, that such a monster, that such a beast occupies the whole bosom of the motherland, that this most voracious vulture plunges its mangled claws into its innermost heart. Alone, sucking on the breasts of the motherland in a non-maternal way [i.e. an unnatural way], he is not able to draw from them milk, but instead draws out blood. He either drives far away the other misbegotten [children] or suppresses them with haughty force.[43]

---

40   Kadłubek, *Chronicle of the Poles*, 326–329.
41   Darius von Guttner-Sporzynski, "Writing History," 12–14.
42   Ibid., 11.
43   Kadłubek, *Chronicle of the Poles*, 186.

Sieciech, though in reality an adult man, in this metaphor is the rebellious son who attacks the fatherland. Furthermore, Sieciech's rapacious acquisition of land is compared to a greedy and ungrateful child who, against nature, draws blood instead of milk from his mother's breast, and drives away the other children who seek nourishment. The sacrality of the relations between parents and children is therefore the backdrop for Vincent's use of the trope to bring to mind the horror of political malfeasance.

This sacrality also extended to relations between older siblings, uncles, and other kinsmen with their respective wards. In 1177, when Kazimierz II rose up against his older brother Mieszko III, and seized the title of High Duke of Poland, Mieszko began to gather allies both inside and outside Poland. He also tried to persuade his brother to respect his wishes:

> He asked him to recall the deep sweetness with which he had been fostered with them while an adolescent, and with what zeal, what esteem he had been educated, and at last with what favor, with what skill, and—if he does not wish to hide it—by the favor of them he not only gained the first fruits of his patrimony, but also the auspices of his rule; and also how childlike [*filiales*], how devoted, how intimate were the warm affections of his heart which always existed towards them.[44]

Even though Mieszko III and Kazimierz II were clearly adults by that time, the memory of how an older took care of a younger brother could serve as a persuasive argument in the dispute. It is interesting to note that Mieszko alludes not only to food, shelter, clothing, and guardianship, but also to education and political (or military) assistance. The relationship between the two is presented as lopsided, with Kazimierz II portrayed as having "childlike" or "filial" feelings toward his older brother. To Vincent and his audience, the experience of raising another human being in one's kin group created a network of expectations upon which one could draw on rhetorically long after all involved parties had reached adulthood.

4   Childishness, a Negative Stereotype Applied to Rulers

Children did not always fulfill the hopes of their guardians, and indeed "childishness" was often used a pejorative concept to express this disappointment. Vincent often employs the concept to describe and denigrate immature or

---

[44]   Kadłubek, *Chronicle of the Poles*, 334–335. The reference to "patrimony" is perhaps a hint at Mieszko III helping Kazimierz acquire Sandomierz and Wiślica in 1166.

incompetent behavior, particularly in the case of rulers. According to him, intemperateness and foolishness were major sins for rulers, who thus behaved like children. Pompilius II became a murderer by acting like a child, both through his own actions and through his passive acceptance of somebody else's control of those actions. Strong rulers like Bolesław III rejected childish behavior and rivaled older men in wisdom. Here, childishness operated as a negative attributes, much like in the hagiographical sources examined in Chapter 5.

To Vincent, a female or a low-class regent was preferable to an incompetent ruler of very young age. Following the story of Wanda, a virgin queen whose innocent beauty could destroy by itself an enemy commander, the narrator John hints at examples of adults ruling as regents for incompetent children. Queen Semiramis of Assyria, for example, served as "king" instead of her immature son (*inmaturo filio*), fighting wars and imitating manly actions, conquering her neighbors with such gusto that she was said to be superior to men in her martial deeds. While Vincent notes that it seemed inappropriate for a woman to rule over men, it was nevertheless praiseworthy that "the good deeds of the dead [father] do not die among his offspring."[45] In other words, a powerful woman ruler was far superior to the disintegration of the patrimony under a weak and incompetent child, who would squander what his father had worked hard to build. Similarly, upon his death, Anaxilaus, the tyrant of Rhegium (who lived in the fifth century BC), entrusted his very young boy (*parvulus*) to a slave named Macalus. To Vincent, it is quite clear that people would rather obey a slave then let the king's legacy die.[46] The problems associated with rulers that are too young are also illustrated by examples from Polish history.

In the final book of his *Chronicle*, Vincent tells the story of what happened in 1194, when Duke Kazimierz II died with only young children as potential heirs. The noblemen, hoping to control a weak government, favored one of those children, the nine- or ten- year-old Leszek the White. Older dukes such as Mieszko III and Mieszko IV Tanglefoot used the opportunity to assert more power over Poland, claiming power over the whole on the basis of seniority. The resulting conflict between the young and the old Piasts resulted in the Battle of Mozgawa (1195), in which Mieszko III's ambitions were crushed. In telling the story, Vincent noted (or concocted) various arguments in favor or against Leszek and his younger brothers. Leszek's supporters argued that "even if they are both small and are of irresponsible age (*pupillares annos*),

---

45   Ibid., 102.
46   Ibid.

it is appropriate to honor the elder with his father's office."⁴⁷ In other words, despite the incompetence associated with young age, the right of birth was the most important argument for selecting the most competent candidate. As a counter-argument, Vincent had a certain noted man (*vir insignis*) reply that "a wizened head does not befit the [beardless] chin of the youth (*inpuberis*), but it is childish (*puerile*) [to let] the ignorance of a child (*puerilis*) command over the experienced. As the words of the wise go, 'Woe to the land where a child is king.'"⁴⁸ Leszek's enemies, therefore, valued experienced and tested leadership over the immediate principle of dynastic succession. Both sides agreed, therefore, that a young child was incapable of ruling well.

When the assembly of noblemen eventually decided in favor Leszek the White, Mieszko III blasted the pronouncement as a "scurrilous laughingstock" (*scurrili ludibrio*) and condemned the decision "no less grievous than ridiculous." According to him, "one cannot help but laugh at the crazy infancy (*infantia*) of such old men. Children have a habit of playing with children [the game] 'even or uneven, riding on a long rod.'"⁴⁹ Childish behavior is attributed here not to Leszek—a child—but to mature adults who had taken the decision to support that child in the first place. In this rhetorical inversion, it is the adult who behaves like a child, when choosing to yield power to a child. It is possible also that this sophisticated use of the trope of childishness is meant to prepare Vincent's audience for the story of how Leszek ended up defying the stereotypes of his age and living as a model youth. Vincent employs the same trope when praising Bolesław III Wrymouth's precocious maturity, in contrast to the childlike, adult leaders of Poland. Likewise, when urging her husband to kill his uncles, Pompilius' wife compares the uncles to children, for they play with the young prince in matters of realm as if they themselves were children. While a child was certainly expected to be fool, a wise child could make a foolish man look like a child.

Although crowned in Kraków, Leszek the White nonetheless ruled with his mother, Helen of Znojmo, as regent until he came come of age (*adolescat*).⁵⁰ Like Wanda and Semiramis, the wise Helen rules on behalf of her son, who is said to have been the closest to maturity (*pubertati*) among all her sons. The use of the word *pubertas* suggests that Vincent associated sexual maturity, but also a certain level of mental maturity, with adulthood. In other words, the ability to rule was a function of physical qualities that came with time.

---

47 Ibid., 380–381.
48 Ibid.
49 Ibid., 382–324. The quote is from Horace, *Satires* II 3. 248.
50 Ibid., 390–393.

Conversely, *adolescat* points to a process by which one reached an intermediary stage (*adolescens*) in which one acquires some of the attributes of adulthood, without the expectations of fully embodying the ideal of a good, mature ruler. The choice of both words strongly suggest a well-developed notion that, in medieval Poland, children matured in several stages. *Pace* Ariès, the evidence of Vincent's *Chronicle* demonstrates the existence of a clear and distinct concept of several stages of childhood.

Leszek the White, the child chosen by the powerful in Kraków precisely because they hoped to dominate him and his mother, eventually received an interesting proposition from his old nemesis, Mieszko III. Concerned with legitimacy, the uncle now wanted to dub his nephew a knight, in exchange for him (Leszek) recognizing Mieszko as senior prince in Poland. Gallus had turned Bolesław III's knighting into the capstone of his proven qualities, and the harbinger of the glorious future. Vincent has a different attitude towards Leszek's knighting at the hands of Mieszko:

> Let your son cede the principate to me, and I shall adopt him. Subsequently, when I present him with the knightly belt, I shall return it [the principate] to him, and render him an heir, on the basis of legitimate custom, so that at the Cracow dignity, and even the entire principate encompassing the whole of Poland, would be confirmed in your family be means of perpetual succession ... it will be safer to respect the uncle as a father than to have in him a constant enemy, and it that it is better to rule by his grace than to be always dependent upon the predilection of the common people ...[51]

While Leszek and his mother Helen accepted the deal, Mieszko III did not conduct the promised knighting before his death in 1202. Vincent's account of this episode suggests that even after four years of his mother's rule as a regent, and as even he approached his teens, Leszek the White had a precarious position in regards to his subjects, most likely because he was perceived as a child. That is probably why the proposal of his former enemy was accepted. That proposal also implies that legitimacy was commonly associated with a respected elder, either the father or, in his absence, with one of his male relatives, according with the principle of seniority adopted at the death of Bolesław III. In exchange

---

51 Ibid., 4:25. English translation from Zbigniew Dalewski, "The knighting of Polish dukes in the Early Middle Ages: ideological and political significance," *Acta Poloniae Historica* 80 (1999): 15.

for submission, respect, and, honor to Mieszko III, young Leszek could hope to attain legitimacy, protection, and dynastic support.[52]

5 Prophecy and Children

Like Gallus and the hagiographical sources discussed in this book, Vincent uses descriptions of a particular ruler's childhood to forecast future accomplishments. This is true both for his historical and for his fictional characters. Jacek Banaszkiewicz has already noted that Vincent highlights Leszko II's heroic life by pointing out that even in his youth he had shown superiority over his peers through his actions.[53] Vincent's remarks are set against the background of the factional strife erupting in Poland at the death of Leszko I. In this story, a popular assembly decided that a horse race should be held, with the winner proclaimed as king. One of the young, noble contenders for the race used the "art of Vulcan" (*artis ope fretus Vulcanie*), i.e., spread iron nails on the trail while leaving a secret passage for himself. However, prior to the race, two young men of low social status (*condicione humillimi iuvenes*) attempted to run the course on a bet, while joking about becoming king. They discovered the spikes and prepared accordingly. On the day of race, when "blossoms of young men are smiling" (*iuvenum arridet uernantia*), one of the two commoners put iron shoes on his horse to survive the nails. That young man won the race after beating out his cheating competitor at his own game, but was killed at the discovery of the nails on the ground. The other commoner, who had become a laughing stock by avoiding the nails through a circuitous route to the finish line, and who thus refused to take seriously a rigged competition, was proclaimed prince by the populace. He took the name Leszko II and went on to become a leader of legendary humility, never raising himself above his people, as well as a great warrior and conqueror.[54] This story contrasts the humility and wisdom of a young man of low status, who can only joke about becoming king, to privilege associated with cheating. The humble spirit and enterprising mind of the mature Leszko II are forecast in this story, which also illustrates Vincent's general point that ducal or royal elections in Poland are always according to God's, not the ruling elite's will.

---

52 Dalewski, "The knighting," 30–34.
53 Jacek Banaszkiewicz, *Polskie dzieje bajeczne mistrza Wincentego Kadłubka* (Wrocław: Leopoldinum, 1998), 155–62.
54 Kadłubek, *Chronicle of the Poles*, 112–16.

Further evidence of childhood employed rhetorically for prophecy comes from the famous vision of Bolesław III, which appears after the audience learns that Bolesław III has announced the division of his kingdom to his subjects. His advisers were dumbfounded by the fact that he had completely left out his fifth son, Kazimierz II:

> He was reminded of his fifth son, who was still a small child (*adhuc infantulo*), and asked why he did not think of him and why he did not prescribe to him a part of the inheritance. He answered 'yes, I certainly thought of him and left something for him.' When they were all astounded, since five portions were able to be made from four parts ... and since he was being accused of being undutiful, he said: 'In the pupil of my eye I saw four streams flow from one tear, and collide with their waves, which crash into each other; and some of these are suddenly dried up even in the midst of the strongest flood. But a fragrant spring bursting out of golden bucket flooded the [empty] riverbeds [of the four dried streams] with the most dazzling gemstones. So let this quarrel over the validity of the will cease, for this is just a matter of entrusting the inheritance of the wards to the guardians and not to the wards themselves.'[55]

This vision is meant to anticipate the later developments in which little Kazimierz II, as the "fragrant spring," will inherit the four parts of the kingdom after his brothers' streams had "dried up." Vincent presents the vision as both authentic and prophetic, a completely acceptable explanation for Bolesław III's actions, and a justification for Kazimierz's later actions. A child born with destiny was not a greedy usurper, or so Vincent wants his audience to believe when thinking on his patron.

A similar prophecy appears in the episode of Leszek the White's ascension to the throne while still a child, a development that angered his uncle Mieszko III:

> Leszek advanced both in age and industrious activity, [and] as a teenager (*adolescens*) he exercised his youthful (*iuvenile*) strength for hunting in as much as [other] pursuits. Among these pursuits, above all he aspired to the exercise of weapons, and though he was not even a squire, let alone a knight, he revealed the glorious signs of knighthood. To crown his glory in all this, it is sufficient to say that, although a youth (*adolescentulus*) he shone like the sun over all the princes of Rus'.[56]

---

55   Ibid., 278–80.
56   Ibid., 392–93.

There is an echo in this of the *puer senex* trope, but also shades of Gallus' descriptions of the young Bolesław III. While Vincent eliminates hunting expeditions and precocious martial activities in his portrait of Bolesław III, he uses both for Leszek the White. Exactly why he did so remains unclear. It is possible that to him Bolesław III was already an almost legendary dynastic icon. Whatever the case, he chose to compare Leszek favorably in relation to his contemporary princes in the region, of all ages, and in this respect Vincent follows his favorite trope, namely making worthy children appear as more mature than their elders.

6 Child(hood) as a Rhetorical Device

On a number of other occasions, children or childhood are solely a rhetorical device to express a concept or an idea. Vincent's John and Matthew refer self-consciously to childhood. At the starting point of their conversation, John asks Matthew about the time of "our" inception (*conceptam*) or that of the "infancy of our laws" (*nostrarum constitutionum infantiam*).[57] This refers of course to Vincent's more general idea about his chronicle being about the people of Poland, not a glorification of the Piast dynasty. The body politic of Poland has its own "infancy" reaching deep into antiquity.[58] On a related note, Matthew compares himself to an infant when it comes to his own knowledge of that ancient history of Poland (*me vero in hac parte infantulum fateor*).[59] This double use of infancy in a rhetorical fashion is placed at the beginning of the Chronicle on purpose. Poland appears as a biological organism, which, like Matthew's knowledge (and Vincent's own chronicle) has a hazy, unformed beginning. In other words, childhood and its characteristics, were fundamental concepts that Vincent and his audience commonly employed to understand the life of any given country.

A similarly rhetorical use of the notion of childhood appears in the account of Bolesław Chrobry's campaign in Rus' (1018), and his defeat of Yaroslav the Wise. According to Vincent, Yaroslav has scorned and underestimated Bolesław I's military prowess, and therefore had to pay the penalty in defeat. In commenting upon Yaroslav's arrogance, John compares him with story

---

57 Kadłubek, *Chronicle of the Poles*, 92.
58 Skibiński sees sexual rhetoric in the rest of this passage, specifically the fact that John is asking "sub quonam" or "under whom" the infancy of the constitution began, implying that Krakus himself was the spiritual father of the Polish people, as he was the first to give them the laws that would make them a nation. see Edward Skibiński, "The narrative ...," 103.
59 Kadłubek, *Chronicle of the Poles*, 92.

of Darius lifted from Iulius Valerius' *Res gestae Alexandri Macedonis*, the 4th-century Latin translation of pseudo-Callisthenes' *Alexander Romance*. In the story, the arrogant king of Persia had only contempt for the young Alexander, whom he regarded as a *puer*. He therefore sent to him a ball to play, a belt with which to be disciplined, and some small coins for support. He then ordered Alexander to return to his parents, for children are unable to rule. However, Alexander choose to give a different meaning to the "gifts" received from Darius. The ball represents the globe (the world that he was about to rule), the thong was the fetters to tie up Darius, and the coins were all the goods of Darius' empire that would eventually be Alexander's.[60] What is the role of this story in Vincent's *Chronicle*? At a quick glimpse, it serves a very clear purpose, namely to warn against rejecting the (social) value of children or young people only because of their age. While most youths may indeed be fools unfit to rule, others such as Alexander the Great, Bolesław I, or Bolesław III, are better than any adults at what they are doing. In whom innate ability, divine favor, fate, and excellence converged, to them belonged sovereignty, even youths.

Another example of the rhetorical use of childhood recalls themes to be discussed below in Chapter 4 in relation to the Henryków Book. In a discussion of the reasons for the dispossession of Zbigniew, Bolesław III's half-brother, John and Matthew tackle the question of whether Zbiegniew was doomed to fail merely because of his low birth, or perhaps because his own actions. In this context, Matthew inserts the biblical story of Abraham's sons, Isaac (born to a legitimate wife) and Ishmael (born to a slave), and concludes that "the son of the slave is not to inherit with the son of the free." Matthew's attitude is akin to that of the authors of the Henryków Book, who reject the claims of low-born children. Matthew then introduces the story of Jephthah (Judges 11), who was born from a prostitute and was subsequently driven out by his half-brothers, thus becoming a bandit. To judge from those two passages, it would seem that Matthew endorsed the idea that Zbigniew failed because of his low birth. In his reply, however, John urges Matthew to look more closely at the story of Jephthah. Despite his low birth, Jephthah later became a judge of Israel, and completely erased his early disgrace by means of his noble and courageous deeds. To support his point, John inserts the story of Hieron II, the tyrant of Syracuse in the third century BC, who was born to a slave girl and was therefore not recognized by his father.[61] However, after a fortune-teller brought word of the boy's future glory, the king brought the boy home to be raised. Later, when Hieron engaged in his first fight, he had an eagle on his shield to represent his

---

60 Ibid., 152–54.
61 Vincent found the story in Justin's *Epitome*.

royal lineage, but an owl on his lance to symbolize his humble origins. From those stories, John concludes that one's birth does not automatically condemn one to misery: "Zbigniew was not so much hurt by the suspicion (*suspicio*) of his birth, as by the crimes of his [own] shame. Because you should not nurse the thistle among the young plants, let alone the asp in the womb."[62] Zbigniew may, therefore, have been treacherous from birth, but this was not because of his birth, but because of his later character and choices, as he took advantage of his position of power to sabotage his father and heroic half-brother. By means of famous children of antiquity, whose shame equaled that of Zbigniew, Vincent provides a conceptual framework for understanding why Zbigniew suffered humiliation and defeat as an adult.

7   Conclusions

Vincent eliminated many of the stories about children found in Gallus (such as Bolesław III's hunting scenes), and minimized (as in the initiation rituals of the early Piasts), or adapted others (such as the story of young Kazimierz I). Similarly, children and youth are constantly berated for their poor decision-making capacity, and Leszek the White is scorned by his uncle as unfit. Utterly bad children are portrayed as a real threat to their parents and to the nation, and a good child, like Bolesław III is presented as not being a child at all, but a miniature man. Furthermore, Vincent has patriotic fathers ready to sacrifice their own children for the fatherland. Finally, it seems that to Vincent the submission of the young to their parents was a crowning virtue, with no room left for a playful childhood.

Nevertheless, at a closer examination, Vincent's treatment of young age is more sophisticated. He often references youth and childhood in both concrete terms and as a rhetorical tool. While Vincent reconfigures Gallus' version of events, he introduces his own tropes of childhood to play on the emotions and expectations of his audience. This is definitely the case of two versions of the young life of Kazimerz II, one of which is cast in the form of a sympathetic fairy tale. Likewise, while the prophetic function of children for the early Piasts appears somewhat reduced in Vincent, children and youths were nevertheless associated with prophecy, as seen in Bolesław III's vision and in the footrace of Leszek II. Vincent expects parents, or even kinsmen, to take care of children, an expectation on which his stories of child sacrifice for Poland are based. The heroism of the parents cannot be understood without the high

---

62   Kadłubek, *Chronicle of the Poles*, 223.

value placed on children. Finally, certain young people, from Bolesław III to Leszek the White are presented as overcoming the limitations of their age and engaging in behavior that is superior even to that of adults. Although this may be regarded as diminishing the social value of childhood, it is nevertheless a mirror image of adulthood. Furthermore, the idea that children need special attention and guidance even in their teenage years, like young Kazimierz II, suggests that the weakness of youth was not necessarily a negative attribute, but a way to point to the importance of familial nurture. While childhood and youth receive seemingly contradictory treatment in the worldview of Vincent, it is impossible to deny that they were present in the text and the intellectual milieu in which that text was written. Childhood represents a major part of his argument for virtue in the *res publica*.

CHAPTER 4

The Henryków Book: The Weight of Future Children and the Threat of Youth

One of the most unusual sources for the history of Poland in the High Middle Ages is the Henryków book. The main part of this text, which is divided into two books, focuses on the circumstances surrounding the foundation and the acquisition of land at the Cistercian monastery at Henryków, located thirty-one miles to the southwest from Wrocław, in Silesia. That monastic community was founded in 1227 by Henry the Bearded, Duke of Silesia (1201–1238), and swiftly acquired supporting territory, as is recorded in the Henryków Book. While the surviving codex was produced by monks of the monastery shortly after 1310, it covers actions and interactions from as far back as the twelfth century. The Henryków book is a record of property owners and their transactions, but, as Piotr Górecki has pointed out, its purpose was to control, to form, and to shape collective memory, particularly in regards as to the reasons for which the Henryków monastery had rights to specific pieces of land.[1]

Like Gallus Anonymous, the Henryków Book might appear to have no relation whatsoever to children. However, at a closer examination, its subject matter is tightly associated to the topic of this book. This is primarily because children, as heirs of landholders and titles, and as inheritors of the present state of affairs, are regarded as the major threat to the monastery, since they are potentially capable of challenging the claims of the monks, while at the same time they are the future benefactors of holy "capital" accrued from donations to the monastery. After all, it was future generations that must be convinced through the judicious use of strategies of remembrance that the monastery still owned its properties legally. In the Henryków Book, therefore, children, feature as a kind of weight on the future, in which hope and threat are intermingled, and in which the individuality of any particular child or youth, or any person for that matter, is subsumed by his or her position within a lineage. In this respect, this chapter will not discuss age category, but instead deal with the position of "sons" and "daughters" within family networks, and with how people in general are understood in the book. Because of that, I will discuss children and youths in the Henryków Books through a number of themes:

---

1 Piotr Górecki, *The Text and the World: The Henryków Book, Its Authors, and Their Region 1160–1310* (Oxford: Oxford University Press, 2015), 55–106.

children as inheritors; the importance of an age of responsibility; the negative and positive association with youth; future generations and the idea of memory; the need to care for young kin. Through this discussion we will see how a text that has been almost exclusively used by historians to explore such "adult" concerns as landholding patterns, the formation of social hierarchies, colonization, law, and social memory has a lot to say about the perception of children in society and their role even on the horizons of adult affairs.

1   The Text and Its Purpose

The first part of the Henryków Book, covering the period from the foundation of the monastery until 1259, was written by an abbot of the monastery, named Peter, and includes many narrative accounts of transferred land and of the lives of previous owners. This first book was written from 1269–1273. The second part deals with transactions taking place between 1259 and 1310, and was composed sometime after the latter date. Its author is not known (hence the conventional name "Continuator"), but he must have also been a Cistercian monk, who had a great deal of respect for Peter (the author of the first part). This unknown author had access to, and incorporated many charters, which by 1300 seem to have replaced a more general reliance on oral testimony.[2] While the purpose of the first part of the Henryków Book is not different from that of the second part, Abbot Peter and the Continuer have slightly different attitudes towards children and childhood.

The Henryków Book does not fit into any specific genre, but draws in fact from different genres.[3] It is a cartulary, for it contains copies of several charters, especially in its second half. It is also a regional chronicle, for it records the events and actions of local individuals and actors. It is a local history of the Cistercian Order, but also *gesta* (history of the deeds of mighty individuals), as well as hagiography (for it contains short biographies of local rulers, monastics, clerics, and holy laity). Nonetheless in its combination of all these ingredients, the Henryków Book remains distinct, a local product suited to local needs. For that reason, it is more difficult to find any direct parallels either in

---

2 Górecki, *The Text*, 1–5. For a discussion of the identity of the Continuator, with the suggestion that it could well have been the second abbot named Peter i.e. Abbot Peter II, see Rościsław Żerelik, "'Ego minimus fratrum' w kwestii autorstwa drugiej częśći Księgi Henrykowskiej," *Nasza Przeszłosc* 83 (1994): 70–74.

3 Górecki, *The Text*, 6–10.

Western or in Central Europe, despite the fact that several analogies are known for individual aspects.

The overall concern of the two authors of the Henryków Book is the transformation of notions of land ownership and of the associated duties, from the "Polish" custom of patrimony to the "German" system characterized by permanent legal alienation of sold land, as well as clearly delineated fees and obligations.[4] What historians have traditionally regarded as the traditional *ius ducale* was presumably a system under which the duke had enormous power over both people and land in the countryside. When the abbey of Henryków came into being, *ius ducale* was replaced with a more hierarchical system in which the church, the monasteries, and the nobility acquired rights over ducal peasants and introduced new systems of obligations. As Robert Bartlett has noted, the introduction of those new ideas from the West was initiated by dukes, lords, and monasteries seeking the development of barren and unprofitable land, but often came into conflict with local traditions.[5] Of all monastic orders, Cistercians played the greatest role in the transformation of the administration of the Polish countryside in the 13th century.[6] Regional customs came directly into conflict with the monastery's aims in the process of land purchase, for the monks wanted permanent acquisitions just as Cistercians sought in western Europe, while Polish law allowed heirs to redeem sold land. The difference is explained in clear terms to the abbot of Henryków by the prior Vincent, who was presumably of Polish descent:

> you ought to know, lord abbot, that it has been established long ago among our ancestors, and forefathers that if anyone from the stock of the Poles sells any patrimony of his, his heirs will be able to redeem it

---

[4] For the origins and development of the special rights that dukes had over peasants and land, see Karol Modzelewski, "The system of the ius ducale and the idea of feudalism," *Quaestiones Medii Aevi* 1 (1977), especially 74–81; Piotr Górecki, "Ius ducale revisited: twelfth-century narratives of Piast power," in *Gallus Anonymus and His Chronicle in the Context of Twelfth-Century Historiography from the Perspective of the Latest Research*, edited by Krzysztof Stopka (Kraków: Polska Akademia Umiejętności, 2010), 35–44.

[5] Robert Bartlett, *The Making of Europe: Conquest, Colonization, and Cultural Change 950–1350* (Princeton, Princeton University Press, 1993), 106–153.

[6] Jerzy Kłoczowski, *History of Polish Christianity* (Cambridge, Cambridge University Press, 2000), 39–42. See also Eugeniusz Cnotliwy, "Osadnictwo w północnej części ziemi pyrzyckiej przed i na początku działalności cystersów kołbackich w świetle nowszych badań archeologicznych," in *Cystersi w społeczeństwie Europy środkowej. Materiały z konferencji naukowej odbytej w klasztorze oo. Cystersów w Krakowie Mogile z okazji 900 rocznicy powstania Zakonu Ojców Cystersów. Poznań-Kraków-Mogiła 5–10 października 1998*, edited by Andrzej Marek Wyrwa and Józef Dobosz (Poznań: Wydawnictwo Poznańskie, 2000), 419–34.

later. But perhaps you Germans do not fully understand what a patrimony is. Therefore, in order that you may fully understand, let me give you an explanation. If I possess anything which my grandfather and my father have left me in possession, this is my true patrimony. If I sell this to anyone, my heirs have the power to demand it according to our law. But whatever possession the lord duke may have given to me for my service or by grace, that I [may] sell to whomever I wish, even against the will of my friends, because my heirs do not have the right to demand such a possession.[7]

The presence of these familial customs created the need for record-keeping such as illustrated by the Henryków Book, in which relevant details of particular acquisitions are remembered. These often included the history of a certain holding, a family history of its previous owners and their relationship to the land, the details of the terms of the acquisition, as well as juicy, often negative, details about the previous owners to be brought up in a legal dispute. From these it was essential that the monastery prove that all viable heirs were alienated from the right of redemption for each purchase and holding.

Various passages throughout the two parts of the Henryków Book establish the first, most famous, and most important donor of land and privilege to the monastery—Duke Henry I the Bearded and his Piast heirs. According to Piotr Górecki, Abbot Peter and the Continuator purposefully cultivated both that special relationship with the duke, and, just as importantly, its image and prestige.[8] Indeed, the first eighteen chapters of the first book meticulously and emphatically describe Duke Henry's patronage of and interest in the foundation of the Henryków monastery, as well as establish his specific interest in the monastery for his own sake and the sake of his heirs.[9] While that earned Duke Henry I undying praise from the monks and the monastery, as we shall see later, his heirs were not exempt from sharp criticism when breaking faith with the monks and denying them their rights. Interestingly, the monastery tried to promote the memory of later "good" dukes, especially in connection with this duke's donation or confirmation of property. For example, Duke Henry II "the Pious" (1238–1241), who died in the Battle of Legnica in 1241 fighting the

---

7   Piotr Górecki, *A Local Society in Transition: The Henryków Book and Related Documents* (Toronto: Pontifical Institute of Medieval Studies, 2007), 125–126.
8   Górecki, *A Local Society*, 21.
9   Ibid., 90–99.

Mongols, "confirmed Rudno for the Cloister."[10] Much like elsewhere at that time in Europe, dynasties were often associated with saints and martyrs.[11]

This cultivation of memory we see in the Henryków Book is an important topic of discussion for medieval historiography, for it is tightly connected with power, landownership, and lordship in the Middle Ages. Patrick Geary writes, "the right to speak the past also implied control over that which gave access to the past—the 'relics' by which the past continued to live into the present. How these tangible or written relics of the past were preserved, who preserved them, and who could therefore make them to disappear were fundamental aspects of power and authority."[12] Memory was, perhaps, the most praised intellectual quality of medieval period, comparable to imagination in the present day.[13] According to Mary Carruthers in her seminal work, even when the written word became more common in later medieval centuries, memory was always considered more than simply recording something in a book: "writing, as we have seen, was always thought to be a memory aid, not a substitute for it. Children learned to write as a part of reading/memorizing, inscribing their memories in the act of inscribing their tablets."[14] In this sense, literacy and oral culture were not opposites, as might be supposed, for great swaths of medieval and early modern culture, and the written word was considered simply on part of the formation and training of memory. The book was not the end of memory, but only part of its beginning. Carruthers also notes how medieval people saw memory and its formation as a dynamic process, one that involved written words, spoken words, the mind and heart of the reader, and the community all in tandem. She summarizes this process thus: "*Memoria* is better considered, in the context of my study, as praxis rather than as doxis."[15]

While perhaps medieval attitudes towards memory changed only slowly, it is undoubtedly the fact that in its careful attempts at shaping social memory, the Henryków Book reveals a shift in the technology of remembrance. This process had occurred in various parts of Europe before Poland, and has received the most attention in Norman and Plantagenet England in the classic work of

---

10   Ibid., 130.
11   Gabor Klaniczay, *Holy Rulers and Blessed Princesses: Dynastic Cults in Medieval Central Europe* (Cambridge: Cambridge University Press, 2002), 295–366.
12   Patrick Geary, *Phantoms of Remembrance. Memory and Oblivion at the End of the First Millennium* (Princeton: Princeton University Press, 1994), 7.
13   Mary Carruthers, *The Book of Memory: A Study of Memory in Medieval Culture, Second Edition* (Cambridge: Cambridge University Press, 2008), 1–3.
14   Mary Carruthers, *The Book of Memory*, 195.
15   Ibid., 15.

Michael Clanchy, *From Memory to Written Record*.¹⁶ In this book Clanchy argues that England not only went through an extraordinary expansion in the numbers of written material it produced, but also a shift in mentalities, namely the creation of a "literate mentality," in which power and authority were increasingly connected to the written word and its record. At the beginning of this process, "when historical information was needed, local communities resorted not to books and charters but to the oral wisdom of their elders and remembrancers. Even where books and charters existed, they were rarely consulted at first, apparently because habits of doing so took time to develop."¹⁷ While in England Latin literary culture began to become important by at least the late eleventh century, and had a strong boost from the kings and government of the realm, Poland's transition began much later, perhaps as late as the thirteenth century, and was often led by the church, as Poland's government was divided and weak into the fourteenth century.¹⁸

In the transformation to written record, Michael Clanchy highlights the rise of cartularies, or collections of charters collected into registers for better preservation, with the first appearing in the eleventh century in England.¹⁹ Patrick Geary notes the importance of charters in even earlier in Carolingian times in Piedmont and Bavaria.²⁰ The need to record the deeds of past ancestors and notables was present everywhere in Europe from 900–1200, as new

---

16 Michael Clanchy, *From Memory to Written Record* (Chichester, West Sussex: Blackwell, 2013), Introduction.
17 Clanchy, *From Memory to Written Record*, 3.
18 The work of Anna Adamska discusses literacy, what it means, how it can be measured, and how it spread in Poland and elsewhere, in the following collected volume, but see especially: Anna Adamska, "The Study of Medieval Literacy: Old Sources, New Ideas," in *The Development of Literate Mentalities in East Central Europe*, ed. Anna Adamska and M. Mostert (Turnhout: Brepols, 2004). As this title might suggest, Michael Clanchy has provided the framework through which many Eastern European scholars have understood the rise of the written word in their countries.
19 Clanchy, *From Memory to Written Record*, 103.
20 Geary, *Phantoms of Remembrance*, 124. Geary nonetheless makes clear that this use of the written word by no means replaced oral culture, and he explains that written records often were designed to refer interested parties to the right person to ask verbally. Geary writes about the importance of witnesses and prominent people connected with events and donations, as well as the constant reference to concrete geographical phenomena, in the written word of the time. In this sense, the Geary argues that even in literate societies collective memory functioned as a "control" on the written word. The Henrykow is similar in this regard, often carefully listing, the prominent people who witnessed a donation, as well as referencing landmarks that would have been recognizable to contemporary people.

forms of inheritance, ownership, and lordship encouraged new strategies of remembrance.[21] In Poland, the transition to use of charters can be seen by comparing the two books written by the monks of Henryków. Few charters are reproduced in the first book, and instead there are stories, lists of witnesses and communal events, and records of perambulations. Those are indications of an oral culture, over which the Henryków cloister had an advantage because it recorded its version of events in the written word, though only to the extent that anyone cared about the authority of the written word.[22] In contrast, the Continuator in the Second Book placed a great deal of emphasis on charters, which seemed to serve as the primary source of evidence in property cases and ownership. Such charters functioned as "weapons" to shape memory and assert the monastery's claims against challengers and usurpers.[23]

Despite much interest in memory in general in the Henryków Book, the rhetorical use of children and of concepts of childhood in order to influence memory have not yet been the subject of scholarly attention for the Henrykow Book, and little has been done on childhood and youth in the Henryków Book at all. Małgorzata Delimata, for example, only mentions that there was a legal responsibility for non-parental guardians to provide education for their charges and care for their assets until the child came of age.[24] Most other scholars of childhood in medieval and early modern Poland simply ignore the Henryków Book.[25] This is not particularly surprising, as previous Polish scholarship has focused on the reality of medieval youth and childhood. Yet young people are present in that text, albeit primarily as an idea, or potential in the minds of the Henryków monks. This chapter will highlight this role for children, showing how the potential that children possessed for good or ill dominated the minds of the Henryków monks.

---

21 Elizabeth von Houts, *Memory and Gender in Medieval Europe, 900–1200* (London, Macmillan Press, 1999), 146. This book focuses generally on the secular development of memory, but similar forces shaped the needs of monastic writers as well.
22 Górecki, *A Local Society*, 28–32.
23 Warren Brown, "Charters as weapons. On the role played by early medieval dispute records in the disputes they record," *Journal of Medieval History* 28 (2002), no. 3: 246–248.
24 Małgorzata Delimata, *Dziecko w Polsce średniowiecznej* (Poznań: Poznańska Drukarnia Naukowa, 2004), 176.
25 There is nothing about the Henryków Book in Dorota Żołądź-Strzelczyk's magisterial *Dziecko w dawnej Polsce* (Poznań: Wydawnictwo Poznańskie, 2002).

2 Youth as Part of Dynasty and Potential Threat

For the monastery at Henryków, the redemption rights according to Polish law were perhaps the greatest constant threat. Since legal action was required to press and dispute those rights concerning past land donations, most actions against the monastery were taken by youths and young adults. Nevertheless, the monks recognized the threat that even the youngest members of a family could represent to them. This was, in fact, one of the major reasons for the composition of the book, namely to prevent future heirs from successfully pressing their claims through a careful record of exactly how property had fallen into the monastery's hands, though even these efforts did not prevent disenfranchised heirs from engaging in mischief.

To provide an example of the sort of threat a child could pose, we look to a story where a priest named Nicholas convinced his brother Stephen to donate land to the Henryków monastery in 1239, and even had a privilege drawn up in the presence of a number of castellans and bailiffs which stipulated that the transfer had occurred on account of their sins and "neither he nor his successors shall henceforth have any power to redeem."[26] Despite such precautions, disputes nonetheless ensued:

> Stephen had a very small son [*filius parvulus*], John by name. As soon as this John reached a responsible age, he often tried by Polish custom to revoke his uncle's and his father's deeds. But because he was always poor and modest in things, his malice achieved nothing of what he wanted.[27]

Despite his noted young age, John is precisely the agent of trouble, the "successor" which the author of the privilege had in mind when explicitly cutting off Stephen's heirs from succession. The charters in the Henryków Book were not just records of events, but instruments against specific, concrete people known in the community. The threat was real, even if those people were small children at the time of the recording. Despite the fact that young children did not engage in property transactions, that by no means implied that their existence was ignored, and their looming potential seems to have caused some hand-wringing. Indeed, the passage clearly targets only Stephen's heirs, as his brother was presumably a celibate priest, for the preposition is in the singular: "his" (*eius*) heirs were barred from subsequent rights. It is nonetheless worth noting that the donation had been made jointly by Stephen and his brother,

---

26 Górecki, *A Local Society*, 116.
27 Ibid.

Nicholas.[28] On another note, one wonders why John ignored the wishes of his father and uncle in his challenge. Perhaps it was John's young age at the time of transfer that prevented him from remembering the intention of his father, or perhaps his own rapaciousness. At any rate, he did not respect the privilege drawn up in the written word when it spoke against his own traditional claim, and the text implies that only the poverty of John's means prevented him from successfully challenging the monks in court.[29] Additional expenditure and an additional charter were necessary in 1259 to settle the claim, which strongly suggests that John had engaged in, and had completed all legal challenges in his 20s.[30]

To continue, given the tendency of children to ignore or circumnavigate privileges issued by their parents, it is not surprising that in time charters became far more specific and comprehensive in their descriptions of the renunciations of rights and privileges to land. Almost twenty years after the charter issued by Stephen and Nicholas, in 1257 two other brothers, Bogusza and Paul, in the presence of Duke Henry III donated land to the monastery. The donation was accompanied by a charter "barring any alteration which might come in the future, by themselves or their children (*liberi*) or any kinsmen whatever."[31] Not only are "children" specifically named, as opposed to a more generic "successors" in the previous charter, but alterations to the status quo after the sale are strictly prohibited. A further step in closing of loopholes may be seen in a charter from 1293:

> We, Bolko, by the grace of God duke of Silesia … by letters patent make it known to present and future that Poltko, our knight … has willingly sold us his village … publicly renouncing all property and right which he and his heirs or any descendants, sons, grandsons, and friends seemed to enjoy in the aforesaid village, so that we may freely put it to any uses of our own, free from all hindrance and doubt.[32]

---

28 Ibid., 115.
29 Anna Adamska, who has studied the introduction of the written word into Poland, has doubts about charters having any real meaning for the general population in the 1230s. This is one reason, she argues, the book goes to great lengths to record the feasts and communal events surrounding the foundation of the monastery. It is indeed in this context that claims to land written through privileges could be so easily challenged by heirs in this early period of spreading literacy. Adam Adamska, "Founding a monastery over dinner: the case of Henryków in Silesia (1222–1228)," in *Medieval Legal Process: Physical, Spoken and Written Performance in the Middle Ages*, edited by Marco Mostert and Paul S. Barnwell (Turnhout, Brepols, 2011), 230–231.
30 Górecki, *A Local Society*, 117.
31 Ibid., 145.
32 Ibid., 167.

Now, even grandchildren are specifically mentioned and cut off from redemption rights, and the alienation is intended to cover every possible eventuality of conflict with the monastery. This gradual tightening of charter clauses came at the expense of lessons learned from children like John in the first charter, whose attempts at wrangling territory from the monastery spawned an atmosphere in which all children, living or yet to be born, posed a threat to the cloister's ambitions.

One of the differences between the book composed by Abbot Peter and the later work by the Continuator is the presence of women as legal actors, a feature that is far more pronounced in the later work. The special role for women, which was unusual by the European standards of that time, extended from the top of society downwards. After 1230, Polish duchesses possessed their own seals and were featured first on witness lists for charters. Their powers expanded in the later part of the 13th century to include the ability of female rulers to issue charters in their own names in order to certify the transactions of others.[33] In the book by the Continuator, the role of women as actors and movers in potential land disputes with their neighbors and the monastery meant that actions had to be taken to alienate them from potential land claims:

> and when Siegfried died, his daughter Hildegund—who remained as a survivor and was married to a certain citizen of Nysa by the name of Siegfried the Tanner—raised a claim against Poltko regarding the aforesaid mill. He made an amicable composition with her, and persuaded her to renounce her right [to the mill], and completely to cease all action [to regain it].[34]

Daughters could inherit claims to land from parents. Hildegund, not her husband Siegfried, was the one who initiated the dispute over the mill, and she was the one with whom the final agreement was concluded. In other words, women, not merely as regents for children or widows, could and would challenge the monastery. This meant that the monks at Henryków also had to keep track of their lineage and doings from a young age.

As with men, much of the power of women originated in the power of their respective families, and the infamy of a family also seemed to be able to travel through daughters. For example, a certain Stephen Kotka, nicknamed "Kotka" ("little cat" in Polish) because of unscrupulous predation on his

---

33 Sébastien Rossignol, "The authority and charter usage of female rulers in medieval Silesia, c.1200–c.1330," *Journal of Medieval History* 40 (2014): 82–84.
34 Górecki, *A Local Society*, 161.

fellow humans,[35] held a modest amount of territory, but was beheaded for his crimes. However,

> he [Stephen] left survivors: one son, Paul, by the nickname of Kotka, and one daughter by the name of Paulina, whom a certain youth from … named Peter took [as his wife]. He was allotted the nickname of his father-in-law and of his brother-in-law, so that he was called Peter Kotka.[36]

Not only did Peter acquire the unflattering nickname through his young wife, but he also acquired her claims to some of Stephen's land, in addition to the duties he owed for it.[37] Like boys, girls were active links in family agency, unlike the situation presented by Gallus, who recorded the fate of girls only in relation to marital status or monastic vows.

Because of the power of daughters to wield legal action, quite a few of them are actually named in the Continuator's Book. For example,

> Cieszybór, together with his two sons Jeszko and Albert, and with his two daughters Obiecka and Bogudarka, thus resigned his inheritance of Nietowice to the abbot and the convent, here at the doors of the cloister …[38]

The act of renouncing claims to Nietowice takes place at the "doors" of the Henryków Abbey, and the daughters Obiecka and Bogudarka are there not only alongside their two brothers, but also with their father Cieszybór. While the age of the two daughters is unclear, the transaction did not exclude women, and daughters were clearly not mere additions to lists of those forgoing redemption rights, Obiecka and Bogudarka were participants in their own rights. Daughters also appear in a passage in which the peasant Peter attempted to make an ill-supported and ill-conceived claim on some territory:

> by the counsel of the wise, sentence was pronounced against Peter, and an eternal silence concerning his accusation about the aforesaid hide was imposed by the rigor of justice on him and on all his sons, daughters, and any descendants whatsoever.[39]

---

35 Ibid., 160.
36 Ibid., 161.
37 Ibid., 161–162.
38 Ibid., 162.
39 Ibid., 171.

Both daughters and sons share the consequences of the decision taken against their father and his rights. In sum, it seems that, as the abilities of adult women waxed in the later part of the thirteenth century, so did the relevance of female children in the mind of Continuator. Daughters joined sons in the family descriptions of purchases of the Henryków Cistercians.

Another distinctive element of the Continuator is the use of Old Testament imagery involving children and descent. As Marek Cetwiński has pointed out, Abbot Peter rarely uses Old Testament imagery (and never mentions Satan). By contrast, the Continuator employs that imagery quite frequently to present the monks of Henryków as children of Israel fighting against God's enemies.[40] Particularly common is the theme of God separating the holy and chosen (in reference to the monastery and its denizens) from the lesser and wicked (secular people and challengers to the monastery). One example is drawn from a reference to the Old Testament story of Hagar and Sarah in Galatians 4:22–26, in which the apostle Paul compares those still practicing Jewish law to the children of Hagar and those under Christ to the children of Sarah. This imagery surrounds the story of how the monastery paid to have the obligation of half a war-horse lifted from some previously acquired land. In describing the reasoning behind that decision, the Continuator wrote:

> because the servitude of the sons (*filiorum*) of Hagar forever clash with the freedman of Christ, the lord abbot, having come up together with the citizens of Munsterberg to the prince, bought out from him the aforesaid service of half a war-horse …[41]

That the monastery should remain detached from obligations to the local prince, and more generally, that secular power should remain separate from that of the church, is an idea expressed in terms of the Old Testament story (Genesis 16). Paul used this story to advise his followers to avoid getting trapped in old Jewish practices, such as circumcision. Using a passage such as this in reference to local secular elites suggests a deep distrust of secular power and its relationship to the monastery. Nonetheless, the fact that the emphasis is placed on descent is significant. At play is clearly the fear that future generations of secular lords, i.e. the "sons" of Hagar, will be at war with the monastery.

Old Testament stories were also used to denigrate those who disrupted the life of the abbey and challenged its claims. This is the case of the Czesławice

---

40 Marek Cetwiński, "Bog, Szatan, i człowiek w księdze Henrykowskiej," *Nasza Przeszłość* 83 (1994): 81–87.
41 Piotr Górecki, *A Local Society*, 188.

holding, for which the monks were tormented with claims by four heirs, namely three sons and one daughter, led by the oldest son, Jeszko:

> But the pious Lord, who does not cease to weed out the Amorite from amongst His children (*alumpnorum*) until today, upon observing with the eye of divine mercy that His humble covenant was repeatedly molested in its forests, crops, rivers and meadows by the aforesaid heirs, by a secret and terrible judgement brought it about that when Jeszko, the oldest and foremost of the aforesaid three brothers, was riding a horse, he and the horse fell, and he broke his neck and died.[42]

In the Old Testament, the Amorites were enemies of ancient Israel, whom they harassed when the Chosen People entered into the promised land. For that reason, as well as for their grievous sins, God ordered their utter and complete annihilation (Deuteronomy 20:17). It is therefore an appropriate metaphor for Jeszko, who as a wicked heir found he had inherited his own destruction. The word chosen for "child" in this passage, *alumpnus*, refers to a nursling, i.e., not to a specific age category, but to someone of young age who needs fosterage from a parental figure. Here, the Lord's providential protection for his loyal children, namely the monks at Henryków, is communicated through the rhetorical context of paternal care.

3 How Many Roads Must a Man Walk Down: What Is a Responsible Age?

One of the most essential components to the life cycle in terms of legal action in thirteenth-century Silesia was the concept of "responsible" or "legitimate" age. There are no references to small children (*pueri*, or some other, similar word) taking any significant public action on their own behalf. In other words, the age of permitted legal activity on one's own behalf is clearly an important stepping-stone into adulthood. Unfortunately, no specific age details exist in the Henryków Book for anyone, so establishing either the exact age or the circumstances in which an individual could first conduct legal action is impossible, and scholars can only project the rules from later centuries backwards. At the same time, as we shall see in later examples, many of those who apparently conducted legal action were, nevertheless, still not thought of as possessing full adulthood and masculinity, for they are labeled as *iuvenis*. Therefore, it is

---

42 Ibid., 190.

important to see what exactly this age of responsibility entails and with what it was associated in the mind of the Continuator. This will allow us to separate different forms of youth from one another and to understand, at least in the negative, what those considered young children were not supposed to do.

The expectation of care for children as an abiding trope in the Henryków Book will be discussed later, but one element that is relevant at this time is the concept that children below a certain age were expected to receive guardianship from kinsmen, if their parents died prematurely:

> After Mencelin died, and his wife likewise, Arnold assumed for himself his small grandchildren (*nepotulos*)[43] with the aforesaid two hides, and was made their guardian (*tutor*). And when the same Arnold's children attained lawful years (*annos legittimos*), Arnold himself bought these hides from them, and later sold them to a fellow citizen ...[44]

The implication is that "guardian" is a more formal concept within an extended family, since the word chosen for that is *tutor*, which is more than just a family member who "ends up" with the children. The guardian was expected not only to provide nurture, education, and protection for the children, but was also to keep the childrens' inheritance intact until they reached the age of legal action. Arnold, although a guardian, did not transfer the property onto his own name until after his wards came of age, which suggests that such a duty was taken very seriously in Poland at that time. It is unknown whether this was typical, but we can conclude that the ability to transfer property was considered acceptable only for those of a certain age.

As a corollary to the need of a certain age for the transfer of property is the connection of adults with the writing of charters and privileges to document and certify property transactions:

> The noble lord Herman of Baboy ... who was at that time guardian (*tutor*) of his sister's sons, the princes of this land Bernard, Henry, and Bolko. Because the margrave was then outside the boundaries [of Silesia], and the princes of the land were below age (*sub annis*),[45] a privilege concerning the aforesaid inheritance could not be obtained at the time ...[46]

---

43 The Latin version of the text is from Roman Grodecki (ed.), *Księga Henrykowska* (Wrocław and Poznań: Instytut Zachodni, 1949), 328.
44 Górecki, *A Local Society*, 161.
45 Grodecki, *Księga*, 330.
46 Górecki, *A Local Society*, 163.

Underage children, even princes, were unable to issue charters, even through the mediation of their noble guardians. The best that could be arranged in such a case was the witnessing of the property transfer by powerful men of the realm. This suggests a lack of power and authority of young children, and the nebulous power vacuum that was created in the legal sphere for their subjects when their rulers were unable to put their mature adult power behind their actions. Indeed, as will be discussed later, doubts were raised even about youths who had the ability and right to engage in legal action.

Reaching legitimate age was also correlated with the tendency to find a spouse, which often went hand in hand with a reorientation of landholding strategy and location of residence:

> There was a certain youth (*iuvenis*)[47] in Munsterberg, Gobelo of Watzenrode, who held the bailiwick of the aforesaid village by paternal succession. But upon taking a wife in Wrocław, and permanently moving to her there, he publicly sold the aforesaid village bailiwick to the lord abbot.[48]

This passage suggests the impermanence that the coming of age of youth could impose upon landholding in the countryside. Gabelo, who held this land from "paternal succession" was more than happy to see the territory and all its rights definitely and completely transferred to the monastery.[49] This was a fortuitous occasion for the monastery, but the desire of youths to alter their situation, and the status quo achieved by their parents, generally worked against the stable strategy of the monks. Indeed, no one could tell what the next generation would do.

The dangers that the next generation may bring about is illustrated by a passage about the role of the young Henry III (1247–1266) in the damaging succession crisis after the death of Duke Henry II the Pious in 1241.

> Knights captured their lord Bolesław, the said duke, and this was done supposedly in the name of Henry [III], his brother born after him. But let it be known that at the time this young lord, lord Henry, had not attained the years of responsible age. Hence, because the disorder and damage of the entire province of Silesia began at this time, let it be known that this

---

47 Grodecki, *Księga*, 339.
48 Górecki, *A Local Society*, 171.
49 Ibid., 171–172.

captivity was perpetrated not by the council of the young lord Henry, but of certain others, whose names shall not be inscribed in this book.⁵⁰

This passage is a perfect example of how the Henryków monks supported the dukes to affirm their special alliance and connections with legitimate secular power embodied in the local branch of the Piast dynasty. Henry III indeed confirmed many transfers of land to the monastery in privileges and in person, and this personal authority was essential in a time of transition from oral culture to the written word. Childhood here operates as a "legal shield" to protect Henry III from blame for the disaster that descended upon Poland after the death of Henry II at the hands of the Mongols.

As a child, Henry III was in need of care and guidance, and could therefore not have been responsible for the evil deeds of others. However, the association of Henry III with youth is not always positive. The Continuator believes that young Henry III misbehaved:

> Let it thus be known that when this Duke Henry confirmed in rule, began to revoke his first-born brother's deeds in diverse places, he removed from us and from this cloister the village of Jaworowice, among others. He said on every occasion and at every gift, that was sat aside, "I wish to regain my forefathers' inheritances." Upon hearing this, lord Bobo, abbot of the place, said with a certain sadness, "If this holding ... should be granted to some powerful knight, the cloister will have nowhere to procure sand for work. The cattle pastures around this cloister will also be greatly diminished." So for six weeks, with whatever strength he could muster, he continuously worked around Henry, the said duke, by [the intercession] of the nobles and by himself ...⁵¹

The young duke behaves here like an errant child.⁵² Gabelo's youthful desire worked to the benefit of the monastery, but Henry III's did not, and instead required enormous efforts on the part of the monks, and in this case their abbot, to persuade the duke, with a paternal "sadness" to stick to the policy of his forebears.

---

50 Górecki, *A Local Society*, 119.
51 Ibid., 119–120.
52 As Górecki, *The Text*, 162, notes, there are no parallels to or other examples in the Henryków Book for the revocations attributed here to Duke Henry. It is unclear what exactly was happening at this point.

4   "Kids These Days": Disappointment in the Next Generation

When there are unambiguous moral judgements of the young in the Henryków Book, they are often negative. In a world where the ability and resources to act made one powerful,[53] the young, who had not yet received the esteem of their peers and dependents and who often had partial inheritances of a larger estate appeared lesser versions of their parents. The death of Henry II the Pious in 1241 was an especially tumultuous experience, as not only were his heirs young, but they also had to live in the shadow of their martyr father and deal with the tumult of the Mongol invasions. Duke Bolesław II (1241–1278) is especially singled out for derision:

> In those days, after the pagans, our young dukes first began to reign, many things occurred which were unheard of under the glorious ancient dukes (*antiquos gloriosos duces*).[54] Hence the firstborn among them, lord Bolesław, did many juvenile (*puerilia*) things at tournaments and in other amusements (*lecticiis*) during his youth (*iuventute*) …[55]

In this passage, the celebration of the old and the denigration of the new go hand-in-hand. The "ancient" dukes were "glorious" and had supposedly passed into revered memory, to the convenient benefit of the monastery's propaganda. The clear idiocy of duke Bolesław is not blamed on any particular moral failing of his own, a wise strategy as the monastery wanted to propagate the idea concept that the Piast dynasty had a special connection with the monastery. Instead, his inability to rule is explained in reference to the time of his life. The trope of the young being occupied with games and tournaments is present here, and his actions at these events are described as *puerilia*, connecting them to boyishness. It should be remembered that in Gallus' narrative young Bolesław Wrymouth is said to have avoided similar activities, and he in his virtue occupied himself with martial deeds of prowess in defense of his subjects and kingdom.[56] Not only did Bolesław II disappoint in his youth, but some events during his rule were "unheard of" in the golden age of his forebears. The

---

53   Piotr Górecki, "Words, concepts, and phenomena: knighthood, lordship and the early Polish nobility (c. 1050–1150)," in *Nobles and Nobility in Medieval Europe. Concepts, Origins, Transformations*, edited by Anne J. Duggan (Woodbridge/Rochester: Boydell Press, 2000), 115–55.
54   Grodecki, *Księga*, 269.
55   Piotr Górecki, *A Local Society*, 117.
56   After the death of Bolesław III Wrymouth in 1138, the kingdom was divided up into provinces by his sons, and these regional duchies, in varying levels of alliance and unification,

concept that sons were often their fathers' epigons, at best, and their antithesis, at worst, appears frequently in the Henryków Book.

The monastery and the subjects of the young Bolesław had reason to fear theft and chaos. Without the steady hand of a powerful duke, property rights and inheritance had no strong enforcers and often rightful owners were cheated. Immediately after Abbot Bodo returned to the devastated remains of the monastery burned by the Mongols, he discovered that a valuable landholding, the village at Schönwald, had been seized by a local man. Abbot Bodo:

> was distressed with at great sadness and very disturbed, above all because in this days the land was ruled by Duke Bolesław, son of Duke Henry killed by the pagans, which young (*iuvenis*)[57] Bolesław then occupied himself with nothing but foolish deeds (*fatuorum opera*). At length, continuously for five years, in every general assembly before Duke Bolesław himself and his barons, the abbot claimed that his house was exposed to violence from this Peter, son of Stosz. But the more often the Abbot complained, the more the duke occupied himself with his juvenile pranks (*iuvenilia ioca*) ..."[58]

The image of Bolesław is not only of utter ineffectiveness and inability, but also an unwillingness to help his subjects suffering loss and violence in their need after a national disaster. What is worse, his time is occupied instead with other, unspecified, but frivolous activities. While unfortunately these youthful actives are not described in this passage, they probably included tournaments and hunting, as the previous passage reported. It is also strongly implied that Bolesław did not take his public offices seriously and perhaps made false promises that he retracted later, as the passage mentions five years of effort on the part of the abbot in front of the duke and his assembly with nothing to show for it. The monks at Henryków could not expect quick and decisive justice under a youthful leader.

While the youthful and immature behavior of duke Bolesław II hurt his subjects, the young duke himself suffered loss from the unscrupulous. Without effective power himself and without a powerful guardian, those in the land with access to military and financial power stripped away large portions of ducal land:

---

ruled their own branches of the Piast dynasty. As a consequence, the numbering of their rulers begins again after the division.
57   Grodecki, *Księga*, 291.
58   Górecki, *A Local Society*, 133.

> this land was dominated by knights, each of whom seized whatever pleased him from the duke's inheritances. Hence the said Albert procured for himself from the boy (*puerilem*)[59] Duke Bolesław two ducal inheritances adjoining his estate, Cienkowice and Kubice, for a modest sum of money ..."[60]

Apparently Bolesław did not know the value of his own estates or could not resist the threats or charms of his knights. Perhaps his youthful lifestyle and constant extravagance required ready money. At any rate, part of being a boy or youth meant that one did not know the value of goods, and could thus be easily cheated and deceived.

Dukes were not the only ones to behave foolishly in childhood in regards to property. This often led to the poverty of once wealthy families. The best example of that is the story of the grandsons of Boguchwał, a deceitful Czech who usurped more ducal land than he was given in reward for his service:

> when these two youths, Bogusza and Paul were still in a youthful state (*iuvenili etate*),[61] their father Racław died in the land of Opole. After his death, these two ... were foolish and thought nothing of their future welfare, but offered their holdings for sale to various people for a long time ...[62]

These youths are later forced to sell their inheritances to the monastery as testified in a series of charters after they deplete their reserves. At first the abbot at Henryków attempted to help them in their poverty, but later became disillusioned: "I with my brothers have fulfilled your wishes in everyday, beyond the point I was obliged to do. I would be well disposed toward you if you were worth it."[63] A later section will discuss the assumed right of care for children and youth, but what is essential to this passage is the concept that youthful recklessness was associated with prodigality and stupidity, and that even the generosity of monks could be worn out by their irresponsibility. However, Piotr Górecki suggests that, since the Henryków Book notes that the youths' father had died only as the boys attained adolescence, trauma and lack of a a responsible parental figure may have been considered the reason for their unwise

---

59   Grodecki, *Księga*, 257.
60   Górecki, *A Local Society*, 106.
61   Grodecki, *Księga*, 300.
62   Górecki, *A Local Society*, 141.
63   Ibid., 142.

behavior, and this explains why the monastery tried to help them despite their threats and uselessness.[64]

Most of the stories of negativity associated with youth is in regards to boys and young men. However, one of the most entertaining stories of the Henryków Book, involving the selling of Nikłowice to Michael, actually features German girls, and focuses on the danger of their female sexuality:

> Because Michael repeatedly tried to disturb the cloister, he settled his inheritance with Germans. For which reason, while this was going on, women (*mulieres*) and girls (*puellae*)[65] danced in our orchard on holy days. Upon noticing this, lord Bodo, abbot at that time, became distressed with a great affliction, saying in his head, "If over a long passage of time this dancing ripens into a habit here that will lead to a most dangerous loss of many souls in the Cloister."[66]

Beyond the comic aspect of this passage, in which sly Michael uses sex as a weapon, the true terror and threat of the sexuality of young women to souls of the monks of Henryków is considered so dire, that the abbot hastily works to sell the aforementioned land to Michael. While male youthfulness was associated with stupidity by the monks, female youthfulness was connected with lasciviousness.

Despite the fact that the majority of passages referencing childhood and youth have negative associations, this is by no means universal. Heroes of the Henryków Book are described in ways similar to the heroes already described in Gallus and in the hagiography. An example of that comes from the very foundation of the Henryków monastery through the efforts of a cleric named Nicholas. Nicholas immigrated to Silesia and served the duke while amassing his own personal fortune, then instigated the foundation of the monastery at Henryków, until the project was coopted by Duke Henry I himself. Abbot Peter heaps praise on his character, and this includes the description of his virtue at a young age:

> As those who knew him in his youth (*iuventute*)[67] have testified, from the beginnings of life (*a primevo etatis*) Nicholas strove for discipline with an unceasing exertion, and after reaching mature age, was distinguished by

---

64   Górecki, *The Text*, 20.
65   Grodecki, *Księga*, 273.
66   Górecki, *A Local Society*, 121.
67   Grodecki, *Księga*, 239.

an honesty of habits, and, because of his constant uprightness, was much cherished by the noble, the mediocre, and the base.[68]

Perhaps unsurprisingly, much of this unfortunately brief description of Nicholas' early years matches a number of features we will observe in the next chapter on hagiography. First, Nicholas' virtue in his childhood is seen as part and a symbol of a future life lived well. Like the saintly children, he strove hard for excellence even in his earliest years, showing his inborn virtue. These efforts at discipline and holiness in his youth produced a fruit of virtue later in life, and so both nature and nurture are mixed for the maximal glorification of the saint. Nicholas was born with enough discipline to shape himself into a man worthy to do the work of God. By emphasizing the perfection of virtue in Nicholas' earliest through latest phases of life, the monastery roots itself in the works and efforts of a saintly founder, alongside its main eventual patron, Duke Henry I. Piotr Górecki notes that Nicholas' childhood narrative is in the context of a larger panegyric for the life of Nicholas that included many tropes typical of "medieval laudatory biography," and his childhood virtue should be interpreted within this context.[69]

Another interesting passage features the meeting of the Henryków monk Peter (probably the Abbot Peter, who wrote the first book) with the notary Conrad. The passage links boyhood experiences and memories with positive adult actions:

> in his boyhood (*puericia*),[70] this same Conrad had been a school colleague of a certain monk of this cloister by the name of Peter. The Peter quite often visited the courts of the princes together with the abbot. Hence it happened that one time Conrad said to Peter at court, 'I have seen you before, but I do not know where.' In return, Peter answered, 'And I hold a likeness of your person in my heart, but cannot at all bring back to memory where I've seen you.'[71]

The boyhood friendship of Abbot Peter with Conrad sparked old memories, and they eventually recognized each other and "were talking about this and many other similar things among themselves concerning their old friendship."[72] Eventually abbot Peter told Conrad about his purpose at court,

---

68 Górecki, *A Local Society*, 92.
69 Górecki, *The Text*, 34.
70 Grodecki, *Księga*, 291.
71 Górecki, *A Local Society*, 133.
72 Ibid., 134.

namely to reclaim the village at Schönwald. Conrad promises to help and eventually received a favorable settlement. The youthful friendship of these two virtuous men is contrasted with wicked youth of Duke Bolesław II in this same passage, who is accused of wasting time engaging in boyish behavior (*puerilia*).[73] The resulting pun—*puericia* for the "good" Conrad and Peter, and *puerilia* for the misbehaving Bolesław—is meant to highlight the contrast between the virtuous demands of boyhood friends and the whims and injustices of the duke.[74]

5 Memory and Youth, a New Kind of Remembrance in Poland

As the story of Peter, Conrad, and Bolesław II just illustrated, memory of friends, events, and transactions from long past have enormous significance in the Henryków Book. The Henryków Book is all about memory and shaping future remembrance of events in the monastery's interest. As the written word was part of the establishment of new strategies of remembrance, it is reasonable to ask whose memory is the target of those strategies. While sometimes living adults were the target, the memory the Henryków Book was attempting to shape was often that of future generations. In this sense, children and grandchildren, both real and projected, were key to thinking about memory and its preservation over time.

The importance of memory of future generations is so critical to the book that the very beginning of the Henryków Book elaborates about it:

> Because the deeds of the mortals grow old and are dimmed by a fog of oblivion in the course of time and with the long succession of posterity (*longa posteritatis successione*),[75] it has wisely been decreed to entrust them to the memory of succeeding generations (*posterorum*) by the record of letters … and because through succession of diverse times and persons the good deeds of the faithful are sometimes violated by the malice and iniquity of those who come after them, we have expressed in the present booklet, by truthful narration, how … the gifts of all the

---

73 Grodecki, *Księga*, 292.
74 It should be noted that while "puericia" in the Henryków Book is not clearly defined by age categories, in France, many 13th century texts refer to "pueritia," which extended between ages 7 and 14 and was initiated with dental development, namely the coming of "dentum plantatura" see Dieder Lett, *L'enfant des miracles: Enfance et société au Moyen Âge (XII–XIII siècle)* (Paris: Aubier, 1997), 26.
75 Grodecki, *Księga Henrykowska*, 237.

inheritances which this cloister had peaceful possessed since the beginnings ... have accrued to this church, and have been confirmed in eternal possession"[76]

A number of themes in this passage are repeated, reaffirmed, and elaborated in the rest of the text. Fear of oblivion and forgetting, as one generation succeeds another, is perhaps the most prominent of all. Something similar may be found in Gallus, and in the works of other medieval authors, but Abbot Peter has a particular fear, namely that descendants of his contemporaries would forget the pious donations of their parents and dispute their legitimacy. In this sense, the Henryków Book was to serve an educational purpose to the young, so that they would come to understand the actions of their remote ancestors. The means of this memory is the written word and the "record of letters."

The theme of "letters" and the written word is elaborated on in the books written by Peter and the Continuator in which they reproduce charters. One of the most relevant is found in a charter issued by Duke Henry III, in which the abbey exchanged land with Bogusza and Paul, the two youths previously mentioned:

> We prudently escape many evils when we commend the affairs of our age to the memory of letters. For the things established by our predecessors come to our knowledge by the service of letters; for as long as the letter lives, so also lives the act committed to the letter, whose declaration sustains memory and perpetuates temporal acts ...[77]

It seems more than merely coincidental that this passage, perhaps the longest exposition on the power of the written word in memory, is connected with a transaction with two *iuvenes*, who, as noted above, were particularly atrocious examples of wastrel youths. Distrust of their desperation and the observance of their irresponsible behavior probably contributed to these particular reflections accompanying the charter. Bogusza and Paul were living examples of an inheritance squandered, and the damage that a succeeding generation could inflict on the works of their parents. The brothers were a living embodiment of the "many evils" that the monastery hoped to avoid through the "memory of letters." Other charters make clear that their intended target included those far beyond living adults.

---

76 Piotr Górecki, *A Local Society*, 91.
77 Ibid., 141.

Another revealing part of this passage is the concept of living memory, specifically how the written word is said to "perpetuate temporal acts" and keep the "act committed" alive. In the context of the passage, this ability of eternal memory inherent in the written word is a parallel and a counter to the rise of new generations. While human successors, perpetuating a human lineage, arise in time and often commit evil deeds, the monastery employs the power of the written word, which perpetuates not only the memory, but also the very fact, existence, and force of what is done in the past. For childless monks, written words are the closest they will come to physical immortality on earth and the extension of their wishes and rights in time. An example of that may be found in the ducal privilege concerning the liberty of Dalebor's holding: "Hence it is that we … desire it to be known to all—those living as well as well as those who will live …" Here the written word is to be a companion even for the unborn.[78]

The Continuator records charters featuring the trope of letters as a defense against future forgetfulness. A significant example of this is found in the ducal privilege concerning the liberty of Raczyce:

> One generation passes, another arrives and nothing is permanent under the sun, for which reason the ingenuity of the ancients has decreed the efforts made by mortals should be made eternal by worthy witnesses and by the inscription of letters …[79]

Impermanence of memory among succeeding generations is a recurring theme, but here the focus is not so much on the written word as a living continuation of a historical deed, but more on the eternal quality of the word, and its ability to remedy the impermanence "under the sun," a citation from Ecclesiastes, a book of the Bible replete with references to the the passage of time and the meaninglessness of things. One of the most famous passages of the book (Ecclesiastes 2:18–20) criticizes the hope in posterity, for one cannot tell if the offspring will be wise or foolish. As was discussed in a previous section, the problem of the wicked or foolish child is exactly the problem that plagues the Henryków monastery and all landholders described in the book, and this passage suggests that that issue was strongly colored, understood, and rhetorically framed through the Bible and especially the book of Ecclesiastes. It is important to note, however, that this is a reference from a charter, which suggests that such Biblical references were not only on the Continuator's mind.

---

78   Ibid., 189.
79   Ibid., 183.

While charters and the written word countered the claims of the future, some charters suggest that even these attempts were not enough to secure the memory of "future persons." By the time the Continuator wrote Book 2, charters betray a need for further strengthening:

> We, Bernard and Henry, dukes of Silesia ... by tenor of the present privilege—may it be strong forever—make it known to the memory of future [persons], and publicly declare the lord abbot and convent of Henryków hold in their village of Wiesenthal ... in order that oblivion may not erase, nor an evildoer's shrewd desire infringe upon, this present grant of liberty of ours, we took care, in the witness of truth, to strengthen this writing with our deal ... in the presence of the witnesses listed below ...[80]

Not only are the usual list of witnesses meant to give credence to the document, presumably to convince the living of the charter's robustness, but the duke's seal perhaps served as another material witness, alongside the written word, for future generations. But the stated desire for the charter to be "strong forever" suggests a doubt whether even those efforts were sufficient. Indeed, the brief, perfunctory nature of many of those charters, as well as the tendency for their authors to overlook inconvenient details (along with the need for the Henryków authors to add supporting details) suggests that they were, in themselves, not enough.[81]

Poland was not the only place in the High Middle Ages, where people wished to strengthen charters. In England, at that same time, charters were often placed on, in, or near altars on churches to mark their value to witnesses.[82] In fact, the very wording of charters in Poland is extraordinarily similar to what is found in the west. Michael Clanchy writes that "posterity" was the constant target of English monastic charters, and "oblivion," "proof of gift," and "frailty of memory" appeared again and again as concerns for the authors, and he concludes "the fact it illustrates in the present context is that for monks the

---

80 Piotr Górecki, *A Local Society*, 172.
81 Marek Cetwiński, "Formularz dokumentów a opis rzeczywistośći w 'Księdze henrykowskiej,'" in *Formuła, archetyp, konwencja w źródle historycznym: materiały IX Sympozjum Nauk Dających Poznawać Źródła Historyczne, Kazimierz Dolny, 14–15 gr 2000 r.*, ed. Artur Górak and Krzysztof Skupieński (Radzyń Podlaski: Radzyńskie Stowarzyszenie Inicjatyw Lokalnych, Instytut Badawczy "Libra," 2006), 78–81.
82 John Hudson, *Land, Law, and Lordship in Anglo-Norman England* (Clarendon Press, 1994), 182–184.

primary purpose of writing was to inform, or misinform, posterity."[83] In fact, the first cartulary in England, written in the late eleventh century by Hemming of Worcester, is almost indistinguishable from the Henryków Book in tone:

> I, Hemming, monk and priest have composed this little book concerning the possessions of this our monastery, so that it may be clear to our posterity which and how many possessions in land pertain to the endowment of this monastery for the sustenance of the monks, the servants of God; or rather which [possessions] ought by right [to be ours], although we have been unjustly dispossessed of them by force and fraud.[84]

After even a brief glance at this passage, it is evident that despite the differences between Poland and England in culture, politics, land holding patterns, social context, and circumstance, there is still a remarkable similarity in the acknowledgement of the danger lurking in subsequent generations.

6 The Care for Children

Despite the fact that, much like the adults, children and youth appear only in the context of property transfers, the care given to children of all ages is also mentioned frequently. There are two particular contexts in which that care receives special attention. The first concerns the gifts to monasteries given on behalf of the souls of one's children. This was a very common practice in the Middle Ages throughout Europe, and the fact that that practice was recorded for Poland in the 1220s is an indication of the degree of elite Christianization. The second context concerns the need for guardians of young children after the deaths of their parents. Both concerns connect with themes discussed in other chapters, such as the father's care for children mentioned in Gallus and the care of parents for the well-being of their children expressed in the saints' lives.

The most important example of the care for one's children and descendants is the story of how the Henryków monastery came into being. After Nicholas had initiated the foundation of the monastery, Henry I took over the project, and ordered that the merits of its undertaking accrue to his lineage so that:

---

83   Michael Clanchy, *From Memory to Written Record* (Chichester, West Sussex: Blackwell, 2013), 151.
84   Ibid., 103.

the authority of the foundation of this cloister be ascribed to me and to my son (*filio*)[85] and to our successors (*nostrisque successoribus*), because when Nicholas first entered our province, he had not property in it. Thus, let present and future persons know that whatever is accomplished or done here in Henryków, occurs within our property and inheritance. Hence, the authority of this cloister's foundation shall not be ascribed to anyone more justly to me and my successors (*posteris*). Truly, by a spontaneous will I permit and with that a cloister of grey monks be founded in this place, Henryków, for the eternal salvation of myself and of my successors.[86]

The use of two different words for "successors," probably for emphasis, has a clear purpose, namely to associate the abbey with Henry I's branch of the Piast dynasty through time. Whether that expressed in any way Duke Henry I's mode of thinking remains unknown. At any rate, it is clear that the foundation of Henryków is presented, to both those living and those yet to come, as a boon for both the temporal fame of founder's dynasty and also a remedy for their souls. Assuming that he was born ca. 1200, Henry I's son, Henry II, was probably 20 to 30 years of age when the Henryków abbey was founded. To refer to him as the chief "child" target may seem a bit of a stretch, but he had in fact not inherited yet his full title, and he had not reached what could be considered full manhood, as suggested by our discussion of Gallus. Nevertheless, there are examples of donations for younger children.

One telling example of a donation for what were certainly younger children as that of Wiesenthal by Duke Bolko recorded by charter in 1293:

> all of that we carefully add to the eternal alms of the house of Henryków and of the brothers, for the glory of Almighty God and of His Mother the Glorious Virgin, in order to cleanse the sins of ourselves, of our beloved wife Beatrice, and of our children (*liberorum*) who now exist or who might arrive in the future] ...[87]

Since Beatrice became regent for her underage son upon Bolko's death in 1301,[88] it is safe to assume that any children mentioned in the charter would have been very young indeed. Interestingly, all children, living and wished for,

---

85   Grodecki, *Księga*, 244.
86   Górecki, *A Local Society*, 97.
87   Ibid., 168.
88   Ibid., 168 with n. 71.

are called *liberi*, suggesting the love and hopes Bolko and Beatrice had for their young family.

The expectation that, should a child's parents die, he or she would receive protection and education from a kinsman is repeatedly marked in the Henryków Book. Despite the fact that, as mentioned above, women famously acted as regents for ducal heirs in medieval Poland, the role of guardian, protector, and educator of a young child (*tutor*) was often a male, even if the child was related to his or her guardian through the mother's family. The boys Burchard and Jeszko were taken under the care of the knight Stosz, whose wife was the boys' aunt.[89]

Men cared for their kinsmen and kinswomen in a wide variety of circumstances. The need to protect powerful male kinsmen was crucial for the preservation of patrimony, for even young dukes could be the victims of theft:

> Duke [Henry IV] the Righteous had taken away the village of Szydłow ... about which village the same duke claimed that John had unduly usurped it from himself during his boyhood (*puericia*).[90]

Even when the property involved was not extensive, children still received protection. For example, upon the death of Mencelin and of his wife, "Arnold assumed for himself his small grandchildren with the aforesaid two hides, and was made their guardian."[91] Not only grandparents, but even those with no blood ties to the children could become their protectors, such as in the case of James, whose father died when he was 10 years old, and whose mother married another man, who agreed to raise him until he reached adolescence.[92] It seems that an adult man in practically any position could end up being called on to manage the property of children, even those with only a loose relationship to him, though it is hard to extrapolate from the available evidence how common this practice was.

7 Conclusions

The fact that the Henryków Book is removed from any general notion of children and their daily life does not mean that childhood as a concept was absent

---

89 Ibid., 149–150.
90 Ibid., 150.
91 Ibid., 161.
92 Ibid., 146.

from the minds of its authors. In fact, children constitute a fundamental reason for the creation of this book, which is designed to influence the memories of following generations. The power of the written word was waxing, but not yet ultimate, in thirteenth-century Poland, and letters were seen as a way to combat the ignorance and cupidity of future heirs, and to allow deeds and ideas to continue even as new generations of children were born. Coming of age, and the rights and responsibilities that it entailed was thus crucial to the issues addressed in the Henryków Book. This also brings in the role of legal guardians, who cared for and managed children and their inherited assets until they came of age. Not surprisingly in a book whose authors feared the rise of acquisitive, aggressive heirs and simultaneously needed the protection and patronage of a strong, mature ruler to secure their claims, childhood and youth are generally not portrayed in the kindest light, and youth is associated with weakness, laziness, and stupidity. Nevertheless, the right kind of childhood was seen as a benefit to a future life, as in the works of hagiography. In a book about provisions for the future we should not be too surprised that children and appeared frequently and in many contexts.

CHAPTER 5

Children and Childhood in Hagiography

Beginning in the mid-thirteenth century, the lands of Poland produced both a flurry of saints, such as Hedwig, Salomea, and Kinga, and hagiographical accounts to celebrate their lives. At the same time, saints from the past, particularly Stanisław and Adalbert, experienced new popularity and received new treatment by biographers. The rush for the elevation of narrowly regional cults to full sainthood in the thirteenth and fourteenth centuries, as described by Michael Goodich, certainly aided this trend, as well as sparking demand for lists of miracles as evidence for a saint's holiness.[1] These sources provide valuable information about the meaning of childhood in a number of respects, despite the fact that these accounts of childhood play little role in the narrative of the lives.[2] This lack of role in the larger narrative may actually be a bonus for a study of childhood, for as Sally Crawford notes "writers of tales based on real life have an obligation to be true to the minutiae of day-to-day existence in order for the web of fiction to succeed, and it is on the minutiae of the Lives that we can draw for real evidence: on the details that are small enough to be necessarily accurate."[3]

First, this chapter will demonstrate that the stories of the saints themselves, though written within the highly stylized and repetitive genre of medieval hagiography, nevertheless provide an image of what a young holy life was supposed to be. Indeed scholarship now focuses on the underlying perceptions about children that these accounts convey.[4] Second, we will observe how the lists and descriptions of miracles provide a window into the daily life of less exalted children who otherwise might be completely invisible in texts, though of course these sometimes colorful accounts cannot simply be taken at face value. Third, it is important to note that some of the precious little that is

---

[1] Michael Goodich, "Childhood and adolescence among the thirteenth century saints," in *Lives and Miracles of the Saints: Studies in Medieval Latin Hagiography* (Burlington: Ashgate, 2004), 286.
[2] Maciej Michalski, *Kobiety i świętość w żywotach trzynastowiecznych księżnych polskich* (Poznań: Poznańska Durkarnia Naukowa, 2004), 181–190.
[3] Sally Crawford, *Childhood in Anglo-Saxon England* (Gloucester: Sutton Publishing, 1999), 38.
[4] Donald Weinstein and Rudolph Bell, *Saints & Society: The Two Worlds of Western Christendom, 1000–1700* (Chicago: University of Chicago Press, 1982), 218.

known about young girls in medieval Poland is found in these texts, especially due the proliferation of holy women in the region.[5] Despite the reputation of the High Middle Ages as a time of narrowing horizons for women in the political, social, and religious spheres, or at least according scholars such as Jo Ann McNamara,[6] in Eastern Europe and Poland in particular, this period was a time for the flourishing of powerful women in religion and politics.[7] A fourth dimension to this chapter comes from a revaluation of the *puer senex* trope, from the Lives of St Adalbert, St. Stanisław, St. Hedwig, St. Kinga, and St. Salomea, with a particular focus on the emphasis on the inborn qualities of saintly children and the relationship of these qualities to the child's upbringing. Finally, we will consider the value placed on infants and the very youngest children, note the rhetorical use of childhood in the narrative leading up to the canonization of St. Stanisław, survey the miracle stories of the saints statistically and qualitatively for insight into their treatment of children, and point out the sometimes surprising and seemingly contradictory Latin words choices to designate children and young people. Fundamentally, this project is about seeing how children function within the texts themselves. I will not decontextualize references to childhood, but instead will analyze how children and childhood flow with the aims of the texts. This will make it possible to show that children did play a part in the arguments for sanctity for the saints, as well as to explore what this might tell us about how people thought about medieval childhood in a hagiographical context.

---

5   Gabor Klaniczay, *Holy Rulers and Blessed Princesses: Dynastic Cults in Medieval Central Europe* (Cambridge: Cambridge University Press, 2002), 195–294.
6   Jo Ann McNamara, "Women and Power through the Family Revisited," in *Gendering the Master Narrative: Woman and Power in the Middle Ages*, ed. Mary Erler and Maryanne Kowaleski (Ithaca: Cornell University Press, 2003), 20–23. The situation in Poland, with the prominence of women among the 13th century Polish saint contrasts with the general paucity of women in the French hagiographical sources from roughly this period. See Simon Gaunt, *Gender and Genre in Medieval French Literature* (Cambridge: Cambridge University Press, 1995), 185.
7   Many scholars have questioned broad narratives of improving or declining opportunities for women in the Middle Ages, and instead chose to focus on the vastly differing situation and perception of women, and instead not only point out difference in region and time, but also note how different authors even within one region in a narrow window of time and even writing within he same genre differ in their portrayals. For more on this see: Jaqueline Murray, "Thinking about Gender: The Diversity of Medieval Perspectives," in *Power of the Weak: Studies on Medieval Women*, ed. Jennifer Carpenter, and Sally-Beth MacLean (Chicago. University of Illinois Press, 1995), 1–15.

1 Are Good Children Serious Children?

When discussing children in medieval sources, especially hagiography, authors often highlight the trope of *puer senex*,[8] in which the hero, usually a young saint, displays the attributes or actions of a much older person, though sometimes imperfectly and often comically. This trope is used to highlight the child's future promise and uniqueness by showing him or her to be not only unique beyond other children their age, but even possessing traits that put adult actions to shame.[9] Some authors have seen this sort of valorization of adult virtues in children as a denigration of "childish" attributes and a lack of any real concept of childhood beyond the lack of adult virtues.[10] As far as can be told from the texts themselves, sometimes this is indeed the case. At the very least there is a tension in medieval hagiography between "the saint as innocent child alternated with the 'old child' who shunned immature sinfulness.[11] Nevertheless, sometimes the virtue of the hero-child is shown *through* the childlikeness of the protagonist and not merely *despite* it. That much has already resulted from the analysis, in previous chapters, of how Gallus noted that Bolesław Wrymouth would rebel against his father by sneaking off to fight in battle, or how he fought ferocious animals even to his own youthful exhaustion. In such cases, it is the very youthful impetuousness of the child that made the manifestation of heroism possible. In other words, the *puer senex* trope can manifest itself in a variety of ways, sometimes seeming to lessen the value of the childlikeness of the protagonist, while other times affirming childlikeness as a kind of sign of, or even preparation for things to come which could only be performed by a child.

The most famous instance of the *puer senex* trope in the medieval Polish hagiography is the description of the early life of the thirteenth century St. Hedwig, written by an anonymous author in the mid-thirteenth century. In fact, some authors writing about other, very different saintly figures in other

---

8   Małgorzata Delimata, *Dziecko w Polsce średniowiecznej* (Poznań: Poznańska Drukarnia Naukowa, 2004), 37–38. Michalski, *Kobiety*, 188.
9   Phyllis Gaffney, *Constructions*, 74–77, for an example of this trope for Gui in the *Cycle of Guillaume d'Orange*.
10 James Schultz, *The Knowledge of Childhood in the German Middle Ages, 1100–1350* (Philadelphia: University of Pennsylvania Press, 1995), Introduction.
11 Donald Weinstein and Rudolph Bell, *Saints & Society: The Two Worlds of Western Christendom, 1000–1700* (Chicago: University of Chicago Press, 1982), 30.

parts of Europe, have used passages from her *vita* to illustrate the *puer senex* trope.¹² Her childhood virtue is described in such terms:

> For from her childhood (*puericia*), bearing the heart of an old person, she strived to avoid levity, accustom herself to good morals and flee the insolences [intemperateness] of youths. She worked diligently always to foster the cleanness of an innocent life of honesty and discipline.... Never did she mix with reprehensible pastimes, neither did she participate with those who walk in levity.¹³

There is a direct comparison of the young saint with the aged, while at the same time marking Hedwig off from the assumed behavior of others of her age, who are presumed to partake in levity and pointless pastime activities while lacking temperate and constant behavior. Passages such as this one seem to take a dim view of childhood in general as a time which is often wasted and is only good in so far as a child does not act like his or her foolish peers, i.e. act like a child at all. Furthermore, given the fact that Hedwig is portrayed as behaving well because of her internal characteristics alien to other children, namely through her old "heart," it seems that the author did not expect other children to even be capable of similar actions.

The description¹⁴ of the boyhood of St. Stanisław shows a number of the same themes found in the *Vita Hedwigis*:

> For he was born elegantly, trusty [richly provided for] in things, educated in the cult of the Christian religion, devoted to God, modest in mind, chaste in body, reverent in habit, mature in morals, acute in genius, discrete in words and prompt and able to do all good things ... he avoided the games of boys, he fled the lasciviousness of youth ...¹⁵

---

12   David Tinsley, "Reflections of childhood in medieval hagiographical writing: the case of Hartmann von Aue's der Arme Heinrich," in *Childhood in the Middle Ages and the Renaissance*, edited by Albrecht Classen (New York: Walter de Gruyter, 2005), 232.
13   "Life of St. Hedwig," in *Monumenta Poloniae Historica* (= *MPH*), T. 4 (Lwów: Lwowska Komisya Historycznej Akademii Umiejętności, 1884), 512.
14   St. Stanisław's life was later written by Wincenty of Kielcza, a Dominican serving in Kraków, in the mid-thirteenth century.
15   "Life of St. Stanław, vita minor," in *Monumenta Poloniae Historica*, T. 4 (Lwów: Lwowska Komisya Historycznej Akademii Umiejętności, 1884), 255–256.

Again, we find the explicit rejection of the activities that are associated with other boys, including games and intemperateness, as well as sexual immorality. Stanisław's holiness seems to flow from, or at least have its origin in, his birth, and this places him in a different category from normal children. Furthermore, we find that even the youthful Stanisław struggled with the intellectual and mental limitations of his age in his zeal for God but was delivered from that:

> And he was not cheated from this desire, as he was aided by the grace of the divine master. For what the period of boyhood was denying to him, the omnipotent grace of God was supplying in him.[16]

In other words, God's grace could make up for the failures of his stage of life. Having the passages about Hedwig in mind, this seems to be a negative impression of the age of childhood, which the saints only escape by divine intervention. One must be cautious here, however, about drawing any general conclusions about childhood from that, for the saints in adulthood are portrayed as categorically superior to other adults, practicing chastity, enduring painful discipline, and performing miracles. The negative image of childhood and the gap between child-saint and normal child may just be a parallel to the gap between adult-saint and normal adult.

In contrast to the examples examined so far, sometimes the childish characteristics of the saints served to highlight their sanctity rather than work against it. In a humorous passage from the life[17] of St. Adalbert we read that

> on a certain day when he was returning from school, he encountered a girl on the way, and a colleague on the route pushing him to ground threw her on top for the cause of frivolity. And so very quickly getting up, from so much naivety he believed himself to have been married and flowing with bitter tears he pointed the colleague saying: "This one made me to marry!"[18]

Childhood ignorance and naiveté are clearly the vehicle through which young Adalbert's sanctity, especially chastity, are highlighted. While his young friend's

---

16 "Stanisław, vita minor" MPH, 256.
17 While Adalbert was martyred around the turn of the millennium, his cult was revived in the thirteenth century by two texts. The smaller of the two was written in 1227 by an anonymous Dominican monk near Gniezno, while the larger life appeared in 1285, also anonymously written and connected with Gniezno.
18 "Life of St. Adalbert," in *Monumenta Poloniae Historica*, T. 4 (Lwów: Lwowska Komisya Historycznej Akademii Umiejętności, 1884), 210.

wicked and lascivious youthfulness is displayed in a pointless prank, the serious but hapless Adalbert's virtuous boyhood shines through even his comedic mistake.[19]

Interestingly, Kinga,[20] as a young girl, has the most telling examples of a virtuous childlikeness in her *vita*. Whether this is due to her gender or the unique proclivities of the author is not immediately clear. While her *vita* does not always follow a strictly chronological pattern, one should begin the discussion of Kinga's special childlike behavior reported in her youngest years. In one instance in a particular custom, a mass celebrated in the presence of infants:

> in the custom of the realm, to celebrate a special mass for the children ... whenever the blessed Kinga heard "Jesus," this very sweet name raised up in salvation through the Virgin Mary for the whole world, from the affect of devotion she was stirred up inside herself and having been filled with abundant joy, in contrast to the usual ways of children lying in the cradle, she was moving her tongue diligently as if yawning, for her mouth was not able to bring forth words, so that with these signs she seemed to honor the saving name and ... because she was not able by nature [to speak], she demonstrated its effect [i.e. the movement of the mouth].[21]

---

19 This story of Stanislaus raises the question of sexuality of saints and whether there were different emphases for men and women. Some scholars, such as Simon Gaunt argue that the control of the body and the suppression of sexuality is primarily the obsession of female saints, with virginity far more essential to holy women. See Simon Gaunt, *Gender and Genre in Medieval French Literature* (Cambridge: Cambridge University Press, 1995), 185–191. The story above concerning a male saint would thus seem rather out of place in this paradigm. Other scholars, such as Ruth Mazo Karras, see things somewhat differently, arguing that male monastics and saints were actually very often engaged in a struggle for purity, and that this effort was encapsulated in martial imagery. See Ruth Mazo Karras, "Aquinas's Chastity Belt: Clerical Masculinity in Medieval Europe," in *Gender and Christianity in Medieval Europe: New Perspectives*, ed. Lisa Bitel and Felice Lifshitz (Philadelphia, University of Pennsylvania Press, 2008), 52–67. Other scholars suggest that holy people were trying to overcome the perceived weaknesses of their sex to achieve an Edenic wholeness, which caused a difference in emphasis between men and women but not in final outcome. See Jacqueline Murray, "Flesh, Two Sexes, Three Genders?," in *Gender and Christianity in Medieval Europe: New Perspectives*, ed. Lisa Bitel and Felice Lifshitz (Philadelphia, University of Pennsylvania Press, 2008), 24–51.

20 The origins of the hagiography surrounding Kinga are dubious, but seem to be connected with the nunnery she founded in Sącz and in 1329 a collection of miracles and a life were compiled by anonymous admirers and followers.

21 "Life of St. Kinga," in *Monumenta Poloniae Historica*, T. 4 (Lwów: Lwowska Komisya Historycznej Akademii Umiejętności, 1884), 687.

Kinga's attempts to respond in words to the utterance of "Jesus," while stated to be unusual for a child, nevertheless mention a very infant-like behavior, moving the mouth and tongue to try to speak. Again, this story is in a passage extolling the miracles and virtues of the young Kinga, and this childlike and seemingly imperfect act only seems to enhance an argument about her sanctity, even in her infancy.

In a similar way, while avoiding misbehavior, Kinga nevertheless spent time with other girls of her age, luring them to church and teaching them how to behave in a Christian way:

> the holy child invited all her comrades to the entrance of the chapel under the pretext of childish comfort, herself avoiding lascivious games, and entering the aforementioned chapel ... summoning forth all the girls, she was solicitously inciting them now to genuflecting, and now to the prostration of the liturgy, so that all her acts before the age of reason commended her to the Director of All.[22]

This passage is interesting as it shows Kinga as a leader of, or at least an example to, other children towards holiness. She is not commanded to do these things, or even taught to, but instead acts in imitation of the behavior of holy adults. This is in some sense a harbinger of her role with her monastic sisters in the future, but also, in another sense a very childlike behavior of imitation. It is also a sort of holy game, in which she gathers girls and leads them in the words and motions that she and they do not seem to fully understand, as the passage notes she had not, in fact, reached the age of reason. Similar activities, whereby peers are brought into church and instructed in the faith, appear in other hagiographical works, as early as the late sixth-century life of Radegund, a princess of Thuringia, who led a procession of children into church,[23] and are typical of hagiography in succeeding centuries.

Kinga even engages in, what I would call, a sort of "holy play," which is to some degree a great caution to scholars who might be too quick to conclude that the *puer senex* trope in hagiography leaves no time for behavior other than study and praying.[24] For example, when Kinga had reached a slightly later stage of childhood, we read that:

---

22 "Kinga," MPH, 687.
23 "St. Radegund," in *Sainted Women of the Dark Ages*, edited by Jo Ann McNamara, John E. Halborg, with E. Gordon Whatley (Durham and London: Duke University Press, 1992), 70–86.
24 A much earlier example would be in Venantius Fortunatus' sixth-century Life of Radegund. He describes her childhood as including marching with friends in faux processions with a cross.

> When indeed permitted to play, [and] she was dressed in precious clothes, she destroyed them by various movements and in diverse ways, so that on such occasions she would be able to give them out more easily to paupers.[25]

First, it should be noted that even a saintly child like Kinga was presumed to play on some occasions. While other passages in her *vita* make utterly clear that, like the other medieval Polish saints, she spurned frivolity and lascivious games, this clearly does not mean that she never engaged in recreation. Furthermore, the behavior in this passage betrays a childlike willfulness at the destruction of parental gifts for the sake of the child's own desired activity, which in this case happens to be not for selfish reasons but instead for the benefit of the poor.

This passages continues to elaborate on the leisure activity of the young Kinga:

> Indeed in all pastimes she chose the most difficult for herself, so that she would train the body with labor to serve the spirit, [for example] she would pull carts with her friends [inside] over the mountains ...; in all things putting herself under others for service and preferring others to herself ...[26]

Along with the delightful image of the small Kinga dragging a cart with laughing or yelling children up the mountain, which is in some sense another sort of holy play, this passage connects with another important trope from hagiography, the "athlete of Christ," with roots in the New Testament. Kinga is, even in her young age, training herself for a life of exertion on behalf of Christ and his church. Michael Goodich notes this same sort of training behavior in the childhood of Elizabeth of Thuringia, which is considered a model for the later Central European saints like Kinga, in which young Elizabeth would use betting games to convince children to say their prayers. Goodich concludes that "every puerile deed represented an outer expression of inner virtue."[27] This expression of inner virtue in childhood was especially important for they female royal saints of Poland, as they were required to produce heirs. As Jennifer Carpenter writes, "the problem of children ... is clear: they were living reminders of the

---

25   "Kinga," MPH, 689.
26   Ibid.
27   Michael Goodich, "A Saintly Child and a Saint of Children: The Childhood of Elizabeth of Thuringia (1207–1231)," in *Lives and Miracles of the Saints: Studies in Medieval Latin Hagiography* (Burlington: Ashgate, 2004), 19.

saint's failure to remain virginal, and were solid links to the earthy, mundane aspects of human existence."[28] By providing a saintly and miraculous childhood for their hero, the hagiographical author establishes holiness before the, often briefly and dismissively covered, birth of any children to the saint.

Clearly the concept of childlike behavior in the saints of Poland is more complicated than a simple denunciation of all things connected with being a child. While certain negative qualities are associated with this period of life, nevertheless there were certainly some sorts of behaviors and actions that only children could or would do that were considered valuable and signs of a holy life. When one looks at the hagiography for descriptions of playful behavior in those who were not saints themselves (and who were thus beyond the immediate rhetorical need of contrast with other children as a foil for their own sanctity), namely conducted by children healed by the saints in the miracle stories, one finds a number of examples of childlike "play" behavior shown in a positive light—as evidence that the child is happily healed from sickness.

The Life of Salomea[29] contains a telling miracle story that illustrates the acknowledgement of positive childlike behavior in the life of a rather older child. In this account, Vlasca, a 12-year-old, lame girl was exhorted by her mother to call upon Salomea and "crying, she made the vow that she would visit her tomb; and at once she was cured from all disability. Getting up immediately, she began to play (*ludere*), running with other girls in the street praising God in the presence of all the populace."[30] The playful joy demonstrated by Vlasca in this account must exist for a purpose beyond sheer storytelling. Miracle accounts were designed to bolster the credentials of the related saint, not to provide entertainment, and thus these miracle accounts are often brief and formulaic. This means that added details of social and cultural life are very likely included to make a point. Perhaps this passage is designed to recall healing in the Bible, such as Peter's healing of a lame beggar resulting in "walking and jumping and praising God,"[31] or perhaps retellings of this story in the other

---

28 Jennifer Carpenter, "Juette of Huy, Recluse and Mother (1158–1228): Children and Mothering in the Saintly Life," in *Power of the Weak: Studies on Medieval Women*, ed. Jennifer Carpenter and Sally-Beth MacLean (Chicago. University of Illinois Press, 1995), 58.

29 Salomea supported the Franciscan order and her own foundation in Zawichost was dedicated to St. Clare. The editor of life of Salomea, Wojciech Kętrzyński, believed that the author was not anonymous. He attributed the text to Stanisław, a Franciscan living in the 13th century.

30 "Life of St. Salomea," in *Monumenta Poloniae Historica*, T. 4 (Lwów: Lwowska Komisya Historycznej Akademii Umiejętności, 1884), 794.

31 Acts 3:8.

vita. But what is clearly important for my purposes is to note that not only the healed girl, but other girls were also participating in the celebration of this miracle, and this was recorded right before the mention of witnesses, in the place where pious praise to God is recorded, in stories about adult sufferers. Indeed, Vlasca herself was praising God and she ran and played in the streets. This story thus clearly seems to feature a positive association with play, in which a healed girl worships God by it.

While it might (implausibly) be argued that playing in the streets could be conceivably be an adult form of joyous expression and not exclusively childlike behavior, the story of Vitozlava in the Life of St. Hedwig leaves no such doubt. The girl (*puella*) Vitozlava, the daughter of a knight, had seriously deformed and defective eyes. When she had received her sight after devotion and pilgrimage "at once in the custom of children (*more puerile*), because it was summer time, she stood up and picked flowers standing in the field nearby."[32] In this passage, there is a clear reference to a presumed custom or behavior of children which is presented as the natural outcome of the healing. There is no indication that this behavior is considered inappropriate because of its youthfulness. On the contrary, it is linked to the joyful praise given to God and St. Hedwig on her behalf.

Another miracle attributed to Hedwig features, a scholar, Nicholas, on his way from Kraków to Rome to promote the case of Hedwig for sainthood. After being deeply saddened at his unnamed niece's suffering and unspecified languishing, he prayed for her through the merits of St. Hedwig and asked for a special sign to promote her canonization. Afterwards he happily discovered that the "girl had recovered from her sickness and was frolicking, clapping her hands happily with her mother, and this struck down the previous sad spirit with movements of joy."[33] In this case, the serious scholar and future bishop of Poznań, was overjoyed through the saint's ability to demonstrate her powers and return the girl to a childlike state of being—and her childlike behavior triggered his joy rather than earned his righteous condemnation for unbecoming behavior.

Not all the stories of children playing after miracles involve girls. A final example, coming from the Life of St Hedwig, involves an 8-year-old boy named Henryk, who had been born with shrivelled legs, so that he could not walk. In Trzebnica, the center of the cult of Hedwig, the miraculous healing occurred:

---

32   "Life of St. Hedwig," in *Monumenta Poloniae Historica*, T. 4 (Lwów: Lwowska Komisya Historycznej Akademii Umiejętności, 1884), 591.
33   "Hedwig," *MPH*, 628.

in the presence of many others, the boy suddenly got up from the tomb and standing erect, took hold of an egg placed there in his presence and was running around the sepulcher rejoicing. When the Lady Petronilla, then custodian of the tomb, took up another decorated egg and threw it before the boy on the location of a further tomb, the boy chased after the egg to take hold of it and returned to his mother rejoicing.[34]

What makes this story of play particularly interesting is the presence of the egg. Painted eggs appear in some child graves and also in a great deal of Polish ethnography from the Late Middle Ages and beyond, usually symbolizing life, birth, and nourishment from supposedly pre-Christian times.[35] In Christian times, these had connections with the resurrection and healing in Christ, and this passage seems to be tapping into these themes.

In conclusion, childlike/childish behavior can be viewed both positively and negatively in hagiography, both in reference to the saints and normal, un-saintly children. Indeed, the *puer senex* trope should be approached carefully, noted for the various, nuanced ways in which it is employed, and not assumed as the final word on play and pastime in any text or genre. While childlike behavior is never valorized in and of itself in Polish hagiography, it does seem to serve as a conduit for conveying meaning about the activities of saints. Saintly children are undeniably set apart from their peers and all of their activities are contrasted with the negative behavior of other children. Even when a saintly child, like Kinga, does engage in childlike behavior, it is special and meant to emphasize the saint's efforts for the sake of God.

2   Education Issues: Nature vs. Nurture, God as Teacher, Male vs. Female

This section will deal with three important aspects of the process of growing up as a saint as presented in the *vitae* of the Polish saints. First is the question of nature vs. nurture: namely, to what extent did medieval authors consider an education, whether monastic or military, to be essential for developing the talents and qualities of children and later adults? As with the discussion of

---

34   Ibid., 601.
35   See Joanna Wawrzeniuk, "Symbolika jajka w grobie dziecka w okresie wczesnośredniowiecznym," in *Dusza maluczka, a strata ogromna*, Funeralia Lednickie spotkanie 6, edited by Wojciech Dzieduszycki and Jacek Wrzesiński (Poznań: Stowarzyszenie Naukowe Archeologów Polskich, Oddział w Poznaniu, 2004), 143–54.

the "*puer senex* trope," evidence from Polish hagiography suggests a balanced approach to this problem, in which the child-saint is praised from both angles rhetorically, both for their inborn qualities which set them apart from others from the beginning, but also for their hard work and diligence in study, and for the value of that study for making them better Christians. The second important issue involves the participation of God or the Spirit directly in the education of the young saint, the process of which combines elements of both nature and nurture. All of the saints receive divine aid in their development to some degree, but the proportions and emphasis of God's help vary. The third issue is that of gender. Is the maturing and education of female saints described differently from those of male saints? What, if anything, characterizes their process of growth when compared to their male counterparts?

The first example one could draw for this balance between nature and nurture comes from the "new" life of St. Adalbert. The saint himself was destined for a career in the church after a miraculous healing in his own childhood had terrified his parents into offering their son to God in prayer if He should save him from a crippling ailment. Afterwards, we read that:

> And when, with his boyhood years with his parents completed, he had learned to read and heedless with modesty he seemed to himself to understand nothing by reading ... Having set out to the Parthenopolis (Magdeburg), he was committed to the teacher Othrich for education, under the discipline of which the boy accomplished so much, relying on his inborn sense, his nature, and his reason, in which he excelled, indeed more carried by divine help ... At that time indeed, with the whole intention of his mind he was pressing on to live well, so that the talent of intelligence entrusted to him by the Lord, he did not waste by hesitating, gaping at the pleasures of the earth.[36]

In this passage there is a heavy emphasis on the nurturing effect of education on Adalbert, namely through his teachers at Magdeburg. His own efforts as well are duly noted, as Adalbert accomplishes much even before he leaves his parents and home. Nevertheless, inborn abilities are also present helping him to succeed, and they provide an important foundation for all that he does. Nevertheless, is is implied that "divine help" itself is the greatest factor in Adalbert's achievements, more important than his own efforts or those of any human teacher or education. For God's help is working within Adalbert secretly and deeply, and is not related to his choices or environment; at the

---

36 "Adalbert," *MPH*, 210.

same time, however, God is the ultimate teacher and nurturer. The last sentence of the passage raises an interesting question: could Adalbert have chosen a different path? Was he actually tempted by "the pleasures of the earth" to relax his zeal for scholastics? Or is this passage simply intended to contrast him with normal children? Perhaps holiness was with him from the beginning, or perhaps his avoidance of worldly diversions came from the noted constant influence of God on his life and studies.

The other major male saint of medieval Poland, St. Stanisław, also had great gifts of intellect and engaged in advanced study. Nevertheless, there are some subtle differences in the portrayals of the source and origin of those virtues. We will begin with his early childhood, before he was sent away for study:

> He by the gift of the Creator arrived with blessings by chance having a good spirit of sweetness from God, because he found grace in the eyes of God; he also received blessings and mercy in the gifts free and natural, which were learned to have been instituted very well from his beginning. For he was born elegantly, trusty (or richly provided for) in things, educated in the cult of the Christian religion, devoted to God, modest in mind, chaste in body, reverent in habit, mature in morals, acute in genius, discrete in words and prompt and able to do all good things. For as just as the liquid wax receives the impressed image of the seal and preserves it, thus the boy easily taught boy Stanisław committed to memory all the good which he was able to hear and to understand. Hence his parents, seeing the aforementioned reason of the boy, studious in spirit, they decided to place him under the discipline of scholastics.[37]

An emphasis different from that in the *vita* of Adalbert is detectable, as a there is a much greater focus on Stanisław's natural capacities, which are repeatedly noted to come from his birth. This includes not only powers of mind such as good memory and natural intelligence, but also great inner virtue (such as chastity, a devoted mind, and a studious spirit) and outer virtue (good habits and morals). Even his essential "spirit" is described as receiving goodness and sweetness and studiousness from God. When his learning process is described, it is through a metaphor of wax and seal, which emphasizes the ease with which young Stanisław absorbed and retained information due to his inborn abilities. At the same time this metaphor de-emphasizes any personal efforts of the saint in acquiring his knowledge, for wax is impressible because of its essential characteristics and it does not "strive" to achieve a shape. James

---

37 "Stanisław, minor," *MPH*, 255.

Schulz notes this sort of metaphor in the German medieval literature as well, whereby education is the tool which shapes the raw material of nature into greatness.[38]

St. Stanisław's time under the scholastics' tutelage shows more reasons for the boy's unearthly progress in his scholarly endeavors:

> having been handed over to the study of letters the boy took hold of his inborn good and did not do things half-heartedly ... he was commended with zeal, to exert (himself) ... These things indeed the acute boy did, so that he could complete them and, completing more and more he would improve himself and arrive at the knowledge of truth. And he was not cheated from this desire, as he was aided by the grace of the divine master.[39]

While in the life of Adalbert at least a degree of credit is given to his teachers, there is little mention of them for St. Stanisław, whose own efforts are the center of attention. Importantly, the excellence of study is presented as the result of Stanisław's, choice to take "hold" of his "inborn good" and to work hard to make himself into a great master of the arts. Despite the gifts of nature, indeed, both passages concerning Stanisław's education imply that the youthful saint in fact does have much to learn that is of value beyond knowledge and goodness they already possess. The agency of human teachers might be minimized, but a saint still needs to be nurtured. In this regard it is important to stress that despite Stanisław's original superiority in all things, he still had to apply himself strenuously, seemingly athletically, to his own self-improvement. In this regard, like Adalbert, the agency of God as teacher is present, for He allows both boys to overcome their moral and intellectual inadequacies. Finally, it is important to note briefly what exactly Stanisław is achieving and mastering in his studies. We find that he succeeds in developing skills in the "liberal arts" and "canon and divine law." and becomes a "man of letters."[40] This will be important for comparison with the female saints.

A number of similar themes appear in the Life of St. Hedwig. In the passage quoted above about the orientation of Hedwig's heart towards the behavior of an elderly person, we see some parallels to Adalbert and Stanisław. A strong emphasis is placed on the strivings and efforts of the young saint as well as a

---

38 James Schultz, *The Knowledge of Childhood in the German Middle Ages, 1100–1350* (Philadelphia: University of Pennsylvania Press, 1995), 98.
39 "Stanisław, minor," MPH, 255–256.
40 Ibid., 256.

sharp demarcation between the behavior of the saint and those of other children at that stage of life. Likewise, the natural tendencies towards excellence apart from any human teacher are evident:

> In all these and others of her works contrary to men, who have teachers bestowed upon them by their ancestors for the learning about correct morals and behavior, she had the education of the Holy Spirit, who from infancy taught her with the fear of God to abstain from all sins in such a way that she would preserve her soul clean from all desires … For in the age of childhood she learned the holy Scriptures in the cloister of Kycingo, in which she spent zeal and time in her youth usefully and afterwards in her understanding she drank the grace of inner consolation and devotion abundantly.[41]

The Holy Spirit is just as active in the life of Hedwig, but while the Spirit gave Adalbert and Stanisław powers of intellect, understanding and knowledge, Hedwig is taught "morals and behavior."[42] The objective of this exercise was to achieve a "clean soul," something that is not at all emphasized in the childhood exertions of the male saints. Interestingly, Hedwig's moral education is the most markedly delineated from the efforts of any earthly teacher of all the saints' accounts, and its perhaps the focus on purity of heart rather than books that causes this to be. Hedwig's intellectual education was also distinct from that of the male saints, for while the schooling of the male saints was centered on instructions in the liberal arts and canon law, Hedwig's was focused on the Scriptures and she did not gain knowledge of an ecclesiastical or scholarly kind, but instead was transformed spiritually, gaining "consolation" and "devotion." This difference perhaps reflects the fact that the education she receives is from a cloister and not from scholastics, but this itself is a result of Hedwig's gender. In this way Hedwig and the other female saints of Poland are firmly within medieval European norms for education. Joanne Ferraro writes that medieval education, including monastic education, for men was considerably different from that of women. With most career paths in administration, education, and the church closed to women, their education in convents focused on the Bible, hagiography, moral character, and good manners. The classics and a general

---

41 "Hedwig," MPH, 512.
42 Note that while Stanisław is praised for his morals and behavior as inborn qualities, they are not described as part of a spiritual education and are not the focus of his early life.

liberal arts education was rarely available to women, at least in their places of formal education.[43]

The childhood education and development of Kinga are more difficult to piece together, but it shares many similarities to that of Hedwig and female saints generally, namely in the emphasis on moral development as opposed to scholarly learning:

> A child of good inborn quality, when Kinga was five years old, under obedience to her mother-in-law, proceeding from virtue to virtue ... for the foremost intention of her devotion was for a good position and for chaste purity, so she with all her body and mind, even to the end of her life, she stressed to observe (this) with all the intention of her heart.[44]

Again, many similarities to the male saints are here, including the mention of her qualities from birth, as well as her athletic striving for advancement. Nevertheless, similar to Hedwig, there is no mention of intellectual or scholarly interests or abilities before formal schooling, as in the case of both male saints. Furthermore, Kinga's life also parallels Hedwig's in that the qualities that are mentioned in her early life are morality and virtue. Little is said by the author about any formal education for Kinga before her twelfth year, when she is married to Bolesław of Kraków. Most of what she learned about Christianity came from her constant attendance at mass, where she listened very attentively to the sermons.[45] Otherwise, as noted in the stories mentioned above, Kinga immersed herself in holy activities and training for bodily castigation. For example, we read that before Kinga reached 12 years of age she had made herself a garment of horse hair which she wore to bed, so that bleeding and pain would toughen her soft body, despite the fact that she wore nice court clothing in public.[46] In short, the gendered emphasis on morality for Hedwig and Kinga rather than scholarly education in the Polish female saints does not diverge from patterns elsewhere in Europe.

The life of St. Salomea provides precious little detail about her early years and education. All that we have is one small passage about Salomea being "always found in the tenderness of her youth illuminated by the holy spirit, with inborn goodness, with holy way of life, in the service of God in the act

---

43 Joanne M. Ferraro, "Childhood in medieval and early modern times," in *The Routledge History of Childhood in the Western World*, ed. Paula Fass (London: Routledge, 2015), 61–77.
44 "Kinga," MPH, 686–689.
45 Ibid.
46 Ibid., 690.

of giving mercy."[47] This description is in line with what has already been discussed, as she has inborn qualities like all the saints, but she also embodies the particular focus of the child female saint on virtue and Christian morals. Her education in her younger years was conducted alongside that of her young husband Coloman, and in the description of this we have the closest example of a female education of intellectual rigor:

> when both were given over to the discipline of scholars, the blessed Salomea advanced in all the sacred literature of the sacred Scriptures, as well as asking for an individual gospel from the teacher, by day she wanted to hear, to interpret, and expound on it.[48]

Not only is Salomea getting an education alongside her husband, but she is excelling at it—not merely learning the Scriptures and other literature, but also learning how to analyze and reason. This is still, of course, not the type of liberal education described for Adalbert or Stanisław, but it is still of more substance than what is said about Hedwig or Kinga. Other female saints in the early Middle Ages, were also described as having devotion to the study of the scriptures, such as Leoba, an Anglo-Saxon nun who later traveled with Boniface to Germany. She is described as being educated in the scriptures from infancy and for showing a zeal for listening and reading them in her girlhood.[49] Despite her Biblical training, Salomea's education does not really result in a mastery of learning, for the rest of this section of her *vita* describes her and her husband's fanatical forays in self-mortification. Unlike Stanisław or Adalbert, who are described as becoming very learned men after their education, Salomea's simply becomes a more devoted ascetic.

There is a tension in all medieval Polish hagiography: the authors want to present saints as models of excellence, but to mention growth and education, while showing character and devotion in the saints, also implies imperfection. The solution is that the saints are completely devoted to the process of overcoming their imperfections and limitations. Thus the the nature vs. nurture problem is in some sense an illusion, for hagiographers stress both learned and inborn behavior at different times for the rhetorical purpose of glorifying the saint and passages like those should be hesitantly approached as any sort of guide to contemporary ideas of childhood. The role of God and the Spirit as the ultimate teachers of the saints was an important part of this glorification

---

47 "Salomea," *MPH*, 776.
48 "Salomea," *MPH*, 777.
49 Monumenta Germaniae Historicae, Scriptores, ed. Waitz (Hanover: 1887): 127–131.

process, for who could be a more perfect teacher than God? Finally, there is a clear gender difference in the hagiography, with young female saints preoccupied with moral perfection and mortification of their bodies while the male saints were lauded on their prowess in scholarly pursuits. Even Salomea, who was rigorously trained alongside her husband in Biblical interpretation, nonetheless did not study beyond religious topics. This gendered education is typical for the time and reflects Poland's general reproduction of educational norms found elsewhere in Europe.

3 Precious or Burdensome? Children Three Years and Younger

Despite the fact that all the lives of the five Polish saints under examination contain descriptions of each saint's childhood, however brief these may be, the earliest days of those children are often either ignored or given the briefest of treatment. Salomea and Hedwig, for example, appear only as girls. The lack of emphasis on the earliest childhood years is not only a phenomenon that appears in texts, but also archaeologically across Europe, or so it is argued from the very low incidence of grave goods in children under three years old. Sally Crawford and Lotta Mejsholm, for example, note this phenomenon in both Anglo-Saxon England and Sweden respectively, and Tomasz Kurasiński and Kalina Skóra have noted it for medieval Poland as well.[50] Sociological explanations are often posited for this lack of treatment, namely that the inability to speak, little mobility, the need for constant parental care, and low self-awareness mean that children of such age have little ability to contribute to society, and initiation rites that reflect full inclusion into society are reserved for later periods in life.[51] Does the lack of visible concern for infants in text and archaeology equate to a general disregard for that age group in the past? A few hints from the lives of the saints suggest that there were at least some moments of significance for those under three, and much more of this level of care can be detected in the miracles ascribed to those saints. However, general conclusions on the basis of these highly stylized and crafted texts must only remain at the most tentative level.

---

50 Crawford, *Childhood*, 27–29. Lotta Mejsholm, "Constructions of early childhood at the syncretric cemetery of Fjalkinge—a case study," in *Youth and Old Age in the Medieval North*, ed. Shannon Lewis-Simpson (Leiden: Brill, 2008), 41. Tomasz Kurasiński and Kalina Skóra, "Children's burials from the early medieval inhumation cemetery in Radom, site 4," *Fasciculi Archaeologiae Historicae* 28 (2015): 46–48.

51 Tomasz Kurasiński and Kalina Skóra, *Cmentarzysko w Radomiu, Stanowisko 4* (Łodz: Wydawnictwo Instytutu Archeologii i Etnologii PAN 2016), 96–98.

Before proceeding, it is important to note that there is a general scholarly consensus, both in Poland and outside of it, that baptism was the defining ritual of early childhood in Christian medieval times, and much of the following discussion will be intertwined with this reality. Nevertheless, it is difficult to know exactly what medieval people understood this ritual to mean. From Augustine in Late Antiquity through Carolingian authors such as Jonas of Orléans, lack of baptism was uniformly thought to result in eternal damnation due to original sin.[52] With the emergence of scholastic thinking in the High Middle Ages, however, the concept of limbo, in which unbaptized children were suspended between heaven and hell in painless but joyless eternity, as epitomized by Thomas Aquinas in the mid-thirteenth century, took over the official position of the church. On the contrary, late antique and early medieval authors assumed the complete purity and innocence of baptized children and their prized place in the heavenly kingdom.[53] Stanisław Rosik questions the degree to which Augustinian or the new scholastic ideas percolated into the thinking of people in the twelfth through fourteenth centuries, when the *vitae* under discussion were written. Old folkloric traditions and even supposedly old fears of revenant children could well have been on the minds of parents when thinking of baptism and its effects.[54] Because of the possibility of misinterpretation of what past people were thinking when it came to baptism, it is important to avoid hasty assumptions and follow where the sources lead as much as possible.

For the male saints, Adalbert and Stanisław, the events of early childhood, whether baptism or otherwise, provided a forecast for what was to come. For Adalbert,[55] the son of the powerful duke Slavnik, baptism brought his name "Wojciech" (or "joy in war"), which was considered "honest enough." Under this name he quickly advanced in qualities and abilities beyond his siblings. But a childhood event "in the time of the weaning of the child," after his baptism, caused major change in the young boy's life:

---

52   Daniele Alexandere-Bidon and Didier Lett, *Children in the Middle Ages: Fifth–Fifteenth Centuries* (Notre Dame: University of Notre Dame Press, 1999), 27.
53   Ibid.
54   Stanisław Rosik, "Vitoslava infantula primo nata mortem accepit ... Dylematy wokół śmierci dziecka w średniowieczu na przykładzie żywotu św. Jadwigi śląskiej," in *Dusza maluczka, a strata ogromna*, Funeralia Lednickie spotkanie 6, edited by Jacek Wrzesiński and Wojciech Dzieduszycki (Poznań: Stowarzyszenie Naukowe Archeologów Polskich, Oddział w Poznaniu, 2004). For more concrete examples of how these fears may have manifested themselves see Crawford, *Childhood*, 77–87.
55   Note, "Adalbert" was the name given to Wojciech by Adalbert of Magdeburg, who was his mentor and teacher and second father.

a very grave infirmity entered his life. When they observed him laboring [in his disease] with great difficulty and in imminent peril of death, and they were hardly satisfied that they would be groaning and crying in anguish, since they despaired for the life of the boy, they laid out a vow to God with a plan for health saying: Not for us Lord ... may this boy live, that he should be occupied in worldly business, but so that he could be transferred to your service, ordained in the holy church in obedience to you ... as the almost dead [boy] was placed on the altar ... God, infused [him] with the medicine of divine piety, he was returned healthy to his parents.[56]

This passage shows a number of important themes. First, the emotional anguish of the parents is almost palpable. Despite the young age of Wojciech, his parents are nevertheless grieved by his illness and terrified of his impending death. Of course, whether this was actually the case or not is unknowable, but what is important is that parents were expected to act this way by the author, or at least noble and good parents were. Significantly, we will see below that in a discussion of infant death in the miracles of the saints, beyond the immediate need to show the sanctity of the parents or the child in the *vitae* proper, the same emotional attachment even to the youngest of children is evident. Another important point is the promise of the dedication of Wojciech to God, should he be healed and how this dedication led to a transformation of the life trajectory of young Wojciech, and seemingly changed his destiny away from being a warlord and noble leader (as indicated by his name at baptism), and despite his abilities over his siblings: "the parents did not in the least choose him as heir of their possessions, and with very great honesty of devotion they chose (him) to be an imitator (of Christ)."[57] In other words, key points and events at even the earliest parts of life were considered important and transformative, at least in hagiography.

St. Stanisław did not experience a great moment or transformation in his earliest life, but instead his biographer chooses to elaborate on the meaning of his name, chosen at baptism, and on its meaning for the future: "Stanisław, as we said before, descended from worldly dignity, not only born from honorable parents, but even his name was a sign that he would be a man of nobility and illustrious. For the word Stanisław, given to him in the sacrament of baptism was divinely inspired, from the Latin word and from Poland: 'standing praise'

---

56 "Adalbert," *MPH*, 209.
57 Ibid.

or 'station of praise' or ..."[58] In fact, the author offers multiple other interpretations of the name and goes on to explain how each of them applies to the future Stanisław. The explanation of the etymology of a saint's name was a common trope in hagiography in western Europe.[59] What is important to note, however, is that the event of baptism and the name connected with it was considered highly significant for the future life of the child, and the author clearly say the naming as "divinely inspired."

A similar motif of prophetic events and words is associated with the young Kinga, though in this case connected with her birth and actions of infancy. This began when her mother, Maria, felt terrible heaviness in her womb, and feared for her life, and she fled to a church where she entreated the Virgin Mary for help in her distress. Miraculously, she heard a voice in heaven telling her, not only would she escape death from giving birth, but she was also told "you will give birth to a girl who will be a great solace to you and a rest for many souls and a special remedy."[60] While still in the womb, Providence had foreseen her pious acts and her future works for God. Furthermore, we are told that, notwithstanding God's punishment of Eve with pain in childbearing, Kinga's birth was, indeed, painless and bloodless, as she came forth shining and pure, a characteristic she would exhibit for the rest of her life. Pre-natal miracles and prophecies are common in hagiography, and were often used to suggest future attributes of the relevant saint, such as in the lives of late 13th century Franciscan Francis Venimbene or Joan of Aza, St. Dominic's mother.[61]

Similar to Stanisław, Kinga's baptism also featured special signs: "with the hands of the bishop seeking to baptize her, not without a great, miraculous portent" was she brought into the family of God.[62] Specifically, after the baptism liturgy had begin she was completely silent, neither crying nor stirring, until the end of the service. After she was weaned, during mass she never desired food or sleep, but steadily looked to heaven. Neither was she diverted by games designed to amuse infants, but "she truly overcame, inspired by the Holy Spirit, all the vanities of temptation."[63] A further miracle is mentioned above, when during the special, customary mass said in the presence of infants Kinga tried

---

58   "Stanisław, vita minor," MPH, 254–255.
59   Michael Goodich, *Vita Perfecta: The Ideal of Sainthood in the Thirteenth Century* (Stuttgart: Anton Hiersemann, 1982), 82.
60   "Kinga," MPH, 686.
61   Goodich, "Childhood and adolescence", 287. Weinstein and Bell, *Saints & Society*, 24.
62   "Kinga," MPH, 687.
63   Ibid.

to mimic the name "Jesus," albeit unsuccessfully.[64] The existence of this custom, with infants present in the mass in a special way is itself important for the understanding the importance of infancy. The fact that it was considered a time when saintly children, like Kinga, could set themselves apart from others suggests another way in which infancy was considered a time of portent.

A broader point from this account of Kinga's life is that her signs of miracles were manifested at a series of significant points in her life cycle. Starting from pregnancy and childbirth, she showed signs of uniqueness at her baptism (initiation ritual), at her weaning, and at her first attempts at speaking. This suggests at least some degree of knowledge on the part of the author of a series of stages of development for even the youngest of children, and the fact that he chose to attach miracles and signs to each of these hints that he could have been matching tropes of early childhood stages with the revelation of Kinga's character and future.

While the lives of the saints use earliest childhood for the means of prophecy, the saint's miracles are more closely linked to mourning parents, with rhetorical effect when the child is miraculously healed, or for pointing out the importance of baptism in saving young children from an unenviable afterlife. While often terse and vague, these accounts provide some of the only textual representations we have of young infant and child death outside the circle of the ducal families in Poland and Hungary. One of the difficulties, however, in discussing these miracles is that the age of the victim is not always clear. Sometimes only *puer* or *puella* are used to describe the child. I shall show below that, these terms are not always used in accordance to particular age categories, for they could cover anything from a newborn to a young adult.

One of the most telling stories features a funeral for a small child, "the son of Stronislaua the wife of Vrotslay a knight from Policarciz, named Vicherus, who is in his third year."[65] The passage uses the present tense when referring to the boy's age, and furthermore this is followed by a favorable description of the boy's physical appearance by those examining the family about the details of the miracle, suggesting that the age given is the age at the time of the examination, not at the time of the miracle. When the child, whatever his age, did become sick and died, his mother, also gravely ill, prayed to St. Stanisław for healing, and an old man appeared to her and told her that through Stanisław her prayers had been answered, and that she should dedicate the boy to St. Martin in response to his resurrection. At this point we find out about what the rest of the family had been doing in the meantime:

---

64   "Kinga," MPH, 687–688.
65   "Stanisław, vita minor," MPH, 302.

And the mother, having opened her eyes, and seeing no one she returned into her house, where the boy was lying. She narrated this vision to her husband and the sister of her husband and many others who had gathered there for the purpose of a funeral ...[66]

This passage is from the earlier and more laconic Vita Minor, but the Vita Major adds a few more details about the funeral. First, we are told that relatives had gathered both for the funeral AND for "consoling the parents."[67] Second, we are given the setting and position of the audience: "with all those sitting and watching above the bier."[68] From this account it is apparent that despite the young age of the deceased child, a proper funeral was in order, with at least the boy's aunt, and presumably his extended family congregating in order mourn the boy's passing and comfort the grieving parents. While, as shall be discussed later in my archaeology chapter, children at this age rarely received many, if any, grave goods and often were buried in shallow pits, passages like this suggest that, at least for the lower nobility, their deaths did not go unnoticed or unfelt by the community.

Another salient passage suggesting the emotional bond between parents and the youngest of children comes from the miracle of St. Salomea. "A small girl, perhaps two years old, the daughter of count Iaxichonis, whose wife was called Sophia, with a vow having been made by her parents for her, was resurrected from death through the merit of the holy Salomea, to whom they humbly entrusted her (their daughter) with great tears and crying."[69] Whether the tears of the parents were due to a feeling of loss from the donation of their child to the church or to their joy at their daughter's miracle, they are clearly noted for their intensity (*magno fletu*).

Many of the passages describing the affliction and death of infants and small children are connected to baptism, or more specifically, the death of the child before baptism and the dolorous reactions of parents fearing for the soul of the child. This miracle category is common in Polish and, indeed, general European hagiography, therefore, I will only discuss one miracle in the category which has comparative relevance to another chapter.[70] From one story in the Vita Major of St. Stanisław there is a glaring phrase and word choice in

---

66   Ibid.
67   "Life of St. Stanisław, vita major," in *Monumenta Poloniae Historica*, T. 4 (Lwów: Lwowska Komisya Historycznej Akademii Umiejętności, 1884), 402.
68   Ibid.
69   "Salomea," *MPH*, 794.
70   Didier Lett, *L'enfant des miracles. Enfance et société au Moyen Âge (XII–XIII siècle)* (Paris: Aubier, 1997), 72–77 and 205–210.

regards to a baptism following resuscitation. After two twins were born on the feast of St. Florian, tragedy struck, for "the boy on the day following his birth died without the grace of baptism. When this was announced to the father, a great pain seized him not for the death of offspring (*pro defuncta prole*), but for the death of the soul."[71] As mentioned in Chapter 3 above on the Henryków Book, in medieval Poland, offspring were exceedingly important both in reality and as a social concept. As a consequence, the author did not use the word for boy or son (*puer*) to refer to the deceased is in and for itself relevant. Since the author of the account was a churchman, it is impossible to know whether the father had some other reason for mourning. Whatever the case may be, this passage indicates that the death of offspring was truly a tremendous loss, given that the author uses that fact to argue for the even more devastating loss of the soul. Without the audience understanding how essential heirs were, it makes little sense to value the loss of an heir less than the loss of a soul from lack of baptism.

The resuscitation of young children is an outstanding feature in the miracles attributed to St. Hedwig. In fact, in the section of her miracles concerning the resuscitation of the dead, four out of seven involve children.[72] Nevertheless, these stories suggest that, while deep mourning and sadness for children and fear of death before baptism was often connected with the death of young children such as in the case of Vitoslava,[73] fear of punishment for negligence was also an expected reaction. Stanisław Rosik draws attention to one of these passages with a rather singular story, in which 5-week old Pietrucha is left in the care of a nurse, who leaves the baby briefly in the cradle, which is then disturbed by a pig coming into the house and knocking it over, thus causing the young girl to suffocate in the linens, in which she is wrapped.[74] The parents' reaction is very different from all the cases discussed thus far:

> The mother wailed over her dead daughter and fear doubled her pain, for not a little did she fear to be castigated by her husband for this negligence. The said husband arriving mourned the death grievously, but he did not regret so much about the death of his daughter, but rather about being charged with the sin of negligence, for he was fearing that the death would be blamed on himself and his wife.[75]

---

71 "Stanisław, Vita Major," *MPH*, 400.
72 "Hedwig," *MPH*, 621–626.
73 Ibid., 623.
74 Rosik, "Vitoslava infantula", 115–7.
75 "Hedwig," *MPH*, 623.

The mother, at least, in the passage, is at least partly distraught by her loss, but the husband seems entirely absorbed with his image in the community and fears of punishment. While to some extent this sort of passage could be used to argue that parental emotional attachments to very young children were not always assumed to be present, one is left wondering why the parents themselves would have been so concerned about the opinions of friends and family if children were not, at least by some, deemed to have value. The fate of the negligent nurse is not clear from the passage, but other guardians of young children were presented as fearing the wrath of parents. This is illustrated in the story of Wilhelmus, whose guardian decided to go swimming in a river while the two-year-old was placed on its bank. After the boy fell in and drowned the guard "returning to the house with the boy he wanted to hide the deed from the parents, but he was not able to hide it, for when the boy was warmed up by his mother, he vomited a residue of water and suddenly died. The parents of the dead and the family were mourning ..."[76] In this instance, the parents are indeed grieving for their child's death, but the guardian is in terror for his future. These two passages suggest that the death of small children, vulnerable and always supposed to be under supervision, could result in feared condemnation and prosecution.

Children three years of age and younger, while only briefly mentioned in the lives of saints and only receiving treatment in certain kinds of miracles, nonetheless play some part in the rhetoric of those texts. This is reminiscent of Gallus Anonymus, though of course for him the focus was on older children, signs from naming, baptism, and early behavior served to prophetically prefigure later glory. Furthermore, the emotional anguish of bereaved parents serves to highlight the mercy of the saints in the miracles. Baptism is presented as the most grievous loss in a young child's death, though perhaps parents were more afraid of the end of lineage. Finally, death of infants resulted in deep fear of condemnation. In fact, infants and the youngest of children in the Infans I category were comparatively well-represented in European medieval hagiography. By contrast, the Infans II category—children of 4–7 years of age—appear under-represented for reasons that remain unknown.[77]

---

76   Ibid., 622.
77   Lett, *L'enfant*, 31.

4 Children, Childhood, and Descendants in the Canonization Story of St. Stanisław

While it seems evident that authors like Gallus Anonymus used childhood in a self-conscious way and employed words and themes of childhood to weave a compelling narrative, this is much less sure in the other texts under examination in this book. The narratives of childhood in the Vita Maior and the Miracles examined so far certainly work with childhood rhetorically, but these have been confined to only certain, small parts of these texts, namely narratives clearly about children or childhood and often are expressed in tropes, such as *puer senex*, which were common in medieval Europe.[78] Nevertheless, there does seem to be at least one instance in which images of childhood play a larger role in a narrative not explicitly related to children or childhood. This is in the story of the elevation and canonization of St. Stanisław found in the Vita Maior and the attached miracles. In fact, this canonization section works not just with tropes of youth, but also with those of age in general and perhaps even with gender. In the end, the reader is left with the impression that thirteenth century Poland, a generation far removed from the sins of the older generation that murdered Stanisław, has received a blessing from God in the later, younger age and are set for restoration and rebirth in both kingdom and religion if they hold true to God's purpose for their own time and place.

Before the canonization narrative of the Vita Maior begins in earnest, there is a chapter containing a prophecy linking the impending canonization of St. Stanisław with the reunification of Poland politically. The lack of a kingdom is blamed on the sinfulness of tenth- and eleventh-century Poles, affirmed by the fact that Pope Sylvester chose to send a crown to Hungary, but not Poland. This was a clear sign of Poland's wickedness. However, there was hope:

> Truly in the end of days I will show mercy on those peoples and I will illustrate this with the glory of a kingdom. For God having foreknowledge of the future, visiting the sins of the parents on the third and fourth generation of children, because only he himself knows, when he ought to be merciful to the people of Poland and to restore their ruins ...[79]

---

[78] This Vita was written by Vincent of Kielcza from 1252–1261, shortly after the canonization of St. Stanisław. Aleksandra Witkowska, "The thirteenth-century Miracula of St. Stanisław, Bishop of Cracow," in *Procès de canonisation au Moyen Age. Aspects juridiques et religieux*, edited by Gábor Klaniczay (Rome: Ecole Française de Rome, 2004), 150–151.

[79] "Stanisław, vita maior," *MPH*, 392.

This passage, using a Biblical reference, confirms that God's wrath had long been on Poland, and that the new generations had been living under the curse of the older. But God's anger is not eternal, so better days were ahead for a younger set of children, at the time of God's choosing. This concept, the divine redemption and reunification of Poland, after the punishment for its collective sins, especially the murder of St. Stanisław, is considered by Witowska to in fact be the central argument of the Vita Maior.[80]

In the canonization narrative itself, there are six chapters before we are informed about the proceedings of the curial deliberations. Three of these chapters contain deliberate and essential nods to children. Perhaps related is the fact that elite men in their prime are the center of only one of these chapters: the first story in the canonization arc is about the vision of St. Stanisław, experienced by a very pious noble woman; the second story features two ancient men who also claimed to have seen a vision of St. Stanisław celebrating mass and causing a mysterious ringing of bells without human hands.[81]

The first chapter to mention childhood specifically is the third chapter, which is the logical culmination of what preceded it. In it "Master Benedictus, a teacher from the same church, a man of good morals and devoted to God"[82] was remembered, along with the two old men mentioned above, to repeat a prophecy to younger generations

> They were accustomed to say these words to school boys and others from piety and devotion: "O boys, o youths! Listen to us, decrepit and senile! In your time will be revealed the greatest treasure of this church, clearly Stanisław, who we saw with our eyes circling the altar of God and in pontifical ornaments handling the divine elements.[83]

The fact that this warning is specifically issued by a teacher and two elderly men to a younger generation is revealing, and this passage serves as a connection to the aforementioned reference about God's wrath and Poland's restoration. The wisdom of older generations foresees the "treasure" of the next. We also noted in a previous section how prophecy and foreshadowing is connected with youth, and this single explicit prophecy in the canonization section is directed at children.

---

80   Witkowska, "The thirteenth-century Miracula," 162.
81   "Stanisław, vita maior," MPH, 393–394.
82   "Stanisław, vita major," MPH, 395.
83   Ibid.

The final two chapters before canonization contain the most intriguing and relevant mentions of childhood. In the fifth chapter, a German woman, Adelaide, becomes ill and her only daughter, Willebertha, is the only person who stayed by her side. Adelaide has a vision of St. Stanisław in which he offers her healing if she should tell the custodian of the church in Kraków where Stanisław was buried, that he should clean and elevate his bones to keep them from decay. The age of Willebertha is unclear, but she appears to be young, for we read "the infirm lady called called together her daughter, who was present, and all the boys (*pueros*) of the house and she narrated to them what she had seen and heard and so that she might be led to the tomb of blessed Stanisław."[84] In this passages, Willebertha is grouped together with the "boys" of the house as one of the dependents that Adelaide uses to transfer her body to the said church and tomb. Moreover, the fact that Adelaide must rely on youths (perhaps her sons, but more likely the poor youths under her care, or young servants) and on no husband of Willebertha suggests that the latter is unmarried. Finally, that later Willebertha is said to be sleeping while Adelaide is praying during Matins suggests youth. Whatever the age of Willebertha, the truth of St. Stanisław's holy identity is again told to "boys" and to a younger generation (for Willebertha is always referred to as "filia"). When Adelaide fails to tell the custodian the command of Stanisław, her healing evades her until she has another vision, which she promptly tells to Willebertha, after waking her from sleep. The younger generation hears and participates in both mandates to reveal the wishes of Stanisław to ecclesiastical authorities in this passage.

The final miracle before St. Stanisław's canonization is the healing of a young boy. This story begins with the nobleman Sulcro, who, while he is convalescing from an illness, is visited in three successive visions by St. Stanisław. In these visions a "bishop appeared to him, a very venerable man, dressed in pontifical robes and said to him: I am Stanisław bishop of Kraków. Proclaim to all having need, that, whoever, troubled, should come to my tomb, will be liberated and received consolation."[85] As soon as he had fully recovered, Sulcro proclaimed this message to all who would listen. It turned out that Sulcro had the opportunity to practice what he preached, as within a year his own son was stricken with a terrible sickness and was unable to speak. The father called upon Stanisław praying:

---

84 "Stanisław, vita maior," MPH, 397.
85 Ibid., 398.

> Through the intercession and merits of blessed Stanisław the martyr, help me and liberate this boy, which I commit to your sanctity. Then the boy, having turned to his father, said: What did you say about St. Stanisław? And he said: I vowed, he said, that I would commit you to him, my son. And the boy to his father: Make for me to be quickly carried to his tomb and I will be permanently healed.[86]

Not only is the boy eventually healed from his illness at the end of the story, but even before the healing occurs, the son regains his ability to speak, in order to inform his father, through some divine intuition or instinct, that his healing would come at the tomb of St. Stanisław. This closes the circle, for in previous passages older people had informed the young about the coming greatness and power of Stanisław to heal and console. Now, immediately before the canonization process begins in the narrative, divinely healed children are telling their parents that same thing by miraculous means. Stanisław' time had finally come. From the mouths of babes, indeed.

5   The Miracles

While the analysis so far has mentioned individual miracles in a number of capacities, it is time to survey them as a whole. The miracles have been surveyed for several purposes not related to childhood, particularly for understanding medieval health and disease, but have also featured in discussions of childhood. For example, Chołodowska used some of these stories to illustrate methods of medieval care for children,[87] whereas Delimata employed them to discuss demographic and health issues such as gender, age, disease, and fatality rates of medieval children.[88] My goal instead is to look for the rhetoric and reasoning behind the construction of those miracle lists with children. What

---

86 "Stanisław, vita major," 398–399.
87 Małgorzata Chołodowska, "Matka—opiekunka małoletnich dzieci—w Polsce wczesnośredniowiecznej na podstawie opisów cudów Św. Jadwigi i Św. Stanisława," in *Partnerka, matka, opiekunka. Status kobiety w starożytności i średniowieczu* (Bydgoszcz: Uczelniane Wyższej Szkoły Pedagogicznej w Bydgoszczy, 1999), 160–169.
88 Delimata, *Dziecko*, 49. The figures in my discussion below differ slight from hers. While it is unclear exactly why that is the case, there are a number of clear differences in our methodologies that may account for the deviance. First is the fact that, while Delimata is concerned with disease and death, I include instances of demonic possession and physical injury. Second is that the texts are sometimes unclear about the age of the child, and I excluded youths from my counting, as well as a number of instances when words like "filius" were used and the age of the victim was unclear. See also Małgorzata Delimata,

percentage of miracles involved children? Was there a structure or plan behind the placement of those miracles in the lists? What themes and patterns appear in child miracles, and are they consistent throughout the lists?

Before proceeding, it is essential to outline what exactly is under examination and what methods are used. The *miracula* of the saints were records of miracles recorded for the canonization process as a way to establish the merits of the saint.[89] These were highly formulaic accounts though they often included snippets of daily life. I have chosen the *miracula* of three saints—Stanisław, Hedwig, and Kinga[90]—because they are the most complete. I have chosen to focus on miracles of personal danger, where an individual is sick, dying, or afflicted with a demon, and have left out other miracles, such as visions, as this is in line with the methods of the other scholars discussing *miracula* and children which I reference in the Conclusion. This means that when I sum up the totals of miracles of personal danger for a saint, this sum is not the total number of miracles present in the *miracula*. At the end of this section, I will mention a few salient miracles not involving personal danger to make a few points, but these will not be part of the statistics. On occasion, it was difficult to determine the age of the victim, so I marked as "child" miracles only those stories with unmistakable reference to children through words like *puer* or *puella*, or where more vague words like *filius* or *filia* are accompanied by substantial context cues, such as the presence of doting parents, which strongly imply young age.

Out of 42 relevant miracles of St. Stanisław, 18 featured children and 2 were of youths. For Kinga, 12 out of the 20 miracles of personal danger are related to children. For Hedwig, the rate is only slightly lower, 22 miracles feature children and 2 are about youths in a total of 64 miracles of personal danger. There are a number of potential reasons why children might show up so frequently in the *miracula*. It could be that childhood was, or was considered, a time of real danger for children, and these lists are merely a reflection of that fact. Parents may have been eager to tell stories about their children to the delegation examining the miracles. Another possibility is that the *miracula* are not mere records of events, but that miracles involving children were sought after

---

"Choroby dzieci na podstawie średniowiecznych polskich katalogów cudów świętych," *Nasza Przeszłość* 101 (2004): 437–449.

89   For a description of how these proceedings were meticulously conducted on two separate occasions by papal appointees before the canonization process of St. Stanisław, see Witkowska, "The thirteenth-century Miracula," 151–153.

90   These can be found in the *MPH*, for St. Stanisław 400–426, for Hedwig 584–626, for Kinga 732–744. There are other lists available for some of these saints, for example, St. Stanisław, but these lists were chosen for their completeness and full length.

or included for rhetorical effect, showing the saint's mercy though efforts on behalf of the "least of the these." Also possible is the fact that miracles involving children were more likely to have many witnesses, including both parents and members of the community, and therefore were more compelling as evidence of the saint's holiness in the quest for beatification.

Another perhaps surprising point is that St. Stanislaus, a male saint, does not help children any less frequently than the two female saints, despite his gender. In other words, it does not seem that female saints, because of some supposed the medieval cultural connection between mothers and children, were thought to specialize in helping children in need. Despite expectations, this does correlate well to Gallus, where duke Bolesław I's noble behavior was compared to a father washing his children. This might not be as surprising at it first appears, for Małgorzata Chołodowska writes that saintly women in Poland by the thirteenth century were praised for virginity, piety, and religious zeal and that these contrasted with any notion of holy motherhood.[91] This suggests that there would be no special "boon" for female saints to feature more children than male saints.

One of the most intriguing, yet puzzling aspects of the organization of the three *miracula* under examination is that their opening sets of miracles have an extremely high incidence of children, yet in each of the three cases there seems to be no common reason for that organization. For the *miracula* of Stanisław, the first three miracles (chapters 8, 9, and 10) involve the resurrection of deceased children.[92] The first of these miracles, in chapter 8, involves the resurrection of an infant who died before baptism and the misery of the father because of the doom for his soul, indeed the father refused to let the child be buried until this miracle happened. The second resuscitation, in chapter 9, is about a somewhat older child who died and was healed in the presence of many family members gathered for his funeral. The miracle in chapter 10, also a resuscitation, is special in that the parents of the child are Hungarian, and return to their homeland after their son's miracle. The public nature of those miracles should not be overlooked, as people beyond the parents were available to verify the reality of death in the first two accounts, and the final account featured a foreigner, suggesting Stanisław' power to heal all nations, not just those near Kraków. Perhaps these were reasons to mention them first. Furthermore, these miracles in some sense also further the narrative of childhood in the canonization process of St. Stanisław discussed above. Chapter 6 was the final chapter before canonization, in which a child was

---

91   Chołodowska, "Matka", 160.
92   "Stanisław, vita major," *MPH*, 400–402.

healed, chapter 7 is about the deliberation and announcement of canonization, and chapter 8 follows that with the story of the resurrection and baptism of a dead infant. These miracles are therefore a final piece, a capstone, to the rhetorical use of children.

The first five miracles in the *miracula* of Kinga are similarly focused on children, but unlike the miracles of Stanisław, there is no common theme tying these miracles together.[93] The first and fourth miracle involve physical injury, narrating respectively how a girl fell from a tower and a boy was crushed underneath a shifting house. The second miracle involves the healing of deafness and the third and fifth miracles celebrate the recovery from a deadly illness. Despite those differences, four out of five miracles have unambiguous references to a larger body of witnesses than other miracles. In the first miracle servants and the whole household saw the girl dying from her fall. The second miracle, with the deaf child, was witnessed by a number of people who were her companions on a pilgrimage to see Kinga's shrine. The third and fourth miracles, where one child languished in suffering for weeks, and another was smashed under a house, were witnessed by entire villages, respectively.

Unlike the *miracula* of Kinga, which have no apparent organization, and of Stanisław, in which the organization is loose and inconsistent, the *miracula* of Hedwig are rigorously organized into sections according to the nature of the illness. Under the first category, about the infirm restored to health (*de infirmis sanitati restitutis*), four of the first five instances involve children, including the first two.[94] As all of these miracles were long, protracted affairs, there was of course time for everyone in the community to hear about and witness the misery of those involved.

The healing of those children was also portrayed in such a way as to highlight, through heart-wrenching scenes, the mercy and kindness that Hedwig showed to those who loved her most. In the first miracle, we hear the prayer of the soldier Witoslai, who had long served Hedwig when she was alive, on behalf of his son: "with hands raised with tears, he shouted, saying: my lady, blessed Hedwig, I served you, and you loved me, when you lived; this favor I now ask of you, that my son might retain his life through your intercession. Restore to me, my lady, my son to health and this from your generosity will be for me a particular and special reward for my labor."[95] Of course, Hedwig responded to her loyal supporter with his requested boon. Likewise, the second miracle, in which the boy Waltherus had internal injuries after the incompetence of his

---

93 "Kinga," MPH, 732–734.
94 "Hedwig," MPH, 584–587.
95 Ibid., 585.

nurse, repeated attempts by doctors and medicine to cure his illness failed, but Hedwig was able to do what no human could. These two miracles, through witnesses and the sympathy of readers, certainly put the best feet of Hedwig's case forward.

Beyond the clusters of children at the beginning of *miracula*, both Stanisław and Kinga feature clusters of children not related to the kind of disease. As Hedwig's *miracula* are organized by disease, such patterns are not relevant. For Kinga, the most significant cluster appears in miracles 15, 16, 17, and 18.[96] There is no real connection between them, much like the earlier cluster of miracle accounts with children. In miracle 16 a girl was tormented by a demon, in 17 a child was savaged by a wolf, and in 18 a girl was drowned under water. The length of those miracles varies, with 18 including only the most terse recounting, while 16 is full of dramatic description of the demon's torments of the child and even includes some of its words. There is no extensive description of witnesses. Those accounts seem to be a sort of coda for the *miracula*, as the next three, final miracles, are unusual for their context and length.[97] St. Stanisław' miracle clusters require a different explanation. Of all clusters (8–10, 14–15, 24–28, and 47–48), only some, particularly 47–48 which are about drowned children, have a common theme.[98] Miracles in the largest cluster, 24–28, have, as in the case of Kinga, no clear connection amongst themselves.[99] Miracle 24 is about a girl with a swollen tongue, in 26 a girl suffers from vermin in her eyes, and in 27 a boy suffers from putrefaction over extensive parts of his body. Along with these clusters, there is a unique feature, namely double miracles, each with two children receiving safety or healing. Both miracles, 30 and 40, and are about pairs of infirm children.[100] To judge from such evidence, it was inappropriate, for whatever reason, for children to be left alone, even in the text.

When discussing the kinds of mishaps children suffered, it should already be sufficiently clear that these are many and varied, especially across the different *miracula*. While the relatively small number of miracles recorded in these works makes any statistical conclusions suspect, some broad comparisons are recognizable. First, reviving dead children, either for baptism or from a certain mishap, is a trope in all three works, as was noted above. Likewise, water appears to be a great danger for children. Water appears not only in the

---

96 "Kinga," *MPH*, 737–738.
97 Ibid., 737–743. These include a long demon narrative, the story of two youths whose bees are restored after an invasion, and a slave woman bitten by a rabid dog.
98 "Stanisław, vita maior," *MPH*, 424–425.
99 Ibid., 409–412.
100 "Stanisław, vita maior," *MPH*, 414, 420.

above-mentioned chapters 47 and 48 of the Vita Maior of St. Stanisław, but also in the first two resuscitations of Hedwig's *miracula*,[101] as well as in chapter 18 of Kinga's.[102] Moreover, the *miracula* of both Stanisław and Hedwig feature stories of adolescents who, while faking their (lost) virginity with head coverings, lost their hair when approaching the tomb of the saint.[103] These accounts are so similar that even the author of Hedwig's *miracula* regarded it as necessary to note that a similar event had been observed in regards to Stanisław. This strongly suggests that the tropes and ideas found in those *miracula* are interrelated, and that material from one may have been borrowed from another.

Some kinds of afflictions only affect children in some *miracula*. None of the four examples of demon possession in Hedwig involve children,[104] but one of the few demon possessions in Kinga involves a young girl.[105] On the other hand, while foot injuries occur with unexceptional frequency to children in Kinga and Stanisław, in Hedwig 5 out of 7 of the miracles in the foot-affliction section were children.[106] It is not at all clear why that was the case, but there is a clear pattern of associating or disassociating certain forms of disability with children in different *miracula*.

In sum, the *miracula* of the saints Stanisław, Hedwig, and Kinga betray a deep interest in miracle accounts with children. Children are involved in between a third and over one half of all miracles of personal danger present in the vitae. Likewise, the appearance of stories of children at the beginning of these texts as well as in clusters throughout them suggests that authors are not randomly placing stories of children, but carefully introducing them where they would have the greatest rhetorical or emotional effect. Finally, certain tropes and dangers appear in those *miracula*, and there is at least some evidence that this could be related to intertextuality.

6   Latin Words Relating to Children in the *Miracula*: Exceptions and Rules

It is important to examine the Latin words related to youth and used in the *miracula* to see to what exactly they refer in terms of age and stage of development. There are comparatively fewer references to exact ages in the Polish

---

101   "Hedwig," MPH, 621–623.
102   "Kinga," MPH, 738.
103   "Stanisław, vita maior," MPH, 423–424. "Hedwig," MPH, 588.
104   "Hedwig," MPH, 614–616.
105   "Kinga," MPH, 737.
106   "Hedwig," MPH, 600–605.

vitae, which precludes any systematic approach, such as found in Didier Lett's statistics correlating words and age.[107] In the Polish *miracula*, there seems to be very little regularity or standardization, and only loose associations with age. Tadeusz Buliński has in fact argued that such carelessness implies a lack of a concrete and meaningful image of a separate age of childhood.[108] While my arguments have suggested that such a conclusion is rather premature, he is correct that medieval authors had something else in mind rather than biologically and numerically accurate description of childhood stages when they applied age-related words to their subjects.

While words such as "puer" generally describe male children, this is by no means always the case. The first miracle of Kinga, mentioned above, in which Dobroslava falls from the tower and is healed, uses *puer* once before and four times after she is identified by a feminine name and described as a *filia* of certain parents.[109] This, perhaps, is an irregularity especially prevalent in Kinga's comparatively short list of miracles, because there are other instances of *filia Matthie*, who was miraculous resurrected in a very public miracle, to the joy of her unbelieving father.[110] No age is mentioned for the girl, but she is at all times (8 in total) referred to as *puer* (or some variation thereof) The most logical explanation is that in Kinga's *miracula puer* means "child," and not "boy." While there are irregularities in other *miracula* in terms of age, rarely is *puer* used to refer to a girl. This, therefore, is a usage unique to that text, which suggests that different authors within one and the same culture, writing in the same genre employed words of childhood in their own ways. In the *miracula* of Hedwig, in the story of a troubled pregnancy, an unborn child is referred to as *puer* before the gender is discovered after the birth.[111] This seems to be imply that *puer* is simply often the generic form of "child." For a broader comparison, Didier Lett notes that in his survey of medieval European miracles "puer" referred to a male child in 78% of cases.[112] Indeed, Kinga herself is referred to as "puer felix Kynga" at one point in her Vita, when she was five years old.[113]

In relation to words for childhood and gender, one immediately notices wide variation in terms of age, especially for girls. For example, in the *miracula*

---

107   Lett, *L'enfant des miracles*, 5 and 361–364. Even in Lett's study, age is mentioned only in 103 out of 284 cases.
108   Tadeusz Buliński, "Średniowieczny obraz dziecka." *Studia Edukacyjne 4* (1998): 96, but more broadly at 89–103.
109   "Kinga," MPH, 732.
110   Ibid., 735.
111   "Hedwig," MPH, 620.
112   Lett, *L'enfant des miracles*, 42.
113   "Kinga," MPH, 688.

of Hedwig, *puella* describes the youngest of children, but also extends young women. For example, *puella* Milozlava, born with withered legs and calves, was said to have suffered this condition for 20 (*per viginti annos*).[114] This usage may be in reference to the fact that her condition began at her birth, or to the lack of a husband, or perhaps to her exceptional reliance on her parents. Perhaps it is simply in reference to the helplessness and care that she has needed her whole life because to her disability. We find a similar instance of *puella* with Berchta, who was trapped underneath the wheels of a mill in another very public miracle. One learns a bit later that she was 18 years old (*puella decem et octo annos habens etatis*).[115] While the exact age is not clear, something similar happens in the *miracula* of St. Stanisław, in a story of a fake virgin defiled by a youth (*per iuvenem*). She is described as *quadam puella Theutonica iam nobilis et adulta*.[116] The fact that *adulta* and *puella* are not mutually exclusive in the passage is surprising. Perhaps *adulta* refers to her sexual maturity, while *puella* is referencing her unmarried state and pretended virginity. However one interprets this passage, it is unmistakable that a rhetorical meaning must be ascribed to at least one of these descriptors. Words related to children cannot simply be taken uncritically or at face value.

7   Conclusions

Even though the descriptions of the lives of saintly children take up such a small part of the *vitae*, these passages are nonetheless laden with meaning and prophecy for the future role of these saints. As these childhood scenes are the first things the reader encounters after introductions describing lineage and theological musings, and remembering that the *vitae* are constantly trying to prove a point about the saint's beatification, to ignore those passages would be a mistake. In fact, as I have shown, they are highly significant for several reasons. The *puer senex* trope is a subtle tool in which a child can be seen as having the behavior of an adult, but that does not mean that childlike behavior is not also used for rhetorical effect. Similarly, saintly children prove themselves both through their qualities, and through a careful balance of nature and nurture. While the moments of the youngest of children in the *vitae* and *miracula* sometimes receive less ink, they nevertheless appear to be important and valued within their contexts and families. All the saints showed

---

114   "Hedwig," MPH, 604–605.
115   Ibid., 620–621.
116   "Stanisław, vita maior," MPH, 423.

wisdom and control in their behavior, a way that befitted older people. They all received some sort of education in which they learned about God and improved their own morality, while rejecting the pastimes and wastefulness of their peers. They all controlled their sexuality, and instead filled their lives with pious deeds, even if they were childlike and more symbolic than effective. Similarly, we saw in the *miracula* that female children, just as much as male, were thought to engage in a wide range of activities in their surroundings, often resulting in danger or death. Just as we have seen with other chapters, children, even when their role may seem insignificant or is not immediately apparent, nevertheless constantly have a part to play in the purposes and arguments of the hagiography.

The general tropes and descriptions in Poland of the childhood of the saints and the *miracula*, as will be further discussed in the conclusion of the book, is well in line with the hagiographical tradition in Europe during the medieval period. Nevertheless, some unique appear in the Polish texts. For example, in the *vita* of St. Stanisław, the trope of children as a symbol and sign of the future is introduced before his canonization, emphasizing that this was not an event ordained by man, but was long in the making by God. In examining *miracula*, miracles involving children were frequent and often in highly significant places in the text, where they were most able to affirm the holy presence of the saint. In terms of the incidence of miracles, St. Stanisław was no less willing to heal children than the two female saints, Kinga and Hedwig. In terms of the non-royal children presented in the miracula, there are numerous instances of concern for their well-being by their parents and their communities, and the fact that their stories were deemed worthy of *miracula* bespeaks their social value. Finally, words of childhood in the *miracula* do not always have a clear relationship to gender or age and are not used consistently across the entire text, suggesting that, as in the Gallus Anonymous, words relating to childhood have other functions than simply designating an age range.

CHAPTER 6

The Child in the Community of the Dead

Text and material culture, different because of their creation for different purposes, may tell similar stories by different means. Indeed, they both deal, at various levels, with the same social phenomenon studied in this book, namely the care of children, the treatment of offspring and heirs, the process of growing up and the stages of early life development, as well as sickness and death of children. While text and material culture may not be easily put into direct conversation, they can at least be analyzed as different "voices" on intersecting themes, and thus as fragments of a cultural discourse. Thus in this chapter, I will examine how exactly mortuary archaeology, with a specific emphasis on children, functions within the larger archaeological context of early medieval Poland. There are no contemporary accounts of child burials, nor any descriptions of mentalities or emotions decisions went into funerals of children. Neither will this book attempt to illustrate by archaeological means what was found in texts. Instead, my goal is to investigate patterns in the archaeological record, in order to verify possible connections to what may be seen in textual sources. This method is more about finding broad categories and the contours of age relationships than about testing for any particular practice or custom.

Between the eleventh and the twelfth centuries, medieval cemeteries were set up in Poland in ways that were very different from those in western Europe at that same time, although quite similar to those in other parts of East Central, Eastern, and Northern Europe. While western Europe had settled into a mortuary context dominated by the church and organized into parishes and churchyards, the margins of Europe were undergoing a revolution in mortuary practice towards increasing clerical involvement. As Andrzej Buko put it, mortuary practices underwent a long but decisive transformation from the tenth through the thirteenth centuries.[1] While the interpretation of that transformation remains a matter of much debate, especially when it comes to Christianization,[2] it is quite clear that cremation was slowly abandoned

---

1   Buko, *Archaeology of Early Medieval*, 396.
2   Generally Polish scholars today see practices which were once considered simple signs of continued paganism as conscious reinterpretations of old traditions into a more Christian context. For examples of recent scholarship using this approach see for example: Jacek Wrzesiński, "The Dziekanowice Cemetery—Christian Cultivating Venerable Traditions," in *Rome, Constantinople and Newly-Converted Europe. Archaeological and Historical Evidence*, eds. M. Salamon, M. Wołoszyn, A. Musin, P. Spechar, M. Hardt, M.P. Kruk, A. Sulikowska-Gaska

beginning in the tenth century (Duke Mieszko I converted in 966), but and lingered until the eleventh or even the twelfth centuries in some regions. What is now conceived of as a transitional phase comprised the "row cemeteries" outside eleventh- and twelfth-century villages and fortifications, featuring the continuation of such pre-Christian customs as furnished burials, along with the adoption of such new customs as inhumation (instead of cremation) or the west-east (or east-west, for men) orientation of graves.[3] By the twelfth century, churchyard cemeteries began to appear in urban and fortified centers, and were spreading to the countryside after 1200.[4] Early churchyard cemeteries had marked boundaries, and because of that, as well as the desire for burial *ad sanctos* (as near to the relics inside the church as possible), graves were often stacked, which makes difficult both sequencing and chronology. In churchyard cemeteries grave goods disappear, except for personal adornment, and priests most likely controlled the burial ritual. Despite such general characteristics, there is much variation in cemeteries across Poland.[5]

As Michał Pawleta notes, much like gender, the archaeology of childhood was virtually non-existent until relatively recent times.[6] Two reasons have held back the development of a robust archaeology of children. First, bones of children decay more quickly than those of adults in most conditions, and especially because their graves were often shallower and more exposed to the elements. This means not only that fewer bones of children have been found, but also that only a few could be subject to more advanced tests.[7] A second problem regards the program of archaeology itself.[8] Archaeologists in the past, assuming that childhood and its stages were a biological reality and not a social creation, imposed universal categories of interpretation onto children without respect to cultural and temporal variation. This led to circular arguments, as assumptions were made to prove the supposed regularity of the social construction of childhood. A similar problem came from the lack of any interest in children with the major paradigms of the time, namely the obsessive focus on artifact collection (culture history) or socio-political processes (Marxist and processual archaeology). For that reason, archaeological reports from Poland meticulously describe military or prestige artifacts uncovered, but

---

(Warsaw, 2012), or Monika Garas, "Pochówki Atypowe na cmentarzyskach zachodniopomorskich w dobie Chrzystianizacji," *Acta Archeologica Lodziensia* 56 (2010).

3   Buko, *Archaeology of Early Medieval*, 396–397.
4   Ibid., 398–399.
5   Buko, *Archaeology of Early Medieval*, 399–400 attributes that variation to local, tribal custom.
6   Michał Pawleta, *An Archaeology of Childhood*, 11–12.
7   Ibid., 12–13.
8   Ibid., 13–14.

report barely anything related to children. Nevertheless, the appearance in the last decade of detailed site reports combined with a growing interest in childhood has produced of flurry of articles on that topic. This chapter relies heavily on that burgeoning research in an attempt to identify what archaeology can say about the care for, and the value of children, their role as heirs, and their place in society in relation to adults.

I have collected reports and descriptions for 34 medieval cemeteries in Poland that feature children, and could be dated between the tenth and the fourteenth centuries. I have thus created a database, cataloging all relevant anthropological and material data. Despite cultural variation, those cemeteries are located in regions that had at least some Piast presence during the time considered—Greater and Lesser Poland, Silesia, Pomerania, and Mazovia. I started from the premise that besides commonalities, various parts of the Piast dominions would also offer examples of interesting variation. The database includes both row and churchyard cemeteries, allowing comparison between these two "phases" of mortuary practice in early medieval Poland. However, the cemeteries included in the database have been excavated with very different methods and interpretive tools. For example, none of the included cemetery reports from Łódź differentiate children in terms of age, not even between such broad categories as Infans I and Infans II. Conversely, the anthropologists working on the skeletal material from Kałdus have been able to ascertain the age of a child with a margin of error of one to two years.

1 Incidence of Child Burials

One of the questions that concern archaeologists from around Europe is the incidence of child burials in the medieval period. Sally Crawford sees the relative lack of children in cemeteries of early Anglo-Saxon England, especially before the arrival of churchyards, as a problem for archaeologists, considering the expectation of higher numbers based on projected pre-industrial child mortality rates.[9] Many anthropologists believe that that rate should result in at least 30 percent of graves in any given cemetery being of children. As a matter of fact, as Małgorzata Delimata noted, graves of Infans I and Infans II in medieval cemeteries in Poland represent between 20 to 40 percent of the total number of graves.[10] However, while most cemeteries in Poland have numbers of child burials within expectations, certain cemeteries have very few children

---

9   Sally Crawford, *Childhood in Anglo-Saxon England* (Gloucestershire: Sutton, 1999).
10 Delimata, *Dziecko*, 50–54.

or even no children. On the other hand, there are cemeteries with notably high numbers of children. Such variations may be explained as the result of preservation or the specific function of the site, but there may also be social reasons linked to the relative value of children in the community.

One cemetery that has conspicuously few children is Ląd in Greater Poland. The cemetery was located near a major fortified center of the early Piast realm, mentioned in a 1136 bull of Pope Innocent II. The site was occupied as a settlement since the eighth or ninth century, with a castle appearing in the early Piast period at some point during the last third of the tenth century. There are two cemeteries in Ląd, both functioning between the eleventh and thirteenth century, one inside the castle and the other on the plain below it. Both were later given churches dedicated to St. Andrew and St. Peter, respectively, as recorded in sources of the mid-thirteenth century.[11] These cemeteries featured flat, inhumation burials laid out on an E-W axis with few burial goods. The first cemetery had a small number of child burials (15 percent of all graves), but the cemetery below the cemetery featured only 8 child burials—3 Infans I, 3 Infans II and 2 unidentified infants (8 percent out of 131 graves).[12] However, children are by no means the only cohort underrepresented. The most common age of all skeletons was 20 years, with few older adults as well as younger, and there is a considerable anthropological sex imbalance (47 sexed male, 17 sexed female). In other words, it is likely that this cemetery was, at least for some time, connected with the soldiers in the garrison of the fortress at Ląd. The same is true for Lutomiersk, in the region of Łódź. That cemetery was dated to the eleventh century, but has few children (4 out of 104 inhumations).[13] There is a heavy incidence of graves provisioned with militaria (in Lutomiersk this included swords, spears, battle-axes, and arrowheads), as well as a gender imbalance in favor of males.[14] The martial character of this community may have discouraged burial of children. In both Ląd and Lutomiersk, the rarity of children (and women) could potentially be explained not as reflections of their low value to the community but rather the martial character of those sites.

---

11 Lech Krzyżaniak, ed., *Wczesnośredniowieczne cmentarzyska szkieletowe w Lądzie, woj Konin* (Poznań: Muzeum Archeologiczne w Poznaniu, 1986), 7–8, 13–15.
12 Krzyżaniak, *Wczesnośredniowieczne cmentarzyska szkieletowe w Lądzie*, 57–59. On these pages is a chart of the graves, anthropological data, and a listing of the few present grave goods.
13 Konrad Jażdżewski, "Cmentarzysko wczesnośredniowieczne w lutomiersku pod łodzią świetle badan Z.R. 1949," in *Materiały Wczesnośredniowieczne, Volume 1: 1949* (Warsaw: Muzeum Archeologicznego w Warszawie, 1951), 94.
14 Jażdżewski, "Cmentarzysko wczesnośredniowieczne w lutomiersku," 180–188.

A different explanation altogether applies to the poor representation of children in other cemeteries. Bilczew in Greater Poland began in the seventh century as a cremation cemetery, transitioned to an inhumation cemetery in the tenth century and remained in use until the thirteenth century.[15] In a total of 27 burial pits, only two skeletons have been identified as of children, an Infans I and an Infans II. Unlike other cemeteries with low numbers of children, this does not appear to be a military cemetery, as female skeletons outnumber those of men (47.7 vs. 33.3 percent of all graves).[16] A closer look, however, suggests that preservation issues may be skewing the proportion of children. First, out of the 27 discovered and excavated burials, some (S12 and S22–S26) contain no bones. In at least two cases, it may be established that those were small pits, which could therefore possibly accommodate bodies of children, or perhaps are simply reburials.[17] This suggests at least 4 children for the cemetery. Furthermore the excavators blamed extremely poor conditions of preservation for the lack of more child burials, including the sandy soil as well as the physical health of the community in general.[18] The explanation cannot certainly be neglect, as of the two extant child skeletons, the Infans II in grave S16 contained by far the most spectacular assemblage of grave provisions in the entire cemetery. S16, for example, produced 102 distinct grave goods. By comparison, the next most well-provisioned grave, S13 is the burial of a woman between 30 and 40 years of age, with 9 grave goods. S16 was provided with 2 temple rings, a rattle, a finger ring, a bronze chain on the neck (typical not for Poland, but for Scandinavia), and 88 glass beads.[19] The spectacular number of beads given to certain young children in the Infans II category is a phenomenon found throughout Poland.

Unfavorable conditions, especially sandy soil, may also be the reason for the lack of children in Strzemieszyce Wielkie (Lesser Poland), a cemetery in operation between the eleventh and twelfth century. There are absolutely no children in any of the 101 graves.[20] However, soil conditions in the cemetery were terrible, and the excavators report that most skeletons were at best fragmentary

---

15   Lech Stefaniak, Ewa Andrzejczyk, Krzysztof Gorczyca, Katarzyna Schellner, eds., *Cmentarzysko Wczesnośredniowieczne w Bilczewie, Pow. Konin* (Konin: Muzeum Okręgowe w Konie, 2012), 85–89.
16   Stefaniak, *Cmentarzysko Wczesnośredniowieczne w Bilczewie*, 125.
17   Ibid., 99.
18   Ibid., 97–98, 124–125.
19   Ibid., 61–62, 81.
20   Jozef Marciniak "Cmentarzysko szkieletowe z okresu wczesnośredniowiecznego w Strzemieszycach Wielkich pow. Będzin," in *Materiały Wczesnośredniowieczne V* (Warsaw: Panstwowe Muzeum Archeologiczne, 1960), 184–185.

and often the orientation of the skeleton could only be traced through leftover residue in the pit. A similar situation exists in Dębina, in Greater Poland, where not only were most bones so destroyed that age and sex could not be established, but also many artifacts, especially metal ones, were horribly corroded.[21] Out of 58 early medieval burials, only three were determined to be those of young girls (graves 29,[22] 36, and 44), on the basis of the small size of the pit, a few remaining bones, and especially the associated grave goods.[23] Three out of 58 graves may seem like a low percentage of children, but there are no indications that that reflects disregard of children in the local community. First, a number of pits in the cemetery have insufficient remains, and not even a guess may be made as to the age and sex of the occupant. Those pits are nonetheless considerably smaller in size than most others, the average length of which is above 200 cm. These include pits 1 (156 cm), 3 (120 cm), 12 (170 cm), 35 (150 cm), 37 (150 cm), and 43 (150 cm). Those pits could have been reserved for child burials. Three burials determined to be of children contain grave goods similar to those of adults, with grave 29 featuring beads of silver and enameled glass, grave 36 has a bronze temple ring, a glass bead, and the remains of a pot, and grave 44 contains temple rings of bronze and tin as well as a knife.[24]

There are quite a few row graves for which there is no satisfactory explanation concerning the utter lack of children. In Daniszew (Greater Poland), a cemetery in operation during the eleventh and twelfth centuries, out of 33 skeletons that were subject to anthropological analysis, only one is of younger age (number 33), and even that one was determined to be in the category *juvenis*.[25] The bones in the cemetery were described as being from medium to poor condition, and subsequent plowing clearly disturbed the cemetery,[26] which could have destroyed the shallower graves of children, though this is unprovable. The excavators believe that small children were not baptized and thus not included in the cemetery population, but were buried elsewhere. Such an interpretation is not based on any data either from the cemetery or

---

21 Pukuta and Leszek Wojda "Wczesnośredniowieczne cmentarzysko we wsi Dębina, Woj. Sieradzkie," in *Prace i materiały muzeum archeologicznego i etnograficznego w Łodzi Seria Archeologiczna* 26 (1979): 90.
22 Grave 29 is, along with an adult female in grave 30, apparently intentionally placed on the grave of another female in grave 28. All are well-provisioned with grave goods. This is dealt with more fully when I discuss multiple burials below.
23 Pukuta, "Wczesnośredniowieczne cmentarzysko we wsi Dębina," 94.
24 Ibid., 116–118.
25 Jerzy Kozak and Robert Dąbrowski, "Wczesnośredniowieczne cmentarzysko w Daniszewie, pow. Kolski, woj. Wielkopolskie—analiza antropologiczna," in *Slavia Antiqua* 49 (2008): 213.
26 Kozak and Dąbrowski, "Wczesnośredniowieczne cmentarzysko w Daniszewie," 211.

some nearby site, but on the ideas of another archaeologist about burial of children in pots.[27] As it is, the evidence from Daniszew cannot be interpreted in that way, even though similar explanations have been offered elsewhere in Europe for similar phenomena.[28] Preservation aside, improper methods and lack of interpretive imagination may have largely contributed to the lack of any explanation for cemeteries without (or with few) children.[29]

While the relative absence of children in row cemeteries continues to baffle archaeologists, there are clear explanations for the similarly "missing" children in churchyard cemeteries. Their bones may have been accidentally disturbed, or intentionally moved, and collected in other parts of the cemetery. A good example in that respect is the cemetery that was active in the twelfth century to serve the parish churches of St Catherine and St. Stanisław at Kleczanów (southeastern Poland). The cemetery contains 21 intact burial pits, with 2 graves of children in the category of Infans I, 2 in Infans II, and 1 fetus/newborn. In other words, about 24 percent of the cemetery population was made up of children, but the number is deceiving, as evidence for other children originally being in the cemetery comes from a number of sources. First two adult graves (1 and 14) contained fragments of bones of children, most likely from previously disturbed graves.[30] This occurred for the unremarkable reason that the site was in heavy demand and previous burials were often uncovered and their occupants relocated, to make room for new graves.[31] Second, there were a number of skulls found apart from any particular grave. One of them was an early Infans II. Third, and most suggestively, there were five piles of bones found in various parts of the cemetery from 28 different individuals.[32]

---

27   B. Zawadzka-Antonsik, "Pochówki dzieci w naczyniach glinianach," *Wiadomości Archeologiczne* 38 (1973): 165–171. The relevant discussion is on page 370.
28   Sally Crawford, for example, suggested that bodies of children were highly symbolic, and because of that, children were buried under threshold of buildings or in other meaningful locations. Sally Crawford, "Companions, Co-incidences, or Chattels? Children in the Early Anglo-Saxon Multiple Burial Ritual," in *Children, Childhood, and Society*, ed. Sally Crawford and Gillian Shepherd (Oxford: Archaeopress, 2007), 3–92.
29   Kathryn Kemp, "Where Have All the Children Gone?: The Archaeology of Childhood," *Journal of Archaeological Method and Theory* Volume 8, Issue 1 (2001): 1–34.
30   Andrzej Buko, "Cmentarzysko wczesnośredniowieczne przy kościele parafialnym św. Katarzyna i św. Stanisława," in *Kleczanów: Badania Rozpoznawcze 1989–1992*, ed. Andrzej Buko (Warsaw: Instytut Archeologii i Etnologii PAN, 1997), 105–106.
31   Buko, "Cmentarzysko wczesnośredniowieczne przy kościele parafialnym św. Katarzyna," 101–103.
32   Unfortunately, it was impossible from the maps and material provided by the publishers to determine definitively if there was any pattern to the placement of these bones.

Of these, 12 (43 percent), were of individuals aged from fetus to Infans II.[33] Thus, it is quite clear that the number of child burials in the Kleczanów cemetery was far higher than the surviving evidence of intact graves.

This, however, is by no means an isolated example. In the twelfth- to fourteenth-century churchyard near St. Adalbert in Wrocław (Silesia), there was a very small number of children in intact graves. Only 20 out of around 200 graves (10 percent of the whole), contained skeletons of children. None of them had grave goods, but only 5 percent of the total number of graves were given provisions at all. Children were often buried in coffins, including even a 5-month old fetus, buried close to but not clearly in the same pit as a young woman, which was nevertheless treated like any other child.[34] This last piece of evidence should guard against any hasty assumptions about lack of baptism keeping children out of church cemeteries from this phase of Christianization.[35] In addition to the graves themselves, there were a number of bone clusters scattered throughout the cemetery, which occurred due to repeated use of the limited space of the cemetery in later times. While the documentation concerning these graves is by no means complete or clear, there is no doubt that children appeared in at least 10 out of 49 such clusters (about 20 percent).[36] In other words, it seems that the bones of children were far more likely to be disturbed and reburied than those of individuals in any other age category.

While the emphasis so far has been on cemeteries with few children, why others feature a considerably higher proportion of children? The best example is the eleventh- to thirteenth-century row cemetery excavated from 1969 to 1981 in Czekanów (Mazovia). There are 60 children among those buried in 145 graves of the cemetery (about 41 percent of graves feature children). Among them, 42 percent contain graves goods. Of all children, about a third died before reaching the age of one, 23.3 percent between one and two years, and a fifth between

---

33 Buko, "Cmentarzysko wczesnośredniowieczne przy kościele parafialnym św. Katarzyna," 107–109.

34 Magdalena Wojcieszak and Krzysztof Wachoski, "Średniowieczne cmentarzysko przy kościele Św. Wojciecha we Wrocławiu," in *Średniowieczne i nowożytne nekropole Wrocławia, cz. 1*, ed. Krzysztof Wachowski (Wrocław, Uniwersytet Wrocławski Instytut Archeologii, 2010), 60–65.

35 Martin Čechura, "Christian, Non-Christian, or Pagan? Newborns as the Source to Understanding of Medieval and Post-Medieval Mentality," in *Kim Jestes Człowieku?*, ed. Wojciech Dzieduszycki and Jacek Wrzesiński (Poznan, Stowarzyszenie Naukowe Archeologow Polskich, 2011), 289–297.

36 Wojcieszak, "Średniowieczne cmentarzysko przy kościele Św. Wojciecha we Wrocławiu," 100–101.

two and four years.[37] These numbers are extraordinary, especially compared to the cemeteries just discussed. Soil conditions were obviously more favorable for the preservation of the skeletal material.[38] However, there is more than just good preservation in Czekanów. As I will discuss in the next section, children are generally far more poorly provisioned than adults, and younger children are generally less likely to receive anything, with those under two years of age almost never receiving anything at all. However, in Czekanów, a cemetery with a significant number of children who died under the age of two, there are more well-furnished child graves than in any other cemetery with a comparably great number of older children. It is difficult to find grave goods with a child under 2 buried in any Polish cemetery. By contrast, in Czekanów a 9- to 12-month old baby was buried with a bronze ring, three babies under 1 year old were buried with beads, a 6- to 9-month old with a decorated clay egg, and a 5- to 6-month old with a temple ring, as well as with glass and silver beads.[39] This is not just a cemetery with more children, but a cemetery where the treatment of children remains unique without any easy explanation. Regional variation has an undeniable impact on the treatment of children.

Another cemetery of significance for this discussion of how children were treated in burial is that associated with the eleventh-century church in Ostrów Lednicki, a major ducal, military, and religious center of the early Piast state. No more than 19 graves have been found inside and outside the church.[40] Five of them were of children who died at the age of 10 or younger, with two other graves of children aged 14. Some of these children received elaborate treatment comparable to that of adults. For example, grave 2 was for a child (later exhumed), and was one of only two graves cut into the nave of the church featuring sandstone blocks, a limestone plate, remnants of a coffin and fittings, some glass remnants and a finger ring. It seems almost sure that this child was from an elite family, and therefore merited more spectacular treatment. The nave was preferred for burial of the young, but out of four graves outside the church, to the west from the nave, one was of an adult in his or her late

---

37   Barbara Zawadzka-Antosik, "Z problematyki pochówków dziecięcych odkrytych na cmentarzysku w Czekanowie, Woj. Siedleckie," *Wiadomości Archeologiczne* 47 (1982): 25, 33. There was an additional "Infans I" listed which could not be placed accurately beyond that estimate.
38   Zawadzka-Antosik, "Z problematyki pochówków dziecięcych," 49.
39   Zawadzka-Antosik, "Z problematyki pochówków dziecięcych," 51–55.
40   Janusz Górecki, "Nekropola tzw. II kościoła na Ostrowie Lednickim," *Studia Lednickie* 4 (1996): 137–156.

twenties, one was of an individual of undetermined age, one was of 4-year old, and another of a child who died at the age of about one year and a half.[41]

A surprisingly high incidence of children has also been recorded in eleventh- to thirteenth-century row cemeteries from other parts of Poland. In Giecz (Greater Poland), 34.3 percent of the population died before the age of 12, including 20.7 percent that died before the age of 3. This dovetails nicely with the situation in Czakanów, although graves of children have not been published in sufficient detail.[42] In Masłowice near Łódź (central Poland), 20 out of 85 graves are of children, with almost half of them being furnished.[43] In Kałdus (Kujavia-Pomorania), 28.1 percent of all graves are of children under the age of ten. High percentages of "children" obscure the fact that different cemeteries have different child age ratios. For example, in Kałdus, there are over two times more children in the category of Infans I (23.4 percent) than in the category Infans II (9.7 percent).[44] By contrast, out of 123 graves in Stary Zamek (Silesia), there is only one Infans I and one newborn. This stands in contrast with 24 graves of children in the category Infans II.[45]

To sum up, while scholars have been eager to make broad generalizations about numbers and proportions of children in Polish cemeteries, in reality each individual cemetery has its own specific situation. Both surprisingly high and low numbers of children appear in various cemeteries, and the variation cannot be simply explained away by means of soil conditions. Cultural and social factors may well have been at play. In churchyard cemeteries, a very promising explanation for the low incidence of children might be that their bones seem to have been often unintentionally disturbed and later reburied in individually or in clusters. Something similar could have happened in row cemeteries, but evidence of bone piles might have been more difficult for archaeologists to uncover because of the larger area under examination. Moreover, one would have to wonder why disturbance could take place in a cemetery that was not spatially limited. At any rate, even in cemeteries with child burials within the

---

41 Andrzej Nowak, "Badania archeologiczne na Ostrowie Lednickim, pow. Gniezno, w roku 1963," *Sprawozdania Archeologiczne* 18 (1966): 179–189.

42 Hedy Justus, "Initial Demographic Observations of the Giecz Collection: Sex and Age-at-Death Assesment of Skeletal Remains Excavated at GZ4 between 1999 and 2003," *Studia Lednickie* 8 (2005): 199–202.

43 Abramek, "Wczesnośredniowieczne cmentarzysko szkieletowe w Masłowicach," 227–229.

44 Wojciech Chudziak, *Wczesnośredniowieczne cmentarzysko szkieletowe w Kałdusie* (Toruń: Wydawn. Uniwersytetu Mikołaja Kopernika, 2010), 50.

45 Krzysztof Wachowski and Grzegorz Domański, *Wczesnopolskie cmentarzysko w Starym Zamku* (Wrocław: Uniwersytet Wrocławski, 1992), 33–97. There where an additional 4 children in the cemetery that could not be placed in either Infans I or II.

normal range, age distributions vary, with certain age categories being often and significantly over- or under-represented. Generalizations about children in Polish cemeteries are therefore not possible on the basis of incidence statistics alone.

2 The Problem of Grave Goods in Child Burials

A similar, albeit more complicated picture emerges from the analysis of the provisioning of child graves. Archaeologists have noted that in general child graves in Poland were poorly furnished, especially for those under the age of three, with the number and quality of grave goods increasing slowly after the age of three and well into full adulthood.[46] The relative poverty of child burials in medieval Poland is similar to that in other parts of Christian Europe at that same time.[47] Even in cemeteries with well-furnished child graves, children received fewer grave goods than adults. This is certainly the case of the tenth- to twelfth-century cemetery at Lubień, near Łódź, in which almost 70 percent of children were buried with at least one artifact.[48] While only 9 percent of adults were buried without any grave goods, 28 percent of burials of Infans II and 30 percent of those of Infans I burials were found with no grave goods.[49] While adults in general receive more grave goods than children, some children are quite as spectacularly arrayed as the adults, and in some artifact categories children even eclipse adults. For example, children in the Infans I category were buried with larger numbers of beads (items of personal adornment worn as necklaces or found near the neck, made often of glass, but sometimes of precious metals), coins, flints, pendants, and surprisingly, axes than adults. Similarly, children of the Infans II category were buried with larger numbers of of temple rings and beads than the adults.[50] The 5- to 6-year old

---

46 A general discussion of the state of the field in Poland on this regard can be found in Tomasz Kurasiński and Kalina Skóra, "Children's Burials from the Early Medieval Inhumation Cemetery in Radom, site 4," in *Fasciculi Archaeologiae Historicae; From the Problems of Historical Archaeology* 28 (Łódz: Institute of Archaeology and Ethnology, PAN, 2015), 46–48.

47 See for example: Sally Crawford, *Childhood in Anglo-Saxon England* (Gloucestershire: Sutton, 1999). Shannon Lewis-Simpson *Youth and Age in the Medieval North* (Leiden: Brill, 2008).

48 Tomasz Kurasiński and Kalina Skóra, *Wczesnośredniowieczne cmentarzysko szkieletowe w Lubieniu, pow. Piotrkowski* (Łodz: Institute of Archaeology and Ethnology, PAN: 2012), 108–110.

49 Kurasiński and Skóra, *Wczesnośredniowieczne cmentarzysko*, 109 table 23.

50 Ibid., 108–110.

in grave 36 was buried with a hatchet, a knife, a flint, a coin, and pottery, while no less than 180 beads of all varieties were found on the skeleton of an Infans I in grave 41, along with two temple rings (an item of personal adornment worn along the scalp). There were 150 beads of various forms and colors in grave 56, featuring a 3–4 year old, together with three temple rings.[51] Exceptionally rich child burials in Lubień may have been associated with plots of well-to-do families.[52]

To be sure, in most Polish cemeteries, children in general received fewer and shoddier provisions than adults, but a few were provisioned in abundance, on a par or even beyond what was the rule for most adults. For example, in Masłowice, 20 out of 85 burials were of children.[53] While the vast majority of adults were buried with at least one artifact, about half of all child burials had no grave goods at all. However, three children, presumably girls, all aged between 7 and 10 years old, received the most impressive grave goods in the entire cemetery. Grave 21 had six temple rings, 6 beads, one finger ring, and a knife. Grave 48 had 10 temple rings, 160 beads, one finger ring, and a pot. Grave 85 had 4 temple rings, 73 beads, 2 finger rings, a pot, and a coin.[54] By comparison, the highest number of beads found in the grave of an adult woman is 30 (grave 47), while the highest number of temple rings is 7 (grave 20). Unlike Lubień, such extraordinarily rich child burials do not seem to have connected with family plots. While grave 21 is part of a cluster of child graves around a well-provisioned adult (grave 20), the two other outstanding child graves (48 and 85) are in fact located outside the normal rows of the cemetery.[55] The fact that these aforementioned children stood out from nearby graves suggests that there was something special about them, and that their burials were not simply copying styles of their family or their peers.

The eleventh- to twelfth-century row cemetery at Brześć Kujawski (Kujavia-Pomerania) contains 152 graves, 33 of which are of children, the majority without grave goods. Most adult graves in the cemetery have grave goods. Nevertheless, certain grave goods appear most frequently in child

---

51   Kurasiński and Skóra, *Wczesnośredniowieczne cmentarzysko szkieletowe w Lubieniu*, 172, 176, 182–183.
52   Florin Curta and Matthew Koval, "Children in Eleventh- and Twelfth-Century Poland and Hungary: An Archaeological Comparison," in *The Medieval Networks in East Central Europe Commerce, Contacts, Communication*, ed. Balázs Nagy, Felicitas Schmieder, and András Vadas (London: Routledge Press, 2019), 90–99.
53   Abramek, "Wczesnośredniowieczne cmentarzysko w Masłowicach," 227–229.
54   Ibid., 332–333.
55   Abramek, "Wczesnośredniowieczne cmentarzysko w Masłowicach," 229. See cemetery layout on this page.

graves—coins, knives, and egg-related artifacts.⁵⁶ Egg shells have also been found in child burials elsewhere in Poland, in Czekanow, Końskie, Złota Pińczowska, and Jaksice, while decorated eggs (whether natural or artificial) are known from child graves in Kałdus, Czarna Wielka, Dziekanowice, and Lutomiersk.⁵⁷ Brześć Kujawski is special in that it features both eggshell fragments (*skorupki jajka*) and even a whole egg, as well as painted clay eggs (*pisanki gliniana*) in different graves of the cemetery. Although they also appear in adult burials, in most cemeteries eggs and painted (clay) eggs are primarily found with children. According to Joanna Wawrzeniuk, they may in fact been associated with the Resurrection and with hope for the child to enjoy a blessed afterlife, and were perhaps also associated with young life itself, as eggs contained the offspring of chickens.⁵⁸

True to patterns already established above, a few child graves at Brześć Kujawski have remarkable burial assemblages, though unfortunately poor preservation of skeletal matter makes exact age estimates impossible. In grave 153 a bronze and a silver temple ring appeared as well as beads of various materials (including amber), while grave 137 features 30 beads. A very young woman (possibly a teenager) in grave 117 was buried together with semi-precious beads, two silver temple rings, a silver finger ring, and a knife, through perhaps her adolescence perhaps meant that her contemporaries perceived her as an adult. Graves 153, 137 and 117 are on a par with those of any adults. Most interestingly, there is a double grave of a young boy and a girl,⁵⁹ buried together with two knives, 50 glass beads, two bronze temple rings, and a glass finger ring. The excavators explained the sharp differences between child burials in terms of social class, and this suggests that class rather than young age could have influenced burial patterns.⁶⁰

Extraordinarily well-provisioned, individual graves of children have been documented in almost every region of Poland. In Bilczew, grave S16 mentioned above is of an Infans II, who received an outstanding treatment. In Stary Zamek, two children (both Infans II, in graves 70 and 104) were buried with over 25 and over 10 beads, respectively. Those are the only beads found

---

56 Eleonora and Zdzisław Kaszewsky, "Wczesnośredniowieczne cmentarzysko w Brześciu Kujawskim, pow Włocławek," in *Materiały Starożytne i Wczesnośredniowieczne, Volume 1* (Warsaw: Zakład Narodowy Imienia Ossolińskich, 1971), 427–432.
57 Zawadzka-Antosik, "Z problematyki pochówków dziecięcych," 51–55.
58 Joanna Wawrzeniuk, "Symbolika jajka w grobie dziecka w okresie wczesnośredniowiecznym," in *Dusza maluczka, a strata ogromna*, Funeralia Lednickie spotkanie 6, eds. Jacek Wrzesiński and Wojciech Dzieduszycki (Poznań: Stowarzyszenie Naukowe Archeologów Polskich, Oddział w Poznaniu, 2004), 143–152.
59 Note: these are the excavators' designations. Anthropological evidence cannot determine their accuracy.
60 Kaszewsky, "Wczesnośredniowieczne cmentarzysko w Brześciu Kujawskim," 424–426.

in that cemetery.⁶¹ In regards to temple rings, some children, presumed by excavators to be girls, received equal treatment to older women: the Infans II in Grave 3 received 8 temple rings and the Infans II in Grave 97 received 7. The only women who were given a similar treatment are the Maturus in Grave 121 with 7 temple rings and an Adultus in Grave 54 with 6 temple rings.⁶² The cemetery in Radom (Mazovia) is characterized by the deposition of lackluster goods in both child and adult graves. Nonetheless, grave 37 featured a girl aged 12–15 buried together with a coin, two temple rings, a spindle whorl, and shards of vessels.⁶³

So far the discussion has primarily focused on artifacts like beads and temple rings, which one would expect to find in female graves. But there are also child burials impressively provisioned with weapons most typical for male graves. As Tomasz Kurasiński notes, the deposition of arrow heads in graves of Infans I and Infans II children is attested everywhere in Poland, from Pomerania to Great Poland and Mazovia. Nonetheless, because the total number of such graves is quite small, no general conclusions may be drawn about the meaning of this burial custom. Kurasiński believes that the arrow heads provided magical and spiritual protection from malevolent supernatural forces, but does not exclude the possibility that those artifacts were (viewed as) toys.⁶⁴

Kurasiński also brings up the question of whether certain age groups were associated with different burial patterns.⁶⁵ While in Radom and elsewhere, children were buried in graves laid out, positioned, and oriented like those of adults, they were also different from grown-ups in terms of the number and kind of provisions, as well as of the presence of coffins. Then there are clear differences between burials of children of different ages. Children who died before reaching the age of 3 very rarely receive any kind of provisions. The threshold between Infans I and Infans II is also visible with increasing numbers of beads and jewelry for girls and the occasional deposition of weapons for boys. Teenager were often treated as adults in burial. Such conclusions are not particularly controversial, and have been expanded upon and tested

---

61 Krzysztof Wachowski and Grzegorz Domański, *Wczesnopolskie cmentarzysko w Starym Zamku* (Wrocław: Uniwersytet Wrocławski, 1992), 27.
62 Wachowski and Domański, *Wczesnopolskie cmentarzysko w Starym Zamku*, 25.
63 Kurasiński and Skóra, "Children's Burials," 49.
64 Thomas Kurasiński, "Dziecko i strzała. Z problematyki wyposażania grobów w militaria na terenie Polski wczesnopiastowskiej (XI–XII wiek)," in *Dusza maluczka, a strata ogromna*, Funeralia Lednickie spotkanie 6, eds. Jacek Wrzesiński and Wojciech Dzieduszycki (Poznań: Stowarzyszenie Naukowe Archeologów Polskich, Oddział w Poznaniu, 2004), 131–138.
65 Kurasiński and Skóra, "Children's Burials," 43–47.

statistically for the cemetery at Lubień. A clear distinction exists in that cemetery between younger children in Infans I/II on the one hand, and Juvenis on the other hand, with the latter category showing an unmistakable similarity with adult graves. A number of boys in the Infans II category were buried in Lubień together with weapons, as might be expected from a rite of passage for young men in a society where masculinity was defined by participation in war.[66] Despite these speculations about archaeological traces of the progression of children to gendered adults, any final conclusions remain elusive, as the sexes of child skeletons cannot be determined.

3   Multiple Burials

When speaking of exceptions, the cemetery excavated in Czekanów stands out with its large number of furnished child graves and remarkably equitable distribution of grave goods among children. In one respect, however, Czekanów's child population is not unique, namely in the frequent presence of children in multiple burials. In Czekanów, as well as other cemeteries in Poland discussed below, children frequently appear in graves of two or more people. While the meaning or purpose behind this phenomenon remains to be clarified, some patterns are already visible, such as mothers buried with children, children buried with an elderly or well-provisioned adult, or children buried together. Family connections, emotions, and convenience have all been invoked as explanations,[67] to which Kurasiński and Skóra add possible suicide of a grieving parent, the ritual killing of an adult to help care for the dead child in the afterlife, and the killing of a child who would have lacked the support of his or her deceased caretakers.[68] These macabre and grotesque explanations, while very popular in many scholarly circles today, are also very difficult to verify, and these explanations have been focused on the exceptional cases. This section of this project, instead, will focus on the more prosaic circumstances surrounding the majority of double graves featuring children.

---

66   Florin Curta and Matthew Koval, "Children in Eleventh- and Twelfth-Century Poland and Hungary: An Archaeological Comparison," in *The Medieval Networks in East Central Europe Commerce, Contacts, Communication*, ed. Balázs Nagy, Felicitas Schmieder, and András Vadas (London: Routledge Press, 2019), 91.

67   See especially: Leszek Gardeła and Kamil Kajkowski, "Groby podwójne w Polsce wczesnośredniowiecznej. Próba rewaluacji," *Acta Archaeologica Lodziensia* 60 (2014): 103–120.

68   Kurasiński and Skóra, "Children's Burial," 48.

In Czekanów there were no less than 12 multiple burials containing children, eleven double graves and one triple grave.[69] These came in all sorts of varieties including two children together, child with a woman, child with a man, and, in one instance, a woman with two children. In about half of all instances, the two individuals were arranged in opposite orientations, with one to the east and the other to the west, though no clear pattern exists to explain this phenomenon.[70] Interestingly, none of these double graves truly fits into the stereotypical image of women who died while giving birth, and were buried together with the fetus or the newborn. It is of course possible that two individuals—adult and child—buried in the same grave were relatives. However, despite being buried next to each other, they were buried in separate pits, even though some multiple burials occurred at different times and disturbed previous burials. Perhaps the most intriguing case is that of a 2- to 3-year old child buried in grave 24, together with a clay egg. The child was actually buried along with the adult woman in grave 21, which was marked with a guard and with pavement. Some have rightly argued that this particular kind of burial may illustrate that the body of a child was desirable to add to a grave, probably because of family connection, or the body of the child was believed to have healing or other value for the adult.[71] Several other examples in Poland substantiate that interpretation. For example, there was an adult in grave 107 of the cemetery excavated in Złoto Pińczów near Busko-Zdrój (southern Poland). The grave pit, however, was adjusted to make room for the young child. This is hardly a solution for saving energy and room, and suggests purpose behind the decision, namely the desire to have a child buried with the already deceased.

Two remarkable multiple burials in Radom suggest familial contexts, namely graves 82 and 9. Although located in two different parts of the cemetery, both are within larger clusters of graves that include a number of children. Grave 82 is a double burial in which a fetus or a newborn's skull was placed on the pelvic bone of an adult woman aged 20 to 25.[72] The woman was buried

---

69 Zawadzka-Antosik, "Z problematyki pochówków dziecięcych," 40.
70 Different orientation is used in the Baltic region of male and female respectively. See Andris Caune, "Die Gräbertypen und Bestattungssitten im Ostbaltikum in der Zeit vom 1. bis 13. Jahrhundert," in Bestattungswesen und Totenkult in ur- und frühgeschichtlicher Zeit, edited by Fritz Horst and Horst Keiling (Berlin: Akademie Verlag, 1991), 257–74, especially 263. If the skeleton of a child in Czekanów is arranged in a position different from that of the neighboring female, then the child may have been viewed as a male.
71 Zawadzka-Antosik, "Z problematyki pochówków dziecięcych," 40.
72 Agnieszka Kozdęba, Tomasz Kurasiński and Kalina Skóra "Catalog Grόbow," in *Przestrzeń Osadnicza Wczesnośredniowiecznego Radomia, Tom 1: Cmentarzysko w Radomiu, Stanowisko 4*, ed. Tadeusz Baranowksi (Łodz: Wydawnictwo Instytutu Archeologii i Etnologii, PAN, 2016), 155.

together with temple rings, earrings, and pottery. There is also a brass finger ring, which could be associated either with the child or with the woman. It is likely that the woman in question died in childbirth or its aftermath. In grave 9 the remains of an Infans II (5–6 years) were placed amongst the remains of a woman aged 20–30, and of an adult male.[73] The state of preservation of the grave and of skeletons is quite poor, so exact positioning and provisioning is hard to determine, beyond the presence of a knife and another piece iron. Was this a whole family buried at the same time? Interestingly, grave 9 is close to, and very possibly connected to grave 12, which also contains an Infans I aged 4–5, who was buried together with a temple ring. The proximity of the burials and their distinctness from other burials suggests burial together, potentially of a king group.

The cemetery at Kałdus, with 28.1 percent of the cemetery population dying under the age of ten, contains six double burials, three of them with children.[74] In grave 194 a mature, possible female was buried beside an Infans II around 9 years of age.[75] Each grave had its own protective wooden burial guard to protect the shape of the pit, but they were placed side-by-side and with the same orientation. Only the child was buried together with an iron object, possibly a knife. Somewhat different is grave 221, with an adult woman and a newborn.[76] In contrast with Grave 194, in which the separation between an adult and child was pronounced, in grave 221 both individuals were placed together in the same wooden coffin. The woman was buried with a knife, a temple ring, and some beads, and the child was placed next to her right knee. Is the difference in treatment between the two children and the separation between the older child and its accompanying adult a sign of more independence afforded to a child who was almost as a member of the community? Or is that a sign of a different level of relationship between the individuals in the grave? Can this be simply a difference in family burial customs? The situation in the third double burial, Grave 356, strongly suggests that the age of the child mattered. This grave contained the skeletons of a child aged 7–9 as well as of an adult woman. While only the woman received decorative ornaments in death, both skeletons received protective wooden burial guards protecting their graves pits.[77]

Age of a child not only seemed to have an impact on how integrated a double burial was, but could have implications for the number of grave goods

---

73   Kozdęba et al., "Catalog Gróbow," 123.
74   Wojciech Chudziak, *Wczesnośredniowieczne cmentarzysko szkieletowe w Kałdusie* (Toruń: Wydawn. Uniwersytetu Mikołaja Kopernika, 2010), 129.
75   Chudziak, *Wczesnośredniowieczne cmentarzysko szkieletowe w Kałdusie*, 501, 266.
76   Ibid., 510.
77   Chudziak, *Wczesnośredniowieczne cmentarzysko szkieletowe w Kałdusie*, 20, 557–558.

that a child received in comparison to the accompanying adult. This is best illustrated by two double burials featuring children in the twelfth-century cemetery at Pyzdry, in Greater Poland, which is famous for its unusual north-south grave orientation.[78] In grave 9, an infant, no more than 3 months old, was deposited on the breast of a 15-year old, perhaps the mother. While the infant had no apparent provisions, the 15 year-old received a knife, a finger ring, and some pottery.[79] In contrast, the Infans II (12–14 years of age), buried alongside a 35-year old woman in grave 14 was favorably arrayed, with both receiving a number of bronze temple rings.[80]

Several other cemeteries from the Piast realm substantiate the observations made so far. At the southwestern edge of the kingdom, in Stary Zamek (Silesia), grave 48 was of an adult woman buried with a newborn placed on her side. Both received protection on the side of the shared pit by means of a series of carefully arranged stones. The woman was well-provisioned with both finger rings and temple rings.[81] There are multiple burials of similar pattern in Brześć Kujawski (Kujavia-Pomerania), an eleventh- to twelfth-century row cemetery with 156 burials. Four out of five double burials are with children.[82] In Graves 161 and 162, a double burial, an adult man and a boy of undetermined age buried alongside in distinct pits. The boy received the hoops and implements of a bucket, while the man was buried with an iron knife. Not all older children were clearly separated from their accompanying adults in Brześć Kujawski. In grave 146 a 30 year-old woman was laid to rest with the skull of a 10 year-old placed beside her knee below her hips, with a knife and other iron implements nearby. Unlike the similar graves in Kałdus, however, there is no separation between adult and child in grave 146 of the Brześć Kujawski cemetery. Moreover, in Brześć Kujawski, much like in Czekanów, there are two double burials in which both occupants are children. Grave 172 contained an older boy and a "small child" laid out side by side in one pit. The boy was provisioned with a small knife. Graves 64–65 were also stretched out side by side, with skeletons oriented in the same direction. The burials were identified as male and female (though without anthropological confirmation), with the boy furnished with a knife while the girl garnered 50 glass beads, 2 temple rings, a knife, and a glass ring.

---

78   Ilona Jagielska, "Wczesnośredniowieczne cmentarzysko na stanowisku Pyzdry 11," *Studia Lednickie* 10 (2010): 129–150.
79   Ibid., 143.
80   Ibid., 143–144.
81   Wachowski and Domański, *Wczesnopolskie cmentarzysko w Starym Zamku*, 61–62.
82   Kaszewscy, *Wczesnośredniowieczne cmentarzysko w Brześciu Kujawskim*, 427–432. Unfortunately, accurate age data was not provided with the excavation report.

Children could end up in multiple burials with all individuals of both sexes and various ages, but some were buried with the very old persons. In Zawichost near Sandomierz (southeastern Poland) a twelfth-century tetraconch dedicated to St Maurice was surrounded by a cemetery, in which two triple burials have been found. In each one of them, an old person was buried together the young.[83] In grave 323, a male of the age Maturus was buried with an Infans I of 3–4 years of age and with an Infans of undetermined age. More interestingly, in grave 11 an adult of "very advanced age" was buried with an Infans I aged 2–4 as well as another Infans I.[84] Burying the young with the old or the sick is attested in other parts of Europe as well and has many possible explanations, from kin relationship through care and healing of the two vulnerable individuals for each other.[85]

Because of the considerable variety in the burial record, it is appropriate to cast shadow on attempts at over-hasty conclusions. However, a number of patterns emerge consistently. First, children are more likely than individuals of any other age group to be buried in multiple burials. To be sure, such multiple burials with children take many forms—mother and child in some, but in others children are buried with older women, men, the elderly, and other children. This variety has been noted observed in Anglo-Saxon England as well, but burials in Czekanów that feature child with child are exceptional for the whole of Europe.[86] While in some instances the explanation for multiple burials may be convenience, in many more instances the care accorded to the child, both in grave goods and in the construction of the grave, is evident. An important factor in the ritual construction of multiple burials was the age of the deceased child, with older children receiving clearer demarcation from accompanying adults. While it is beyond doubt that, judging from multiple burials, children had a particular value for those who buried them together with adults, the reasons for doing may have varied locally.

---

83   Dariusz Wyczółkowski, "Pochówki dziecięce związane z najstarszą fazą cmentarzyska przy kościele św. Maurycego w Zawichoście," in *Dusza maluczka, a strata ogromna*, Funeralia Lednickie spotkanie 6, eds. Jacek Wrzesiński and Wojciech Dzieduszycki (Poznań: Stowarzyszenie Naukowe Archeologów Polskich, Oddział w Poznaniu, 2004), 161–165.
84   Wyczółkowski, "Pochówki dziecięce," 164–165.
85   Crawford, "Companions, Co-incidences, or Chattels," 3–92.
86   Nick Stoodley, "Multiple Burials, Multiple Meanings? Interpreting the Anglo-Saxon Multiple Interment," 103–121. England and Poland are different, for in the latter males and children were buried together far more often than Stoodley believes to have been the case for England (Stoodley, "Multiple Burials," 113–114).

4 Spatial Features of Child Burials

While the placement of specific children and adults together in the same grave tells us about specific burial relationships within a group, such relationships appeared personal and variable. For a broader reflection of society's thoughts about children in death, it is important to look at groups of child graves within one and the same cemetery. I have elsewhere noted that in Anglo-Saxon England, Scandinavia, and Poland children tended to be buried within one and the same area of a cemetery, most likely because of the spiritual care and love for children.[87] This section will expand on those observations to show that both in rural, row grave cemeteries and in churchyard cemeteries children were placed together.

Many children were buried together at Ląd, in the cemetery located inside the fortress.[88] There were 196 graves in that cemetery, only about 15 percent of which were of children. However, in Area 169 of the northwestern part of the cemetery, there is group of graves with 12 Infans I or II, 7 unidentified individuals, and 19 adults. This section of the cemetery has more children than any other part of the two cemeteries at Ląd, with at least a third of those children dying before they reached the age of 10. A closer look at the plan of this area reveals that 8 out of 12 child graves are together in the center, lined up in two rows. The row to the left has 15 graves, with at least 7 children. Given the very low number of children elsewhere in the cemetery, this concentration is unusual. Why were those children, as well as the accompanying adults buried at the western edge of the cemetery? Unfortunately, it is not even certain that that was an edge, for the cemetery was not completely excavated.[89] Moreover, area 169 appears as isolated, at some distance from the rest of the excavations. Nothing about the graves goods or grave construction would suggest that these graves were in any way marginalized or of low quality. To be sure, there are no elaborate grave goods in any grave of the cemetery in Ląd. The children in area 169 were buried with ordinary artifacts—knives, nails, unidentified artifacts. Another possibility is that this part of the cemetery represents a distinctive time period, in which church teachings or cultural beliefs encouraged the

---

87 For an example in the Anglo-Saxon context, see Christina Lee, "Forever Young: Child Burial in Anglo-Saxon England," in *Youth and Age in the Medieval North*, ed. Shannon Lewis-Simpson (Leiden: Brill, 2008), 17–36.

88 Krzyżaniak, ed., *Wczesnośredniowieczne cmentarzyska szkieletowe w Lądzie*, 55–56. Also, Plan II.

89 Ibid., 60.

segregation of children, or perhaps this reflects religious or ethnic customs of particular families. Whatever the explanation for this collection of children, it is definitely contrasts with the low number of children in the cemetery in general. It may indicate that in Ląd, at least, children were not buried in the central parts of the cemetery, but on the margins.

Other cemeteries have smaller collections of children in distinct groups. One of the more intriguing is in Radom. This was a group of young people buried together with a few adults. Grave 35 contains an Infans I (5–6 years of age and Grave 36 contains an Infans I/II. Both graves contain pottery. Grave 37 contains an Infans II (12–15 years old) and was well furnished by the standards of Radom with two silver temple rings, a spindle whorl, a coin, and pottery. Grave 34 is a badly damaged grave, with what appears to be an adult of unknown age with an Infans II/Juvenis. Two glass and one bronze ring have been found in the grave, but the damage was so severe that it is unclear whether this was double grave or the result of a later destruction. Finally, a young woman aged 20–25 was buried in Grave 40, while Grave 39 was destroyed too badly for analysis. With the exception of Grave 35, which lies somewhat off on its own, these graves are all in the same row, which is heavily dominated by children. None of these children show signs of "bad death" that would have make them unsuitable for proper burial or communal attention. Moreover, grave 37 was well-furnished. To make matters more interesting, Grave 38, also to some degree part of this row, contained the bones of two sheep, one of them young. No other grave in the cemetery contains sheep, or any other animal for that matter. Sheep, while consumed near the settlement at Radom, were not the most commonly consumed food in Poland at that time, but nevertheless was eaten on occasion. They represent 13 percent of all animal bones found in early Piast Radom (compared to 45 percent for cattle, 34 percent for pig, 8 percent for horse, and 14 percent for wild game), a percentage directly comparable to the situation in pre-Piast Radom (at about 14 percent).[90] Pottery was also found at the bottom of that grave.[91] Much could be made of the ritual possibilities of these sheep

---

90   Anna Gręzak and Beata Kurach, "Konsumpcja mięsa w średniowieczu oraz w czasach nowożytnych na terenie obecnych ziem Polski w świetle danych archeologicznych," in *Archeologia Polski* 41 (1996): 147.

91   Agnieszka Kozdęba, Tomasz Kurasiński and Kalina Skóra "Catalog Gróbow" and "Tablice 170," in *Przestrzeń Osadnicza Wczesnośredniowiecznego Radomia, Tom 1: Cmentarzysko w Radomiu, Stanowisko 4*, ed. Tadeusz Baranowksi (Łodz: Wydawnictwo Instytutu Archeologii i Etnologii, PAN, 2016), 133–136.

in the context of Christianization and the survival of pagan ritual.[92] However, much more important is the relationship between the young sheep, children, and pottery. Pottery was found in the same position in grave graves 36 and 38, namely to the east (at the head) and at the feet, respectively. Graves 34 and 38 both contain young and old together, though of different species (humans in 34, sheep in 38). The considerable care to relate young and old, human and animal strongly suggests a very conscious treatment of children.

In other cemeteries clusters of children appear to be connected with certain adults. The cemetery at Brzeg near Sieradz (central Poland) functioned presumably as a family cemetery from the eleventh to the thirteenth century. There are 7 rows with a total of 72 graves, but there is also a cluster of children buried together with some adults in the southeastern quarter. The 16 skeletons in this cemetery that have been identified as children were buried with fewer grave goods than the adults. Out of 16 children, only 7 had no grave goods, while 5 out of 25 males were buried without grave goods (only 1 of 22 women was buried without grave goods). The excavators have interpreted this phenomenon as reflecting the ongoing Christianization of the region, though other explanations could be provided.[93] The southeastern part of the cemetery features seven (or maybe eight) graves, in two rows (graves 10, 9, 42 in one row and 7, 6, 5, 44, 43, and, with a slight space in between, 57 in another) that are separated from the rest of the cemetery. Five of these graves (10, 9, 7, 6, and 44) are of children. Furthermore, unlike the general trend of the cemetery, four of them children have grave goods comparable to those found with adults in that same cluster. The adult in grave 43 has a knife and the adult in grave 5 also has a knife (as well as money, and a bucket). Similarly the children in graves 9 and 10 both have knives (as well as assorted ceramics), while the child in grave 44 has a knife, a belt, ceramics, and charcoal. On the other hand the child in grave 7 has nine bronze temple rings, along with pottery, while the woman in grave 42, who was around 20 years old at her death, has a bronze temple ring of similar fashion,[94] as well as a glass bead necklace, a belt, a coin, and a

---

92   Jacek Wrzesiński, "The Dziekanowice Cemetery—Christian Cultivating Venerable Traditions," in *Rome, Constantinople and Newly-Converted Europe. Archaeological and Historical Evidence*, eds. M. Salamon, M. Wołoszyn, A. Musin, P. Spechar, M. Hardt, M.P. Kruk, A. Sulikowska-Gaska (Kraków: Geisteswiss. Zentrum Geschichte und Kultur Ostmitteleuropas, 2012), 546. In this article the authors question easy explanations of a ceremonial meal, especially when only single bones are found.

93   Anna Kufel-Dzierzgowska, "Wczesnośredniowieczne cmentarzysko w Brzegu, Województwo Sieradzkie," *Seria Archeologiczna* 30 (1983): 309–322.

94   Kufel-Dzierzgowska, "Wczesnośredniowieczne cmentarzysko w Brzegu," Plates X and XVI.

knife.⁹⁵ Interestingly, pottery did not appear in any of the adult graves in this cluster, while coins did not appear in any of the child graves. There is a clear correlation in treatment and kinds of goods between adults and children in this cluster, with the former playing, perhaps, a key role in terms of both position and grave goods.

Another example of a row cemetery with family plots is Maslowice in the same region around Łodz (central Poland). This was a cemetery with 85 graves, of which at least 20 children. This cemetery functioned in the twelfth and thirteenth centuries, and many graves contained fragments of pottery and charcoal, which the excavator interpreted as evidence of surviving pre-Christian practices, such as feasting at the graveside of the deceased. More interestingly, there are three instances where an adult is buried surrounded by two or more children.⁹⁶ Let us look at each of these in turn. The most distinct of these are graves 55, 54, 53, and 52, which, while broadly within the pattern of rows within the cemetery, are clearly separated from the rest of graves in space. Grave 55 contains an adult male of unknown age provisioned only with pottery and knife, while 54, 53, and 52 are all presumably the graves of children due to their size, though the terrible state of preservation in the cemetery due to unfavorable soil leaves nothing of the bones or provisions.⁹⁷ All of these graves are marked by their paucity of goods. Another adult male was buried away from the rest of the cemetery in grave 49, together with a knife, a whetstone, and pottery. He is flanked by child graves 45 and 50, both of which are devoid of skeletal material probably because of decomposition. In both of the clusters focused on an adult so far, an adult male with basic provisions was connected to children who received nothing.

A different situation is another set of graves in Masłowice, this time more closely associated with a row, though still spatially distinct within it—graves 30, 31, 32, and 33.⁹⁸ These graves are also include an adult male with three children. The adult in grave 30 was buried with a knife and flints, but the children also received grave goods. Grave 30 had a knife, grave 32 (of a young child, up to 6 years of age) had a knife and pottery, and in grave 33 there was a temple ring. Knives appear in three of these four graves, and all children received at least one grave good that was also common among adult graves. This is in sharp contrast to the two clusters mentioned above, in which children received nothing. Finally the last cluster is centered on the woman in grave 20, who received

---

95 Ibid., 323–327.
96 Abramek, "Wczesnośredniowieczne cmentarzysko szkieletowe w Masłowicach," 227–246.
97 Ibid., 233.
98 Ibid., 232.

7 temple rings, a finger ring, and a knife. She was buried in a pit connected with grave 19, a child of around 2 years old, who received no goods. To the left and right of that double burial are two very different child graves. Grave 18 received no grave goods of any kind, but grave 21 was of a 8- to 10-year old child buried in a wooden coffin together with 6 temple rings, 6 glass beads, a finger ring, a knife, and another ornament of unclear design and function. While the adult woman in grave 20 as well as the child in grave 21 received similar and relatively rich treatment, the other two children received nothing, and the same applies to the child grave nearby (grave 19). Given the complete or almost complete decay of the child bones, it is impossible to determine whether this difference has to do with the age of the child or some other factor. In Masłowice, children were placed not in family groups, but around individual adults, and whom the children, to varying degrees, shadow in terms of burial provisions. Whether the children were placed there for the "benefit" of the adults or the other way around, remains unclear, but for many children buried in Masłowice, a special relationship to an adult was decidedly worth (re)constructing after death.

The variety of ways in which children appear in groups in the rural and settlement cemeteries just discussed is matched by what we see in cemeteries closely associated to major church or ecclesiastical centers. Around churches, children are often buried together in some special area. For example, in the eleventh-century church in Ostrów Lednicki discussed above, children were buried in the nave.[99] This is the case of the well-provisioned Infans in grave 2, who received elaborate treatment (stone tomb, coffins, finger ring, glass objects, as well as remnants of other unknown things), though was later exhumed. Similarly, of the four individuals to the west from the nave, two were children (aged 4 and 1 and a half, respectively), one was a male adult, and one was unidentifiable. In other words, of the five children who died under 10 years of age, 3 were associated with the nave. Why were (those) children buried in or near the nave? Helena Zoll-Adamikowa sees in this a practice of West European origin, which associated burial inside or close to the church to the most spiritually rewarding place to rest.[100] If true, then children were placed in the nave as a last act of care by their bereaved, but still caring, families.

Elsewhere children were not buried in the nave. In Zawichost, the twelfth-century tetraconch dedicated to St. Maurice was later destroyed to make room for a wooden church. Out of 11 children in the cemetery associated to the tetraconch, all but one have been found on the northern side of the of the

---

99   Nowak "Badania archeologiczne na Ostrowie Lednickim," 179–189.
100 Helena Zoll-Adamikowa, "Frühmittelalterliche Bestattungen der Würdenträger in Polen (Mitte des 10. bis Mitte des 12. Jahrhundert)," *Przeglad archeologiczny* 38 (1991): 109–134.

(eastern) apse.[101] While many relevant details remain unpublished, the excavator regards this area as a child's quarter, albeit of lesser significance than the other areas in which adults were buried.[102] Why were children buried together near the nave, apse or even on the margins of the cemetery? Martin Čechura, writing about similar instances in the Czech lands, suggests that it has to do with the ambivalent attitudes Christian communities had in the twelfth century as new church doctrines such as purgatory coupled with increasing church control of burial made burials of unbaptized children, or even baptized children dying at a young age, something of a quandary for parents and authorities. In some instances, children may have received burial near the church to be near relics or under rainwater from the church, but in other circumstances young children received burial inside the cemetery, but separated and apart from the rest of the population to mark their ambiguous status, perhaps because of lack of baptism, while still including them in the Christian family.[103]

A pattern somewhat similar is present at Czersk, in Pomerania, in a large twelfth- to thirteenth-century churchyard cemetery with 797 excavated pits.[104] A typical churchyard in many respects (such as orientation, position, and layout), 23.5 percent of the graves had grave goods. The excavators have regarded this as surviving pagan rites, though this can be problematized as we will see below.[105] Among the most conspicuous features, they have pointed to amulets, which appear especially in child graves.[106] While children are interspersed in small groups and individually throughout the churchyard, both next to the church and farther away from it, the largest group by far is, as in Zawichost, on the northern side of the apse. These graves form roughly their own row or two at the very edge of the cemetery and extend northwards to almost the very edge of the cemetery.[107] Around 20 children were laid to rest here, and in fact probably more, as many of the graves near this edge of the cemetery were in such poor state of preservation that their occupants could not be analyzed and categorized. The children were of all ages, from a near-to-term fetus to Infans II/Juvenis, and some of the graves received unusual and rich graves goods.

---

101 Darius Wyczółkowski, "Pochówki dziecięce związane z najstarszą fazą cmentarzyska przy kościele św. Maurycego w Zawichoście," *Funeralia Lednickie* 6 (2004): 163.
102 Wyczółkowski, "Pochówki," 164.
103 Čechura, "Christian, Non-Christian, or Pagan," 289–297.
104 Jadwiga Bronicka-Rauhut, *Cmentarzysko wczesnośredniowieczne w Czersku* (Warsaw, Polish Academy of Sciences, 1998), 7–48.
105 Pomerania was long at the margins of effective Piast and/or German control, and Christianity did not come firmly to the region until the missionary effort of Otto of Bamberg in the twelfth century.
106 Bronicka-Rauhut, *Cmentarzysko wczesnośredniowieczne w Czersku*, 22.
107 Ibid., 51–118.

Closest to the apse are a series of graves that are separated in space from the others. These include the Infans I or II in grave 581, the Infans I in graves 530, 560, and 561, as well as the Infans II in graves 523, 531, 555, 548, and 562. All of these children occupy the very edge of the cemetery, with the young adults (juvenis/adultus) in graves 529, 553, and 563 separating them from the rest of the adult population. Two of the children in this part of the cemetery received grave goods, which is only slightly less than the incidence of goods in the rest of the cemetery population. The Infans II in grave 548 received a knife and two beads. More spectacularly, the Infans II in grave 523 received 75 beads, a finger ring, and an amulet comprising a pierced animal fang found with the beads on the child's neck. Separated by some empty ground, this concentration seems to continue to the north, though more interspersed with graves of adults. These include the graves of Infans I 754, 755, 769, and 791 as well as of Infans II 756, 782, and 783. In this group we also find an adult woman buried with a near-to-term infant. Fragments of pottery were found in grave 782 and an iron object was found in 783. The most prolific, however, was reserved for an Infans I in 769, who received 70 beads, a finger ring, and an amulet comprised of 5 animal fangs.

What should one make of these graves? At a quick glimpse they appear to be special, in a negative sense. Not only are they on the margins of the cemetery, but they are to the north of the apse, a place less prestigious than other parts of a churchyard.[108] Furthermore, two of those child graves contained amulets made from animal fangs. Some have been quick to interpret those as related to some magical, perhaps pagan beliefs. However, ever since the conversion to Christianity, the use of animal fangs as amulets had been undergoing a revolution in Poland. By 1100, such amulets disappeared among adults.[109] As Aleksandr Musin has shown, the use of such amulets among children was a thoroughly Christianized practice, so much so that it continued well into the early modern period as documented, among other things by the portrait made

---

108 Wyczółkowski, "Pochówki dziecięce," 163–164.
109 Aleksandr Musin, "Czy król Zygmunt III Waza był w dzieciństwie poganinem? Między pogaństwem a chrześcijaństwem, o fenomenie amuletów z zębów i kości zwierząt," in *Od Bachórza do Światowida ze Zbrucza. Tworzenie się słowiańskiej Europy w ujęciu źródłoznawczym. Księga jubileuszowa Profesora Michała Parczewskiego*, ed. Barbara Chudzińska, Michał Wojenka and Marcin Wołoszyn (Kraków/Rzeszów: Wydawnictwo Uniwersytetu Rzeszowskiego, 2016), 421–40. For a similar conclusion on the basis of earlier materials, see Tivadar Vida, "Heidnische und christliche Elemente der awarenzeitlichen Glaubenswelt. Amulette in der Awarenzeit," *Zalai Múzeum* 11 (2002): 179–209.

in 1569 of the three-year old Sigismund (future king of Poland as Sigismund III Vasa) wearing a necklace with a dog fang as pendant-amulet. In the new, Christian context, the amulets were about conferring and representing certain traits and abilities that parents and guardians wished to bestow upon children. On the other hand, nothing about the position or provisions of the child graves in Czersk would suggest that they were in any way "bad" or inferior, and in fact the two graves featuring the amulets were some of the best furnished in the entire cemetery. It is likely that those children had been surrounded with great care during their lifetime. Finally, even though these graves were at the edge of the cemetery, they were still undoubtedly part of it, with no borders or gaps separating them from other graves, and they were still placed in relation to and in accordance with the church. Though certainly considered distinct from adults, the children in these rows show every sign that their placement was out of care and concern, not disdain or neglect. This is important to point out, because in late medieval and early modern Poland, unbaptized children were stigmatized, and therefore placed in special quarters of the cemetery, in order to cordon their less-worthy bodies off from the Christian family and to put their remains not in holy ground, but in ceramic pots.[110] These later practices, however, have no relation to those in existence at the time of the churchyard cemetery at Czersk.

There is much variety behind the placement of children in groups within cemeteries. Sometimes children were placed in groups in accordance with a central adult. Family relationships were most likely at work in such cases. In other instances, children were placed with children and its was their age category that determined their location within the cemetery. This was most evident in Zawichost and Czersk, where the child's quarter was on the northern side of the apse. In other instances, such as at Ląd, no satisfactory explanation has so far been advanced for the distinct placement of child burials. At any rate, children were placed in groups not thoughtlessly or carelessly, but instead were consciously and beneficently treated in their final rest.

---

110   Elżbieta Kowalczyk, "Chrześcijańskie miłosierdzie. Rzecz o pochówkach dzieci nie ochrzczonych (na przykładzie północnego Mazowsza)," in *Dusza maluczka, a strata ogromna*, Funeralia Lednickie spotkanie 6, eds. Jacek Wrzesiński and Wojciech Dzieduszycki (Poznań: Stowarzyszenie Naukowe Archeologów Polskich, Oddział w Poznaniu, 2004), 103–113.

5 In Search of Pattern: Micro vs. Macro Comparisons

The discussion so far has revealed few rules or patterns that are universally true throughout all of Poland. One can only conclude that what exists in one or a group of cemeteries will be not be by any means necessarily the case in others. This reality has encouraged a number of scholars in Poland, and elsewhere, to seek other ways to analyze the cemetery data. One of these approaches is to use mathematics to explore widespread patterns in the mortuary evidence, either across regions or within individual cemeteries. In the past, information about childhood was usefully gathered about childhood for medieval France and England through statistical methods. A famous example is Guy Halsall's *Settlement and Social Organization: the Merovingian Region of Metz*, which found childrens' graves in the sixth and seventh centuries to be most similar to those of women. Unlike the situation we see in Poland where certain children are spectacularly arrayed, Halsall did not find much evidence that social status of parents was connected to the furnishing of their children.[111] For England, Sally Crawford also made use of statistics to examine everything from age categories and artifact types to funerary contexts, and she uncovered the reality that children and childhood was far more distinct from adulthood and children showed far more signs archaeologically of their societies' care and attention than previously thought for the Anglo-Saxon period.[112] More recently, scholars have turned statistics towards more careful analysis of particular cemeteries. The best of example of this is in Scandinavia, where Lotta Mejsholm uses a particularly useful procedure to discover childhood initiation rituals in the cemetery at Fjälkinge.[113] Mejsholm uses a form of seriation to group different configurations of child burials, uncovering a strong correlation between more traditional burials and the presence of pots containing milk residue. She then correlates this with religious and legal texts which describe the importance of a first feeding ritual in pre- and early Christian society.

In Poland, a number of archaeologists have used statistics in the last 20 years or so in order to understand better the place of children in cemeteries. I have already mentioned Kurasiński and Skóra's analysis of the Radom cemetery, and their conclusion, drawn from the relative paucity of child graves and comparison with other cemeteries, that the age of 3 was the threshold for

---

111   Guy Halsall, *Settlement and Social Organization: the Merovingian region of Metz* (Cambridge: Cambridge University Press, 1995).
112   Sally Crawford, *Childhood in Anglo-Saxon England* (Gloucestershire: Sutton, 1999).
113   Lotta Mejsholm, "Constructions of early childhood at the syncretic cemetery of Fjälkinge—a case study," in *Youth and Age in the Medieval North*, ed. Shannon Lewis-Simpson (Leiden: Brill, 2008).

the deposition of any grave goods in child graves.[114] A great deal of attention was given to the children in the large row cemetery of Dziekanowice by Anna Wrzesińska and Jacek Wrzesiński, who noted the contrast between the generally poor graves of young children contrasted with the extraordinary or special burials of some children, who were buried with large numbers of beads or with amulets.[115]

Despite all the excellent work that has been done both in Poland and abroad on the mortuary archaeology of children, advanced statistics have not been used to address the broader role and meaning of children in cemeteries or indeed anywhere else in Europe, where so far only seriation has been used for cemetery analysis. Recently, however, a model of interpretation and comparison has been advanced, which is based on correspondence analysis.[116] Correspondence analysis is a mathematical tool that uses multivariate analysis to find correlations between many different variables, all at the same time, and its results can be displayed graphically.[117] the study of the two cemeteries, one in Poland and the other in Hungary, identified "family" sections, which resembled each other so much statistically that a family or community ritual was likely in use. Much like Guy Halsall has noted for the region of Metz in the Merovingian age, Infans I and II more closely resembled the graves of women in medieval cemeteries in Poland. However, unlike Frankish Gaul, in 12th- and 13th-century Poland, there was a marked change for children in the Juvenis category, which resembled more male graves, probably due to the deposition of weapons in graves of young men on the threshold of male adulthood.

---

114   Kurasiński and Skóra, "Children's Burials from the Early Medieval Inhumation Cemetery in Radom," 41–52.
115   Anna Wrzesińska and Jacek Wrzesiński, "Pochówki dzieci we wczesnym średniowieczu na przykładzie cmentarzyska w Dziekanowicach," *Studia lednickie* 6 (2000): 141–160. Also see Anna Wrzesińska and Jacek Wrzesiński "Pochówki dzieci najmłodszych INFANS I na wczesnośredniowiecznych cmentarzyskach w Dziekanowicach," in *Od narodzin do wieku dojrzałego: dzieci i młodzież w Polsce, V/1. Od średniowiecza do wieku XVIII*, ed. M. Dąbrowska and A. Klonder (Warsaw, Instytut Archeologii i Etnologii Polskiej Akademii Nauk, 2002), 269–283.
116   Curta and Koval, "Children," 87–122.
117   Establishing a threshold of cases for establishing significance is debated in the literature. For a recent discussion on this, see Giovanni Di Franco, "Multiple correspondence analysis: one only or several techniques?," *Quality & Quantity* 50 (2016): 1299–1315. This article concludes, "in the literature we found no clear guidelines relating to the minimum number of cases required to perform an MCA. Evidently, this number must be directly related to the number of active category-variables. Given the strong sensitivity of the technique to small changes, in order to obtain robust results the number of cases subjected to analysis ought to be decidedly high." Using Di Franco's suggested guidelines a project with my parameters would require need a minimum sample size of at least 100.

The following section will apply the model to a number of other cemeteries in Poland.

6   Age, Sex, and Grave Goods

As mentioned in the introduction to this book, one of the larger theoretical questions surrounding childhood in the archaeological record is whether the treatment of children had some relationship to gender. For the following discussion of this problem, I chose five cemeteries in Poland to analyze by means of correspondence analysis: Czersk, Masłowice, Kałdus, Radom and Cedynia. They have all been mentioned above, except Cedynia, a sizable churchyard cemetery in Pomerania, which was active from the twelfth to the fourteenth century.[118] These cemeteries were chosen for three main reasons. First, correspondence analysis needs a large number of units to achieve significant results. In practical terms, this means that each chosen cemetery had to have at least 80 burials in order to achieve significance and variety in the statistics. It also means that enough burials needed provisions so that simply the presence of grave goods themselves would not skew the results, for then the rare good here or there would be the outlier and determining factor and not the arrangement and distribution of goods. In short, the cemeteries chosen had to be larger and have high incidences of grave goods. Second, the five chosen cemeteries have been well and comprehensively, with good anthropological (i.e. determinations of sex were not made on the basis of grave goods) studies of the skeletal material, which allows for careful representation of the cemetery characteristics. Finally, cemeteries were selected from different regions of Poland—the Łódź region, Pomerania, Kujavia, and Mazovia—in an attempt to detect regional differences. Only Czersk and Cedynia are churchyard cemeteries. This is because most such cemeteries published in Poland are either too small or have no grave goods. The latter aspect fits into Helena Zoll-Adamikowa's description of the last phase of the Christianization of burial, but makes statistical analysis impossible. This means, of course, that only limited conclusions can be drawn from Czersk and Cedynia for the rest of Poland, as they are both from Pomerania.

With this in mind it is now time to say a few words about how the data itself was collected and analyzed. The Bonn software used for correspondence analysis allows input for units and types, which correspond to rows and

---

118   Helena Malinowska-Łazarczyk, *Cmentarzysko średniowieczne w Cedyni* (Szczecin, Muzeum Narodowe, 1982).

columns on a table, respectively.[119] The "units" were age categories. I used as much specificity as I could for each cemetery, within the bounds allowed by the needs of statistical significance. In cemeteries with poor decomposition, "children" had to serve as one distinct category, while in others Infans I and II could be distinguished. The other units were "male" and "female" according to the anthropological conclusions from an examination of the bones. Skeletons of undeterminable sex and age were eliminated from analysis. Likewise, due to the difficulties of assigning grave goods to any particular individual in many multiple burials, these were also stricken from the record. By comparing the graves of sexed skeletons to the graves of children, I expected to shed some light on how children were treated in burial in relation to adults. Each "type," on the other hand, was an artifact category that appeared in at least 2 graves for cemeteries with less than 100 graves and in at least 3 graves for cemeteries with more than 100 graves, in order to prevent outliers from distorting the overall picture. This, of course, occasionally eliminates many objects from consideration, such as weapons or special decorative elements, which are often weighted heavily towards one sex or another. Despite this drawback, it is better not to have a whole cemetery sex category based solely on the fact that one member happens to have, for example, a spear. Another important factor in calculating the types is that they are recorded according to presence/absence rather than abundance. The obvious reasons for that is that a certain grave might have, say 1,000 beads, but few other graves in the cemetery contain any beads at all. If the analysis is based on abundance, then the one grave with 1,000 beads will skew the significance of beads heavily in favor of that unit, thus making it seem more important than it, in fact, may have been in the first place.

With these caveats in mind, we can now analyze and compare the resulting plots for each cemetery. Correspondence between variables is not represented simply by proximity (as correspondence analysis works in multi-dimensional space). The further variables are away from the origin, the more distinctive and influential they are. Likewise, the smaller the angle between imaginary lines linking the origin to each variable, the more connected the two variables are. Angles of 90 degrees or more show no connection, and angles of over 180 degrees betray negative correlations. In other words, two variables that are close to the origin, even if they are close together on the plot as well as in an angle, do not demonstrate strong correspondence, but if two variables are close together and far from the origin, beyond one degree of connection, then they have a high degree of correlation.

---

119   See https://proceedings.caaconference.org/files/1998/CD-ROM/SOFTWARE/PROGRAMS/WINBASP/BASP.HTM (visit of February 2, 2021).

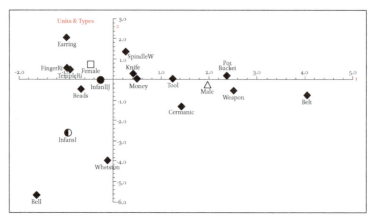

FIGURE 1   CA analysis of Kałdus

A quick glance at Figure 1: Kałdus graph shows a strongly gendered distribution of grave goods. Male graves are highly correlated with belts, weapons, pots, and buckets. On the other hand, the graves of females have correlations to earrings, finger and temple rings. The position of children within this configuration is very interesting. They are clearly more related to graves of females, especially in the Infans II/Juvenis category, but those correspondences are weak, as seen in the proximity of "Female" and "Infans II/J" to the origin, and the 90 degree angle between "Female" and "Infans I." Distinctive artifacts create this skew. For example, bells only appear in graves of children.

Similarly, while present in some female graves, beads are often spectacularly represented in graves of older children. In Kałdus, children in the Infans I category, partly by their lack of goods, but also because of some distinctive characteristics, constitute a separate category. The same pattern is evident at Radom, though the defining artifacts are different. Males are correlated with weapons and buckles, as in Kałdus but belts, buckets, and pots, are not as relevant, or not relevant at all. Females in Radom are correlated with finger rings and beads, which were more ambiguous in Kałdus. Again, children, while slightly more connected to women, are still nonetheless in their own distinctive category. While somewhat distinguished by the deposition of pottery in their graves, children are not exclusively associated to any other artifact category in Radom. In fact, as Tomasz Kurasiński and Kalina Skóra have noted, the most striking characteristic of child graves in that cemetery is the absence of grave goods.[120]

---

120   Kurasiński and Skóra, "Children's Burials from the Early Medieval Inhumation Cemetery in Radom," 42–52.

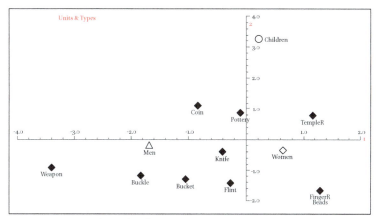

FIGURE 2   CA analysis of Radom

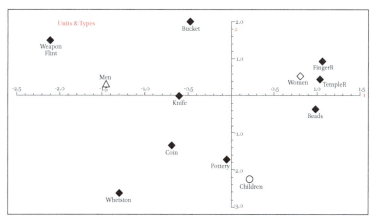

FIGURE 3   CA analysis of Masłowice

If any of the five cemeteries considered for analysis are similar to each other, those are Radom (Figure 2) and Masłowice (Figure 3). While distinguishing grave goods are different, the relationships between age and gender are practically the same. Female skeletons are defined by finger and temple rings, and, to some extent, by beads. Men, on the other hand, are defined by flint stones (used with flint steels for starting fire), weapons, and to a small degree, by knives. Children, on the other hand, are primarily defined more by the lack of grave goods and then by the deposition of pottery.

While in Masłowice and Radom child graves are defined by lack of grave goods, the two churchyard cemeteries, despite all expectations, follow the pattern identified for Kałdus, where children have a number of defining graves goods. In Cedynia (Figure 4), there are only a few weapons, but male graves are defined by spindle whorls, belt fittings and buckles.

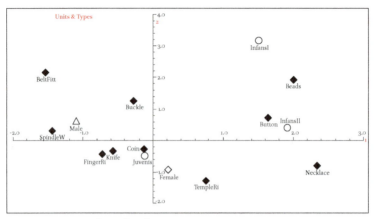

FIGURE 4   CA analysis of Cedynia

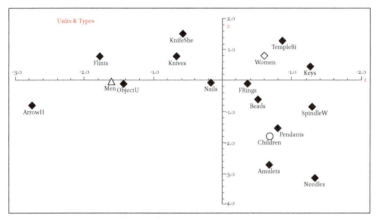

FIGURE 5   CA analysis of Czersk

Women, on the other hand, have stronger connections to temple rings and coins. There was a relatively large number of Juvenis burials in Cedynia, but they do not show any particularly strong relationship to other units, even though, unlike the situation in Lubień, some graves of Juvenis seem to follow the definition of female graves, as they include temple rings but not any of the goods associated with males. sex categories by the presence of beads, which children of Infans I and II are clearly separated from the other age and in larger incidences than the other units. Beads, then, may be regarded as a defining "type" for child burials.

Of all the cemeteries discussed so far, it was Czersk (Figure 5) that offered the best documentation for distinct child burials. Here, as in all other cemetery, female skeletons are typically correlated with temple rings, and male skeletons with weapons (arrow heads), flints, and some other unidentified metal artifacts (possibly tools). Children, on the other hand, are set apart as a category, by the presence of amulets (made of animal fangs, as discussed above), pendants, and needles, followed by beads and spindle whorls. Czersk can therefore serve as an excellent illustration of the fact that even at churchyards of the later stages of Christianization, grave goods could still have significant gendered distributions.

What conclusions can be drawn from the comparison of those correspondence analysis plots? First, in all five cemeteries, children were unmistakably differentiated from both male and female burials. In Radom and Masłowice, this differentiation was mostly based on the absence of grave goods, but in the other three cemeteries distinctive goods set the children apart from the adults—amulets in Czersk, beads in Cedynia, and bells in Kałdus. Whether such constructions of childhood in death reflect and conceptual categories in life is an altogether different question. At any rate, it is clear that, judging from the cemetery data, childhood could not be reduced to a different version of adulthood, as Ariès and others have suggested. Second, while children were undoubtedly separated from adults, what exactly marked that separation was different from one site to another. Weapons in general defined males, temple rings corresponded with females, and beads often lavishly bedecked the graves of children. However, this was by no means a hard and fast rule, for weapons often appear in a few, if any male graves of any given cemetery, while many women were buried without any temple rings. Moreover, in some cemeteries, women often competed with children for the most bedazzling assemblage of beads. Are those differences to be explained in terms of regional customs? To be sure, there are notable differences between the two churchyard cemeteries from Pomerania, even though they are located at some distance from each other. Conversely, Masłowice and Radom are very similar despite being located in different provinces. This is definitely a question that deserves a more detailed study, which would rely on a deeper analysis of cemeteries in one or two particular narrowly defined regions or sub-regions. My own preference when collecting materials for this book was breadth, not depth, for I was interested in exploring and comparing the far reaches of the Piast realm. The question of regional customs for child burial in Piast Poland is an excellent avenue for future research.

7 Final Thoughts

The material presented in this chapter is in a sense very different from that presented in the previous four chapters. What is one to make of the fact that some cemeteries seem to lack children, or that children in some cemeteries receive no, or at least vastly inferior, grave goods, but in other instances the opposite is the case? Even cemeteries with few children or poorly furnished child graves may have one or two such graves that are either the equivalent or even surpass the most elaborate burials of of adults. Where does then the archaeological data fit into the general discussion of childhood in medieval Poland?

First, the archaeological evidence warns against the idea of a single, straightforward framework through which to analyze all children in Piast Poland. Even within a single cemetery children's graves can show a high degree of variance. This does not mean, as we have seen, that there are no results or correlations in certain contexts, but there are no universally relevant results. This is really not so different from what we saw in the other four chapters. In each of these chapters, childhood was constructed and portrayed differently according to the context and purpose of the writer, the class of the child, and the genre of the text. From the kingly childhood of Bolesław Wrymouth, to the saintly childhood of Kinga, the incompetent or threatening children of the Henryków Book, to the reckless and rhetorical children of Vincent, children in texts during this same period, even in the upper classes, appear to have varied characteristics, behaviors, and stereotypes associated with them. There is therefore no surprise that variety also appears in the archaeology of medieval cemeteries of that same time.

Despite the lack of universal regularity for child graves, there were a number of clear trends. Indeed, children were less likely to be buried alone than adults. This is clear both from the high incidence of children placed in multiple burials and from the existence of child's quarters in both row and churchyard cemeteries. Multiple burials, on the other hand, cannot be interpreted simply in terms of convenience, for the children included in such burials were treated with particular attention. Nor were all multiple burials in the context of women dying in childbirth and being buried together with their offspring. In fact, men and women of all ages were buried with children, for it was obviously good not just for the child to be accompanied by an adult in death, but also for the adult to be laid down in the grave together with a child. In other instances, children were buried not with adults, but other children. Exactly why that was done remains unclear, but the context of the burials suggest different reasons in different cemeteries, from family custom and common burial (row cemeteries) to thoughts about the spiritual needs of children in the afterlife, or at least their similar status in death (churchyard cemeteries).

In cemeteries where enough children and grave goods in child graves allowed analysis, children also often seemed to function as a distinct social group, apart from either men or women. This is in spite of the fact that there were always some spectacular statistical outliers who defied general trends.

The reasons for this may have also varied from one site to another. Sometimes lack of graves goods was the unifying factor, but in other times the presence certain artifact categories marked children apart, though in ways different from one cemetery to another. This rhymes well with the textual evidence, according to which children constituted a relevant and distinct social category in Piast Poland, with their own associations, stereotypes, and expectations revealed both in death and in life. Similarly, this distinct social group was constructed differently at various times or places, and in various contexts. In short, the distinct character of children in social terms was as much a factor of local and immediate concerns as it was.

CHAPTER 7

Conclusions and Comparisons

The preceding five chapters should have provided sufficient evidence that each of the sources we have examined has its own descriptions of, language for, and purpose for children and childhood. In these preceding chapters, children have appeared as a threat looming on the margins of a monastery's future (as in the Henryków Book), as a distinct and special group (in the archaeological record), as pupating holy men and women (in the hagiography), as young princes showing their prowess and progressing in their family hierarchies (as in Gallus Anonymus), and even as powerful rhetorical images to chastise the wicked and uplift the virtuous (as in Vincent Kadłubek). All of this begs the question of whether broader conclusions can be drawn about how and why children appear in early Piast sources. This final chapter and conclusion will highlight a number of common themes across chapters, and then note how they fit within the general framework of childhood in medieval Europe in roughly the same centuries.

1   The Child as Symbol of the Future, Prophecy

Children, childhood, and youthful actions were seen in many of the texts we surveyed as harbingers for things to come. This "prophetic" role for children was usually connected to historical children, or at least children believed to have existed, and the significance of their actions could point to both their own personal futures, but also to futures of others or even those of an entire nation. The clearest example of this is the triple hair cutting mentioned in Gallus Anonymus that inaugurated the coming of the Christian Piast dynasty. This coming of age ritual accompanied significant portents for the future of these boys and their country: Popiel's disinheritance was foretold after guests were dishonored, Siemovit through a miracle of Biblical nature was confirmed to be the first of the Piast dukes, and Mieszko I through the healing of his blindness was designated the one to bring Christianity to Poland. This same story was reworked by Vincent Kadłubek, but his version was less focused on Mieszko and the Piasts, and instead was refocused on the sins and blindness of the pagan Poles and the glory of their national awakening, in which metaphors of age were shifted to symbolize the metaphorical youth of the people in general.

Both Gallus and Vincent employed extraordinary boyhood events to bolster the credentials of their heroes, and for both authors Bolesław III Wrymouth was a particular youth of interest. In Gallus, all aspects of Bolesław III's young life, from conception through his teenage years were pregnant with meaning. Bolesław III was miraculously born to infertile parents after the prayer of the monks at St. Giles and the offering of an image of a child, fashioned in precious metals. As a boy, Bolesław mimicked adult martial behavior, and even fought against boar and bear, youthful deeds that were said to excite jealously in others even long after their occurrence. To prove his potency as a warrior and future leader of soldiers, Gallus even concocted for the boy his own literary trope, in which young Bolesław was referred to as a "boy-Mars." Even his eventual knighthood was accompanied by a prophecy, uttered by an unnamed courtier, that he would restore Poland to its past glory. While less obsessed with Bolesław than Gallus, Vincent also included the story of his miraculous birth, and elaborated on the pain and shame of his parents' childlessness and composed a poem on this very topic. Without providing the same level of detail as Gallus, Vincent nevertheless praised the martial seriousness of the youthful Bolesław III in comparison to his peers. Another of Vincent's heroes, Leszek the White, was likewise recorded as possessing these same sorts of mature, warlike virtues in his young years.

Vincent seemed to relish stories that prophesied or presaged the displacement of the privileged and corrupt with the worthy and virtuous. One example of this is from the pre-Piast past of Poland, when the future Leszko II, as an impoverished youth running in a footrace for a claim to the kingdom, refused to take a rigged competition seriously and instead mocked it with out-of-the-box thinking. This behavior was represented by Vincent as pre-figuring Leszko II's pious humility and enterprising leadership. Another example of Vincent's prophetic moralizing is the vision of Bolesław III, which this king relayed to his followers when he was asked why he did not include his youngest son, Kazimierz II, then practically an infant, in his inheritance plans. His explanatory vision metaphorically portrayed the initial vigor, then withering in violent confrontations, of his older sons, then the flourishing of Kazimierz II and how he would supplant his brothers. In the stories of both the child Kazimierz II and of the youth Leszko II, the displacement of those older or more powerful was accompanied by signs associated with the younger years of the hero.

The hagiographical sources were likewise replete with signs that prefigured the holiness of their subjects. This was the very purpose, perhaps, of the inclusion of any part of the young saint's life, namely to show that even in the normally imperfect period of youth the saintly child was more mature than their peers, and even above adults. We will discuss this more when we discuss the prevalence of the *puer senex* trope across all the sources. The actions of the children themselves were not the only symbols of their futures. This is best seen in the life of St. Kinga. The miracles recorded in her *vita* started even before her birth, when Kinga's mother, in agony from pregnancy complications, saw a vision saying that she would not only survive childbirth, but also that her daughter would bring solace to her soul and those of many others besides. Michael Goodich writes that difficult or unusual pregnancies often accompanied saintly births throughout Europe, such as that of Francis Venimbene, whose mother could not feel the weight of the baby within her.[1] Kinga's baptism was also miraculous, for she was silent and serene through it all, and in a later mass in her infancy she was seen trying to move her lips when she heard the name of Jesus. Also in the hagiography is the importance of names, and the hagiographers occasionally speculated on meaning of child's name and how it connected with their future, most extensively with Stanislaus and Adalbert. Every movement of the mouth and every name uttered had significance in the hagiography. There was no unwitting or irrelevant material on any child.

The female saints of Poland, especially Hedwig, have parallels at this time across Europe, from Spain to Byzantium, such as Elizabeth of Thüringen, Isabella of Aragon, and Theodora of Arta. As Petra Melicharova writes, female saints were "destined; the throne (through their family connections, appearance and … education) and/or to sainthood (through miraculous circumstances and humility)."[2] All of these aspects are present in the lives of Hedwig, Kinga, and Salomea, and they were indeed presented as destined to their calling by the occurrences and behaviors associated with them. In this sense, Polish hagiographers are unmistakably participating in a tradition of royal saintliness that had consumed all of Europe.

2 Born Great or Achieving Greatness?

One of the greatest questions involving medieval childhood is the nature versus nurture debate, which was touched upon throughout this book, but especially in Chapter 4. As I noted, the hagiography itself fails to take a one-or-the other

---

1 Michael Goodich, "Childhood and Adolescence among Thirteenth Century Saints," *History of Childhood Quarterly* 1 (1973): 285–309, esp. 287.
2 Petra Melicharova, "Crown, veil, halo: confronting ideas of royal female sanctity in the West and in the Byzantine East in the Late Middle Ages (13th–14th Century)," *Byzantion* 77 (2007): 315–344, esp. 318–321.

approach as to why saintly children blossomed into holy men and women, but instead presented a sort of balance between the two extremes. On the one hand, saints' lives stressed inborn qualities given by God such as holiness, intelligence, chastity, studiousness. On the other hand, the help of teachers, such as Adalbert's in Magdeburg, and the striving and effort of young saints themselves in their sanctifications and educations are likewise given credit. This balance is reconciled, perhaps, to some extent by the usage of a metaphor, namely of the wax and the seal, which is found in the life of Stanislaus. In this metaphor the wax stands for the saint's natural qualities and the seal is the shaping forces of his or her educational environment. In other words, the saints are born with the raw materials of greatness, but these must be put into the right shape. This is why Stanislaus is said to have taken "hold of the inborn good" to advance towards his destiny. Polish hagiography noted a gender difference in how these saints "took hold" of their destiny with male education focused on intellect, knowledge, and the liberal arts and classics and canon law and female saints' education focused on producing pure spirit and behavior, a focus on the Bible or familiarity with the tenets of church sermons, or asceticism. Polish hagiographical tradition is in this sense in line with the hagiographical stereotypes of male and female saints throughout Europe. Last, but not least, it must also be noted that undergirding inherited virtue, educations, and the efforts of the young saints are the irresistible and constant workings of God, who supported and guided every part of the formation of the saint.

The metaphor of the education of the child as a seal leaving its mark on wax might raise eyebrows for those interested in medieval memory, for it is very similar to the metaphor that Mary Carruthers identifies as the primary metaphor for memory formation. In the context of memory, it is a wax tablet that is imprinted with marks that is said to parallel the creation of memory in the mind. Recollection is the process where this material is interpreted, understood, and then used in whatever context they are needed.[3] In this sense, its hard to escape the conclusion that medieval scholars closely associated the education of children with memory and the strategies that it took to create it. Children, as it were, became the living embodiments of memory as they were trained to reach adulthood.

Beyond hagiography, Gallus Anonymus seems to stress that great leaders needed to grow into their roles. This is not particularly surprising, as one of his main goals is to show that even great leaders, i.e. Bolesław III, could make youthful blunders, i.e. brutally gouging out his half-brother's eyes, and

---

3   Mary Carruthers, *The Book of Memory: A Study of Memory in Medieval Culture, Second Edition* (Cambridge: Cambridge University Press, 2008), 18–37.

still serve as excellent rulers. This focus on the growth of leaders begins in the distant Piast past, when Siemovit's growth received praised, since he was said to have made good use of his youth and increased in excellence. As noted in Chapter 2, Bolesław I, Kazimierz the Restorer, Ladislas of Hungary all receive short descriptions from Gallus of their younger years which emphasize the importance of their education and growth. Ladislas of Hungary is even said to have been such a good king in Hungary because he had been so well raised, of course, in Poland. The story of the childhood of Bolesław III himself is crafted so as to demonstrate an upward trajectory of accomplishment culminating in knighthood. This started with his martial activities, followed by his encounters with the boar and bear, then continued with stories of his sneaking out to fight the enemy against his father's will, then proceeded to his participation in minor raids, and then concluded with his defeat of a major invasion of Pomeranians and his knighthood.

Vincent has his own discourse on the nature of birth, deeds, and fate, but from an alternative perspective. Namely, he asks to what extent does the destruction of the wicked have to with their own actions and what is owed to their birth. This debate takes place in the context of the blinding of Zbigniew, who is presented as a despicable, grasping, and deceitful figure whose loss of sight (and subsequently life) was by no means undeserved. After a long debate between the narrators, John and Matthew, their conclusion was that while the nature of his (illegitimate) birth had serious consequences, these were not irreversible, and his own poor behavior and choices in youth brought Zbigniew to his grisly fate.

Education and the shaping of young warriors was an important trope beyond Poland and are considered essential, for example, in the French *Chanson de geste*. Phyllis Gaffney highlights the example of young Aïol, exiled in the forest in poverty with his parents. Trapped in this situation his father bemoans, "Dwelling in these woods is never going to make you wise, You'll grow completely foolish, childish and uncivilized. I don't see who will teach you about steeds or weapons."[4] Just as in Gallus and Vincent, the focus is on the development of the child hero as a warrior. Gaffney notes that in the *chanson de geste*, the "view of the young is centred on those qualities best suited to war, and the subjective life of the individual child is not its chief concern. The epic child is a type, a representative of traits ascribed to him, and only in a limited way can he be said to grow or develop."[5] This lack of development is markedly apparent

---

4 Gaffney, *Constructions*, 91.
5 Ibid.

in Gallus, where Bolesław, despite his limitations and flaws, is practically born with his heroic qualities intact.

On the other hand, the conceptions of the education and growth of a saintly child, likely emerge, as is noted by Valerie Garver, from Carolingian times when monastic thought seeped into broader cultural mentalities. Monks often had the task of honing children towards productive lives both inside and outside the cloister, and this meant that realistic outlooks and methods were needed for the task. Garver writes "although prone to sinful behavior and misdeeds, children could learn through discipline to behave in a Christian manner and become pious."[6] Normal children required tougher measures to ensure a respectable character, whereas saintly children were unique in that they flowered without the customary difficulty.

3   Age and Social Categories

One of the most difficult tasks facing scholars who explore childhood is disentangling age categories, their boundaries, and their expectations and natures. My chapters have suggested that, part of this problem is that, despite the existence of laws, customary rituals, and church practice, there was no single scheme or system for identifying an age category and placing children within it. The Henryków Book well demonstrates these difficulties. Nowhere in this book is a particular age mentioned when one "comes of age" and gains legal autonomy, though it was clearly in the teenage years. Nevertheless, no *pueri* are recorded as taking legitimate action on property. Furthermore, the *iuvenis*, while more legally versatile and able to handle and sell property, were nevertheless still not presented as fully autonomous or free actors, and were often portrayed as foolish, reckless, or easily manipulated. This *iuvenis* stage was especially dangerous for monastic holdings, associated with marriage and the change in land management strategies, and also the time when the next generation could attempt to claim what they perceived as their patrimony. The monks had such a low opinion of the capabilities of youths, that the Henryków Book even uses young age as a way to excuse the horrors that occurred on the watch of young and future dukes. For example, Henry III is exculpated for the disaster and chaos that followed the Mongol invasion by the fact of his youth, though the abbot of Henryków is said to have had to spend weeks working over

---

6   Valerie Garver, "The Influence of Monastic Ideals upon the Carolingian Conceptions of Childhood," in *Childhood in the Middle Ages and the Renaissance: The Results of a Paradigm Shift in the History of Mentality*, ed. Albrecht Classen (Berlin: Walter de Gruyter, 2005), 84.

the young duke to convince him to affirm key lands of the monastery. Youth, even though innocent of real evil because of stupidity, was nevertheless stubborn and in constant need of adult persuasion to do right.

Vincent Kadłubek, as well as the writers of hagiography overviewed in this book, had similar concerns and stereotypes about youth, and presented it both as a phase of moral peril and general incompetence, and constantly tried to show how their respective heroes exceeded the expectations of and behaviors of other youths. Most notably, Vincent takes great pains to demonstrate that Leszek the White was an exceptional child and extremely mature *adolescens*, which is not surprising as Vincent suggests that his path to the throne was contested precisely because of the fears of his nobles about his age. Leszek, with his mother as regent for the early part of his reign, was in a precarious position even in his teenage years, and perhaps this is why his uncle later made the controversial offer to bestow him with knighthood in exchange for homage as the primary prince of Poland, namely to mollify nobles suspicious of the ability of a youthful ruler to guard their interests.

While no specific ages (with the exception of the 7 years old required for the hair-cutting ceremony) are mentioned as definitive turning points in any of the literature surveyed in this book, major events of a child's life were, indeed, considered significant and connected to major narrative events. For example, in the Life of Kinga, miracles were recorded during her mother's pregnancy and at her own birth, at the time of her baptism and weaning, and at her attempts at first words. This suggests that even for the youngest of children, or at least elite children, society recognized a progressive and typical trajectory of development, which could be either ordinary or extraordinary. Gallus Anonymus has a similar path of development for somewhat older children, where a ducal heir grows from *puer* to *iuvenis* to *vir*, with the age category marked by behavior, expectations, and roles rather than numbers. *Puer* was for a child, a youth, or even a young adult whose father still lived and who had not taken the full reigns of power. *Iuvenis* was for one who, while possessing his patrimony and autonomy in military and political affairs, was still emotionally immature and prone to unwise deeds. *Vir*, as the linguistic connection implies, was reserved to describe one with all the manly "virtues."

The use of words related to age to build, explain, and justify social hierarchies, which was present in all the texts from Poland from this time, but especially in Gallus, was, as briefly mentioned in that chapter, especially present and potent in the contemporary church, and especially with those associated with the Gregorian reforms. This according to Kathleen Cushing, was because of "Gregory VII in particular, as well as reformers associated with him … increasingly defining individuals in terms of their function, their suitability (*idoneitas*), and perhaps especially their utility (*utilitas*)."[7] This is precisely what we see with the terminology in Gallus Anonymus, with the function of *puer*, *iuvenis*, and *vir*. For example, Cushing notes that the word *iuvenes* has precisely the same ambiguity of meaning as in Gallus, for it can "denote a position of authority, either in terms of liturgical duties or more broadly in situating this group's place within the monastery's hierarchy. At other times, it seems to refer to individuals who still needed guidance from the *seniores*."[8] The *iuvenis* Bolesław III held the throne in Gallus, but he still made a number of serious mistakes and needed guidance and eventually deep repentance before he could reach his full manhood. Cushing points out that esteemed medievalist Georges Duby created a much more specific scheme with age-related words, in which one remained a *puer* until the cessation of military training (as late as 19), then remained a *juvenis* until he acquired a wife and inheritance, and then finally became a *vir*.[9] Clearly Duby's findings diverge from what is found in Gallus Anonymus, for boyhood (*puer*) for Bolesław III did not end with his knighthood, but only with the death of his father. Nevertheless it is clear that other parts of Europe used such age-related words to construct social hierarchies, much like in Poland. Or perhaps Gallus himself had imported some of that mentality when he arrived in the Piast realm.

If Gallus, indeed, did mold his narrative following western models, especially drawing on the *chanson de geste*, it is not surprising that that hierarchy of masculinity appeared.[10] Simon Gaunt notes that "in the *chansons de geste* male characters are defined as individuals in relation to other men, whilst women are excluded from the genre's value system even, arguably, in poems where the influence of other genres is tangible."[11] With women pushed out of the picture, male bonding, or the breakdown in male relationships, becomes the primary driver of action in the narrative. Gaunt continues, "One consequence of the exclusion of women from the ethical system of the genre and of the foregrounding of male bonding (or its disintegration) is that ideals of the masculine gender are not constructed in relation to the feminine, but in relation

---

7   Cushing, "*Pueri*," 436.
8   Ibid., 440.
9   Georges Duby, *The Chivalrous Society*, trans. Cynthia Postan (London: Arnold, 1977), 112–114.
10 Studies of masculinity in the Middle Ages have surged over the last two decades, and have largely filled many gaps in research, particularly theorizing the concept of multiple masculinities, expanding on the theme of the performance of masculinity and sexuality, and examining the resistance to gender and sexual norms. See Dawn Hadley, "Introduction," in *Masculinity in Medieval Europe*, ed. Dawn Hadley (London: Routledge Press, 1999), 1–18.
11 Simon Gaunt, ed., *Gender and Genre in Medieval French Literature* (Cambridge: Cambridge University Press, 1995), 22.

to other models of masculinity."[12] In Gallus Anonymus, Bolesław Wrymouth is contrasted with his ineffective father Władysław Herman and his scheming half-brother Zbigniew. Along with many of the tropes of contrasting masculinity Gaunt mentions, Gallus uses age-related words and stereotypes to define and advance his own paradigm of virtuous masculinity in his text.

Age categories are one of the topics that archaeologists and historians have often used to find common ground. Unfortunately, considering the imprecision in age estimates that accompany most excavations, this can be rather difficult. The general age of three years for the appearance of grave goods in cemeteries has been posited by others, and while this book has found no exception to that, it is by no means a universal rule. Whether this means that children below three years of age were generally valued or loved less, or whether they were simply not buried with artifacts because they had not begun to use or wear them yet, remains, like many value-judgements related to the past, unprovable. As for older children, while the hair cutting ceremony at 7 years of age for boys might be a threshold, there are only a few notable examples of weapons or other exceptional artifacts in the corresponding graves of such children in the archaeological record, and any broader conclusions about the detectability of this ritual must remain doubtful. The extraordinary presence of beads in what were presumed by the excavators to be girls from the years at the borderline between Infans I through Infans II is one age association that is present across cemeteries throughout Poland, though it was by no means applied to every girl within that age range, and likely is just as much a function of class as of age.

While associations with age, closely related to class and position of the parents, did appear in a number of contexts in this book, the patterns were by no means unequivocal or ubiquitous. This is an important element to point out, for broader guides and handbooks for medieval childhood written in the present day have a tendency to include all sorts of schemes for dividing medieval childhood, drawn from the church fathers to ancient classics to monastic habits.[13] This chapter has shown that, at least for the Polish sources at this time, the numerical, philosophical, and theological schemes of scholars seemed to have little connection to sources, either written or archaeological.

---

12   Gaunt, *Gender and Genre*, 23. Gaunt provides many examples of this contrasting of males for French literature, especially focusing on how Roland is contrasted against Ganelon or even Oliver in the Song of Roland.
13   For example, see Shulamith Shahar and Haya Galai, *Childhood in the Middle Ages* (London: Routledge, 1992), 21–31. This is not to criticize the work of these authors, but to provide an example of a framework established through the study of past thinkers, theologians, and philosophers that does not seem to match uses of age found in Polish texts.

4 Special Care for Children

While by no means every child found in excavations received splendid, let alone any, treatment, it is undoubtedly true that certain children were associated with unusually rich grave assemblages featuring exceptional numbers of beads or temple rings and sometimes even special grave goods such as amulets or bells. Indeed, we saw that children showed up as a distinct category on the correspondence analysis plots. Not only grave goods showed special care for children, but also their placement in cemeteries, both in multiple burials and in their own sectors within the cemetery community. In that respect, the archaeological and textual sources agree, certain children were exceptional and received exceptional recognition.

Medieval Scandinavia, another Christianizing society of this period at a similar stage of development, has a number of relevant archaeological parallels to Poland in terms of the care that some children received in death. Brett Sellevold writes about the great pains taken to provide children with a beneficial afterlife in Norway, especially in the island monastery in Selja, where over half of the burials in the associated church are of children. After considering several possible explanations for this phenomenon, Sellevold concludes that "the most likely explanation for the presence of the child graves in the nave of the monastic church seems to be that the children belonged to wealthy families with special relations to the Selja monastery."[14] These parents paid a premium to have their children receive the most prestigious and spiritually healing places in their death. The Christian context of these spiritual precautions begs the question of what effect Christianization may have had on the ritual treatment of dead children. In Poland especially, this is hard to answer, due to the practice of cremation in pre-Christian times, leaving the remains of few children for analysis. In Scandinavia, however, the existence of some bi-ritual cemeteries offers some tantalizing possibilities. While denying any simplistic categorization of burials as "Christian" or "pagan," Lotta Mejscholm suggests that the practice of infant baptism encouraged the inclusion of children of the youngest ages in cemeteries, where they had not been welcome in pagan times. In her examination of the syncretic cemetery at Fjalkinge, she

---

14 Berit Sellevold, "Child Burials and Children's Status in Medieval Norway," in *Youth and Age in the Medieval North*, ed. Shannon Lewis-Simpson (Leiden: Brill, 2008), 70. Although obviously concerning a different region of Europe (the Balkans) at an earlier time, see Florin Curta, "Church, churchyard, and children in the early medieval Balkans: a comparative perspective," in *Migration, Integration, and Connectivity on the Southeastern Frontier of the Carolingian Empire*, ed. Danijel Dzino, Ante Milošević and Trpimir Vedriš (Leiden/Boston: Brill, 2018), 245–67.

finds a powerful correspondence between children under 3 months of age, east-west orientation, supine position, and lack of grave goods.[15] While slightly older children had signs of both stereotypically "Christian" and "pagan" burial, it seems it was Christian ritual, if not necessarily mindset, that brought newborns into the cemetery in Norway.

Turning to the Polish textual sources, we see that elite children had the right to protection from the older generations, not merely their parents. The Henryków Book, for example, mentions guardians, usually male (especially stepfathers, grandparents, and uncles), for orphans, from both mother and father's side of the family. These guardians primarily had a protective role, for the danger of knights or other kinsmen laying claim to the childrens' inheritance was ever-present, until a child had come of age and could legally and practically defend themselves.

Elite children had not only the presumed right of security and the basics of life, but even to a careful and throughout upbringing. Vincent Kadłubeck provides two illustrative examples of these expectations. In one example, Bolesław IV is recorded to have raising his young kinsman Kazimierz II under his own roof, and specifically to have shielded him from the corrupting influences of the world and form the temptations that seduced other youths, though Vincent notes that cynics might see this overprotectiveness as a way to curb the prospects of this ambitious youth, rather than a desire to keep him safe through the tempests of his tender years. Another story in Vincent has Mieszko III appealing to Kazimierz II through the invocation of the memories of his fostering in childhood to try to persuade him against revolt. In this appeal, likely fabricated by Vincent, Mieszko III notes his provision of all the necessities of life (food, clothing, shelter), but also brings up an extensive education and the military assistance he provided to set the young man firmly in power. Most of all, he appeals to the warm memories that and emerged between the two during these years.

Whatever the truth of Vincent's stories, he worked within a world in which care for young kinsmen, even those who were not your own children was assumed, and this is a phenomenon that is observable in many places in contemporary Europe. The most recent study with parallel results is by Miriam Müller, who likewise had to deal with the lack of sources that dealt directly with children. While Müller's sources, such as the aforementioned manorial records are obviously not the same as the Henryków Book, they nevertheless present a similar image of the treatment of orphans and their tutelage. Similarly to

---

15   Mejscholm, "Constructions of Early Childhood," 54–55.

children in medieval Silesia, "rural children were seen to have roles, age—and maturity-determined responsibilities in their local societies, and, above all, they were accorded a secure and protected space in their communities."[16] This does not mean that rural England and rural Silesia were the same. For one thing, Müller stresses a feudal context where lords wielded great control over peasants, and therefore had great power in, for example, the selection of guardians for their orphaned tenants.[17] Likewise, in the statistical discussion of guardians at Winslow, women were often selected as guardians for children, which was not so common in Silesia, where male kinsmen predominated.[18] Despite these differences, Müller's conclusions are relevant to the examples I have presented for Poland: "Children were already accorded rights as infants, especially if they stood in a direct line towards inheritance, but even if they did not, as potential heirs to be in an age of high child mortality their rights were protected and safeguarded. Children were therefore not figures in the background, and should not be seen by historians as mere appendages to family life. Instead they were central to it, central to their communities and families and kinship networks."[19]

If even distant kinsmen and kinswomen were assumed to provide for their clan's weak and vulnerable children, than the expectations for parents were, if anything, higher. Gallus Anonymus, and other Polish authors, often mention motherly love for children, expressed in descriptions ranging from mothers spoiling their sons to their bitter mourning for a child's death. More surprising, considering early modern and later images of fatherhood, fathers were also

16 Miriam Müller, *Childhood, Orphans, and Underage Heirs in Medieval England* (Cham: Palgrave Macmillan, 2019), 198.
17 Müller, *Childhood*, 130–140. A discussion of the nature of society in early and High medieval Poland, and the absence/presence of feudalism is a complex topic, though a general consensus has formed that neither feudalism nor a strict social hierarchy had formed during this period. For more on this topic, see Piotr Górecki, *Economy, Society and Lordship in Medieval Poland: 1100–1250* (New York: Holmes & Meier, 1992). See also Stanisław Trawkowski, "Spory o feudalizm w polskiej historiografii," *Roczniki Dziejów Społecznych i Gospodarczych* 58 (1998): 91–100; Sławomir Gawlas, "Die Probleme des Lehnswesens und des Feudalismus aus polnischer Sicht," in *Das europäische Mittelalter im Spannungsbogen des Vergleichs. Zwanzig internationale Beiträge zu Praxis, Problemen und Perspektiven*, edited by Michael Borgolte (Berlin: Akademie-Verlag, 2001), 97–123; Grzegorz Myśliwski, "Feudalizm—'rewolucja feudalna'—kryzys władzy w Polsce XI–początku XII w. Punkt widzenia mediewistyki anglosaskiej," *Przegląd historyczny* 93 (2002), 73–102; Marian Dygo, "Czy istniał feudalizm w Europie środkowo-wschodniej w średniowieczu?," *Kwartalnik historyczny* 120 (2013): 667–717.
18 Müller, *Childhood*, 132.
19 Müller, *Childhood*, 198.

portrayed as taking an active role the practical upbringing and care for children. Gallus Anonymus, most notably, compares Bolesław I's treatment of wayward nobles to a that of a father bathing and instructing his own children. Maternal and paternal love have been well documented throughout western Europe in the Middle Ages, as Alexandre-Bidon and Didier Lett noted in their survey of the period.[20] Nevertheless, we should not be too hasty to ascribe modern sentimentality to a father's instruction of and care for children. Juanita Feros Ruys argues, in her discussion of Abelard's writings to his son, that while love and emotion do seem to exist during this period, the focus was always on preparing the child to live "a moral, ethical, and spiritual life," though of course these two goals are not necessarily contradictory.[21]

Parents' care for children was not limited to the physical health of their children. The Henryków Book records a series of donations of land to the monastery for the souls and well-being of children, starting with duke Henry I himself, who founded the monastery and provided it with its initial endowment, in exchange for prayer and blessing for his soul as well as his children's. The donations of the those of lower social class appearing in the Book, such as Wiesenthal's, mention of prayers not only for living children, but also for any that should come in the future.

Parental care was taken so seriously that failure to take care of children was a matter of fear and shame for parents. We see this most poignantly in the story from the *miracula* of the infant Pietrucha, whose cradle, unobserved by a preoccupied nurse, was overturned by a rummaging pig, resulting in the girl's suffocation in her blankets. The mother in this story was as much terrified of punishment from her husband as she was distraught by her daughter's death, while her husband was decidedly more concerned about what charges might be leveled against them for their negligence. In other instances, when they were not directly at fault for the death of their child, parents wept in grief or even trembled, as in the story of two-year-old Wilhelmus who drowned in a river while his tutor swam. This raises the topic of children and emotions to which we now turn.

---

20 Daniele Alexandre-Bidon and Didier Lett, *Children in the Middle Ages: Fifth–Fifteenth Centuries* (Notre Dame, Ind: University of Notre Dame Press, 2000), 53–59.
21 Juanita Feros Ruys, "Peter Abelard's Carmen ad Astralabium and Medieval Parent-Child Didactic Texts: The Evidence for Parent Child Relationships in the Middle Ages," in *Childhood in the Middle Ages and the Renaissance: The Results of a Paradigm Shift in the History of Mentality*, ed. Albrecht Classen (Berlin: Walter de Gruyter, 2005), 226.

5 Children and Emotion

One of the most promising new fields of research into medieval childhood is the study of emotion, to which Albrecht Classen, in his introduction to the groundbreaking collection of essays, devotes much attention.[22] His discussion begins with a careful evaluation of Konrad von Würzburg's *Engelhard*, in which a father must decide whether to kill his own children to save his sick friend, though divine intervention saves both the friend and the children at the last moment. Classen notes how ambiguous a passage like this for historians of childhood. Is the willingness to kill children for a friend a sign that parents were not so emotionally attached to their children? Or is the agony of the father and his anguish in his decision, and his extreme joy at the revitalization of his children, to be interpreted in the opposite direction? Focusing heavily on examples from a wide series of authors, and a series case studies from the everything from German romances to hagiography, drawing on sources from Wolfram von Eschenbach's *Parzival* to the *Later Life of Queen Matilda*, Classen concludes that there is overwhelming evidence for powerful and significant emotions connected with medieval children, though not perhaps in the forms we might expect. He confidently writes that the conclusions of Aries "now can be discarded" and labels James Schulz's arguments that children in medieval times were valued less than adults a "fallacy."[23] Classen even goes so far as to say that "virtually all children were loved from the moment there were born, and parents dedicated much of their energy and resources to raise their children."[24] For this reason, the discussion here should focus not on proving *that* children produced emotions in adults, but rather *how* and in what contexts.

An excellent place to begin this discussion of emotions directed at Polish children is in the hagiography, in which, as we previously noted, there are many instances of parental care. To begin with the obvious, it was sometimes the saintly children themselves who were the triggers for adult grief, the future St. Adalbert, for example. We are told that during the time of his weaning, he grew sick and his parents were depicted as moaning and crying in anguish. They even promised to dedicate him to religious service if he survived, despite

---

22   Albrecht Classen, "Philippe Ariès and the Consequences: History of Childhood, Family Relations, and Personal Emotions, Where do we stand today?," in *Childhood in the Middle Ages and the Renaissance: The Results of a Paradigm Shift in the History of Mentality*, ed. Albrecht Classen (Berlin: Walter de Gruyter, 2005), 1–65.
23   Classen, "Philippe Ariès," 46.
24   Classen, "Philippe Ariès," 47. Classen may indeed be overcompensating in the other direction, namely an over-evaluation of the connection of children and adults. Nevertheless, his assessment of the paradigm shift still stands.

being baptized with the name Wojciech ("joy in way"), suggesting a very different presumed career path for him before his illness. The parents' happiness in the healing of their son resulted in their acceptance of a very different fate for the saint. Michael Goodich observes that the dedication of a miraculously healed child to the service of God is one of most common traits among saints in the thirteenth century throughout Europe.[25]

The *miracula* have numerous emotional stories involving children, and that is not surprising, as children fill the pages of the miracles of the Polish saints. In the *miracula*, 1/3 to 1/2 of miracles involving threat or personal harm feature children. Children seem to appear as those in special need of help, but also those who receive a larger share of divine, and parental, beneficence. Likewise, miracles involving children take a significant place in the organization of the miracles, for example in Kinga's *miracula* the first miracles were for children, which, since her miracles were not organized according to disease or ailment, presumably has the purpose of putting her best case forward, and this best care happens to focus on children.

The emotional connection between parents and even the youngest of children is evident in stories from all the saints. For example, the *miracula* of Stanislaus describes a funeral for the son of Stronislaua, the wife of Vrotslay, who died when below three years of age, and how the extended family had gathered to console the grieving parents. In the *miracula* of Salomea, a two year-old girl, daughter of count Iaxichonis, after being resurrected, was dedicated to the saint's service amidst the great tears of her parents. The hagiography of St. Hedwig shows intense fear, agony, and mourning for souls of young infants and children dying before baptism, and this saint in particular often resurrected them, even if only temporarily, so they could receive eternal salvation through these holy rites.

The most extensive study of children in *miracula* in northern and southern medieval Europe is that of Ronald Finucane, which examines 600 cases of child healing or salvation from harm.[26] This book uncovered many of the broad themes in the Polish miracles stories, including similar kinds of illnesses and accidents, worries about the fate of unbaptized children, the mention of child play and childish behavior before and after miracles, and the deep expressions of emotion form parents and family ranging from abject grief to utter joy. Regional studies of northern European *miracula* have produced similar results to the metanalysis in Finucane, for example, Joanna Skorzewska's depiction of

---

25   Goodich, "Childhood," 287.
26   Ronald C. Finucane, *The Rescue of the Innocents. Endangered Children in Medieval Miracles* (New York, 1997).

children in the *miracula* is found in Scandinavia. She concludes her survey of three prominent saints, who served as bishops, proves "the responsibility of adults for the youngest members of the households as well as a willingness to sacrifice much in order to keep children alive and in good condition."[27] There is an intentional emotional tug of these stories which, "draw the reader's/listener's attention to the disadvantaged whose young age and vulnerability seem to have been the issue which concerned the authors most."[28]

At least in this emotional dimension, the similarities with the Polish situation is remarkable. However, the overall incidence of children in the Scandinavian *miracula* is considerably lower than the case in Poland. While a third to a half of the miracles of personal danger and healing involved Children in the three Polish *miracula* analyzed in this book, the highest recorded percentage of healing miracles involving children in the Scandinavian sources is 24 percent, and others are considerably lower.[29] A similar situation is found in Eleanor Gordon's study of miracle stories for six major English saints (including Thomas Beckett, Wulfstan, and Simon de Montfort) spanning 1170–1500 CE, in which, again, about 24 percent of miracles involve children.[30] These numbers for England and Scandinavia, even allowing for minor differences in methodologies for categorizing stories in the *miracula* according to author and region, are markedly different from those in Poland. Future comparisons and analysis is warranted by these findings, especially since many scholars studying the *miracula*, such as Finucane, have neglected to provide statistics comparing numbers of child miracles to adult miracles.

While the emotional description of children in hagiography is well-documented, one should not assume that the more historical and royal sources show any less. For example, Gallus Anonymus writes how the tears and terror of the *puer* Bolesław III stirred the citizens of Wrocław, and also presumably Gallus' readers, to anger against evil Palatine Siechiech's machinations. Thereby Gallus is able to conceal the ugliness of Bolesław and Zbigniew's seizure and division of the realm. Vincent constantly uses assumed emotional connections to children for both dramatic and rhetorical purposes. Mieszko II's love and tender treatment of his young, dear son Kazimierz is contrasted against the designs of his evil stepmother to tell a fairytale story of the boy's

27 Joanna Skorzewska, "'Sveinn einn ungr fell i syruker.' Medieval Icelandic Children in Vernacular Miracle Stories," in *Youth and Age in the Medieval North*, ed. Shannon Lewis-Simpson (Leiden: Brill, 2008), 120.
28 Skorzewska, "'Sveinn einn,'" 119.
29 Ibid., 113–115.
30 Eleanor Gordon, "Accidents Among Medieval Children as Seen from the Miracles of Six English Saints," *Mediaeval History* 35 (1991): 148.

harrowing origins before he would return to restore the glory of Poland. Vincent also dramatizes the disgrace and agony of childless parents (Władysław and Judith) before Bolesław III's birth, including poetry to heighten the occasion. Finally, Vincent stresses the uncommon valor of his patriotic heroes for putting country even above their own children, such as the willingness of Krak to sacrifice sons for fatherland, and also the defenders of Głogów's decision to fire on their own children, when they were used as human shields by the invading German armies. Whether in their birth or death, or even in the midst of their danger, medieval authors writing for a Polish audience assumed potent emotions for children and used them to further their own objectives, though we must remember that medieval authors speak of a small subset of special children in society and it is unwise to extrapolate too far beyond this to general circumstances.

6   Good Kid, Bad Kid

So far we have discussed conceptions of children, uses of childhood, and adult relationships and treatment of children, but what of children themselves? What might one expect of childhood behavior? Medieval authors usually contrasted their heroic, good children with the general negative stereotype of the average child, using the *puer senex* trope. The *puer senex* trope was universally and extensively used throughout Europe in the High and Late Middle Ages in hagiography,[31] and made its way into other genres. Greedy children were rebellious and grasping, and Gallus Anonymus and Vincent both target Bolesław III's half-brother Zbigniew as the paragon of conniving, ungrateful dishonor, as one who violently and through treachery wrenches an inheritance for himself from his father. Zbigniew is described as a sword that proceeds from his lustful father's loins that turned against him, a bane that then preys on the kingdom and his legitimate, but immature brother. The Henryków Book has a kind of temporal dimension to childish and juvenile behavior, with each generation presented as worse than the last and unworthy of their ancestors. Bolesław II receives special attention as a perfect fool in his younger years, and is disparaged for wasting time at tournaments, in useless activities and on foolish deeds and juvenile pranks because of his "boyishness." This does not mean that he was a particularly bad human being, he grew up to be a decent and respectable duke, but that his age itself was problematic. Later, the boy himself became a victim as he was cheated by his own knights, who stripped away

---

31   Goodich, "Childhood," 288.

ducal lands for themselves. Less exalted youths, such as Bogusza and Paul, grandsons of crafty Czech Boguchwał, embody similar stereotypes. These heirs squander their inheritance through youthful stupidity and prodigality, though this was hinted as caused by their lack of a father to raise them properly and provide them with guidance and wisdom. The failures of children and youths were not always completely their own fault. While there are few discussions of girls outside hagiography in Poland, the Henryków Book does note the danger of young female sexuality, such as in the story of the scandalous use of dancing German girls to push the monastery to give up Nikłowice in fear of their souls.

Medieval Polish hagiography, by contrast, has few examples of naughty children, except as a general negative image presented as the opposite of the hero. Hedwig was said to flee the intemperance and levity of youth. She was serious, engaging in no games, so much so that she seemed to have the heart of an elderly person. Stanislaus received a similar description, with the addition that the grace of God was credited for making up for the deficiencies of his youth. Youth, in general, was considered something to overcome, not to celebrate, at least for the saints. Adalbert's youthful naivety and innocence, nevertheless, was celebrated when his friends hurled him onto a passing girl, and the young saint was filled with shame, thinking that in this carnal act he had married her and given up his virtue. This story broaches an important point, for while "childish" actions were generally considered deficient, this by no means meant that every act or behavior associated with children was negative. Examples of good childlike behavior, as mentioned above, are abundant in Kinga's life, such as when she unsuccessfully attempted to mouth words in mass in response to "Jesus," or when she rounded up children and used childhood camaraderie to coax her friends to go to church and take up religious behavior, or when she destroyed her clothes in play so they could be given to the poor, or even when she would pull other children in carts up mountains, mortifying her body and giving happiness to others above herself. Child play itself was actually celebrated in the *miracula* as it often served as a sign of a healed child and resulted in joy from parents, as their restored children played with eggs, ran through the streets, and picked flowers.

The rise of the royal, saintly princesses, along with their saintly behavior in life, are part of what Gábor Klaniczay calls "the cinderella effect."[32] By this he refers to a new model of sainthood appearing in central Europe and Italy, often following the model of Elizabeth of Thuringia, where sanctity was based on deeds and actions in life, rather than posthumous acclaim or miracles. This

---

32   Gábor Klaniczay, "The Cinderella Effect: Late Medieval Female Sainthood in Central Europe and in Italy," *East Central Europe* 20–23 (1993–1996): 51–68.

new kind of sainthood could be learnt, but also required an extensive list of earthly accomplishments to be recognized. In this context, it was crucial for the saints to put their best feet forward, or at least be thought of doing so, as early in life as possible.

"Old" children also appear in Gallus and Vincent to describe their royal heroes. In Gallus Anonymus, the first Piast ruler, Siemovit, was said to have used his youth well, and to have avoided the behavior of the dissolute, so as to grow into a great duke. Bolesław III, was described in similar terms to the saints in hagiography, and engaged in no silly games, but martial activities and childlike activities of virtue significant, such as fighting wild animals. Vincent takes this parallel to the next level, when he says old men appeared as babies next to Bolesław III. While all authors from medieval times praised obedience in children as virtue, Vincent particularly stressed filial piety as the most important trait of a good child. This is best illustrated in the context of Siechiech's misbehaving attempts to seize power, when Bolesław III supposedly wore a gold plate around neck with name of father inscribed on it, and thus did everything as if his father was watching and to bring his father honor. He even reportedly wore black for five years after his father died.

The description of a good heroic child in Gallus and Vincent bears a remarkable resemblance to the young protagonists in the French *chanson de geste*. Phyllis Gaffney writes "the epic child is heroic because he departs from the conventional view of the child, transcending the constraints of his age."[33] For example, the *puer senex* expectations are apparent in the *Chançun de Willame*, where Guillaume says of the youthful Gui, "You have a child's body and a man's words."[34] The child's body, capabilities, and stage of development is significant, for, as we saw with the hagiography of Kinga, child heroes often copy adult concerns and cares with distinctly childlike behavior. As Gaffney concludes his discussion of this genre "epic youths must accept adult priorities, yet they do this in childlike ways. Physical weakness, hunger and fear are all shared by epic children; the heroic ones overcome these weaknesses and are effective in combat."[35] With the exception of the mention of combat, this trend could equally describe the heroes of both hagiography and secular literature in both France and Poland at this time.

The Henryków Book has an additional two passages that add something to this discussion. At the beginning of the book, Nicholas, the private citizen

---

33   Phyllis Gaffney, *Constructions of Childhood and Youth in Old French Narrative* (Burlington: Ashgate, 2011), 96.
34   Gaffney, *Constructions*, 75.
35   Gaffney, *Constructions*, 97.

and servant of the king, who was the invisible hand behind the foundation of Henryków monastery, was presented as striving for discipline from youth, and indeed the earlier periods of his life. While not a saint or a holy child or a prince, even less exalted persons like Nicholas could live excellent youths. In another instance from the Book, the abbot Peter and notary Conrad met and reminisced about their boyhood days in school, with the result of a favorable settlement of a dispute in the monastery's favor. Even venerable abbots had fond memories of their childhoods and childhood friends.

7 Thinking with Children

When talking about conceptions and constructions of childhood one should not overlook metaphors and imagery taken from childhood that nevertheless have no connection with actual, physical children. One might call this rhetorical strategy "thinking with children" along the lines of how Elizabeth Clark writes about "thinking with women," in which the actions and words of fictional or constructed women stand in for the debates and concerns of men.[36] With childhood, this is occasionally taken one step further, and the associations are abstracted even from the need of fictional child bodies. Vincent was a master of this sort of rhetoric, and he used it to prove or illustrate many different points. Most obviously, bad rulers were constantly compared to children in their fickleness and incompetence and this was used as sign of their unfitness to rule. Most notably, Pompilius was compared to a child by his wife, who pointed out how his uncles kept him distracted like a child with playthings. In another instance, Vincent presented an extensive reflection on the probably fictional female ruler Wanda to conclude that a female ruler was better than a male child, who would squander all of his father's gains. In this instance, the stereotype of childish stupidity was used to support female rule. Supporting a legitimate child as a leader was risky, and one risked being called a child in turn for this support, as when the disappointed Mieszko III likened those electing the child Leszek the White to infants playing games instead of performing statesmanship. Vincent also uses expectations of parent-child love to emphasize his praise of or hostility towards certain behaviors, such as when, in the aforementioned examples, he praises Krak's and the defenders' of Głogów willingness to sacrifice children for nation. On the negative side, Vincent compares

---

36 Elizabeth Clark, "Thinking with Women: The Uses of the Appeal to 'Woman' in the pre-Nicene Christian Propaganda literature," in *The Spread of Christianity in the First Four Centuries: Essays in Explanation*, ed. William V. Harris (Leiden: Brill, 2005), 44–51.

Sieciech's corruption to a monstrous child attacking and drawing blood from the beasts of his mother, i.e. Poland, instead of respecting and cherishing her.

Both Vincent and Gallus Anonymus employ images of childhood when they refer to Poland as an organism with a life cycle. Vincent does this less often and overtly, most notably in two references to the "infancy" of Poland in his opening chapters. He expands on Gallus' rather short pagan pre-history for Poland and provides it with legendary and formative past stretching deep into the past. Gallus himself seems to want to provide a childhood for everything. As pointed out previously, he spends much time on the boyhood of Bolesław III. Likewise, he opens his book with his own version of the formative "childhood" of Poland itself, which is replete with and bounded by, as noted above, three child invitation ceremonies, with each forecasting something about the future.

Much less positive are references in the Henryków Book, where children, even those unborn, are, in essence, the future enemy. Everything in this Book was written with their potential in mind, and children who are described as young and weak at one point are later described as threatening. Charters showed the increasing tendency to list any possible young person who might challenge the ownership of land including little girls. The Henryków Book was concerned with the memory of posterity, and this is constantly referenced in charters and in all actions undertaken. The preservation in "letters" is necessary because of the passing of generations and the rise of those who did not remember past promises, while for childless monks, their words would serve as metaphorical children to stand for their interests. Children and future generations were the purpose of this book, no matter how focused it seems on the world of adults.

Rhetoric related to childhood was popular during the the eleventh and twelfth centuries in Europe, again related to the Gregorian reform movement, often drawing on Biblical and church history themes.[37] Vincent Damian used it to portray "growth in spiritual ability,"[38] Gregory VII and others could see youth as time of danger for young churchmen to avoid or a time for ironing out imperfections, Lambert used words related to youth to blast Henry IV. Gallus Anonymus and later Polish writers, educated and immersed in this linguistic and rhetorical world, clearly adapted these rhetorical patterns to make their own cases. Rhetoric related to the family more broadly, was also common in everything from royal courts to the spiritual family of the monastery. Linda Mitchell, noting how the family was the most fundamental structure in the

---

37   Kathleen G. Cushing, "*Pueri, iuvenes, and viri*: Age and utility in the Gregorian Reform," *Catholic Historical Review*, 94 no. 3 (2008): 441.
38   Cushing, "*Pueri*," 442 (for Damian), 445–446 (for Gregory), 449 (for Lampart).

minds of medieval people, writes that the structures of all medieval institutions "were intended to mimic family relationships. This in turn had an impact on the ways in which people experienced such institutional structures."[39]

The hagiography of St. Slanisław also uses children and family scenes in its mission to bolster his claim for sainthood. This is seen in the Vita Major, where the significance of his life and canonization were framed as a sort of rebirth for Poland, with the sin against the saint bringing death and dismemberment to Poland and punishment to future generations. Not until the saint himself was reconstituted could the country reunite and blessing return to the children of Poland. The events leading up to his canonization use age (contrasting youth and very old age) to build the drama and two miracles involving children are responsible for the elevation of Stanisław's relics and the proclamation of his holiness.

The archaeological evidence also suggests that children were in the minds of medieval Poles. As noted, their graves appear as a separate category from adult men and women in regards to grave furnishings. Likewise, their groupings together and in specific locations either to be with an adult (often old, injured, sick, or unique in some way), or with each other, or in relationship to a church, show that children undoubtedly registered as a distinct and special segment of society, and society consciously worked to physically construct societies of the dead to reflect this thinking.

The alterity of children was noted by various scholars especially for Anglo-Saxon England. Sally Crawford, in her discussion of Anglo-Saxon multiple burial practices involving children concluded that "multiple ritual should be read as having a different form of social identity from other bodies in the cemetery,"[40] though she nevertheless believes that children had the subordinate role in these practices, and were often treated as objects. While it was not so clear that Polish children in multiple burials were always so objectified, nevertheless their high incidence in multiple burials provides a cross-cultural instance of their uniqueness in death. Similarly, Christina Lee writes about a similar connection to Poland, namely the burial of children with old or sick adults. She concludes "in death, children and adults with a disability seem to be given a special place, and in some cases this may be the same plot for both groups. This by no means signifies that they were regarded as lesser people, but that they may have been regarded as belonging to similar categories. There

---

39 Linda Mitchell, *Family Life in the Middle Ages* (Westport: Greenwood Press, 2007), 221.
40 Crawford, "Companions, Co-incidences, or Chattels," 3–92.

is a certain liminality about children and people with a severe impairment."[41] Another unique way children were treated throughout Europe was in their special placement within cemeteries. Children were placed together in relationship to a church in such different churchyards as Lund and Visby, in Sweden[42] to Raunds-Furnells, in England[43] to Göttingen in Germany,[44] to St. Duch in Vseruby in the Czech lands.[45] While a considerable range of explanations exist for the "children's quarters" in medieval churchyards, ranging from physical and spiritual healing from relics to fears of revenant malevolence, their existence implies children had their own place in death in the minds of adults. Children were placed together in rural row graves outside of Poland as well. Christina Lee identified intentional clusters of children in a number of cemeteries in early medieval Anglo-Saxon England in Great Chesterford, Barrington, Edix Hill and Apple Down.[46]

8 Children in a Wider Context

What can one conclude generally from this inclusion of children and youths in so many different aspects of medieval life and thinking? Up to the current day, the literature surrounding childhood and youth has been focused on proving Ariès wrong and attempting to prove that childhood was not an ignored and diminished age category, "colonized" by the concerns of adults, but rather that it had its own inherent value. Louis Haas and Joel Rosenthal point out in their introduction to a collected volume on medieval childhood that scholars,

---

41 Christina Lee, "Forever Young: Child Burial in Anglo Saxon England," in *Youth and Age in the Medieval North*, ed. Shannon Lewis-Simpson (Leiden: Brill, 2008), 36.

42 Maria Cinthio, *De första stadsborna. Medeltida gravar och människor i Lund* (Stockholm/Stehag: Brutus Östlings Bokförlag Symposion, 2002); Gun Westholm, "Infancy and Adolescence, Education and Recreation from the Medieval Period to the 17th century," in *Lübecker Kolloquium zur Stadtarchäologie im Hanseraum VIII: Kindheit und Jugend, Ausbildung und Freizeit*, ed. Manfred Glaser (Lübeck: Schmidt-Römhild, 2012), 478–479. These are from the Bro Parish Church from the 12th century. Many of them are reburials and are in a row in the inner wall of the south nave. Since they were mostly newborns, the author sees their placement here as an act done in concern for their souls.

43 Andrew Boddington, Graham Cadman and John Evans, *Raunds Furnells: The Anglo-Saxon Church and Churchyard* (London: English Heritage, 1996).

44 Betty Arndt, "Archäologische Befunde zu Kinderheit und Jugend im mittelalterlichen Göttingen," in *Lübecker Kolloquium zur Stadtarchäologie im Hanseraum VIII: Kindheit und Jugend, Ausbildung und Freizeit*, ed. Manfred Glaser (Lübeck: Schmidt-Römhild, 2012), 99–101. There are about 80 children placed around the choir at the cemetery of St Nicholas.

45 Čechura, "Christian, Non-Christian, or Pagan," 289–297.

46 Lee, "Forever Young," 26–27.

despite their protestations to the contrary, have continued to be haunted by the ghost of a theory that was long ago supposedly discredited, and scholars of childhood have failed to concoct anything like a theoretical or methodological consensus on how to discuss childhood in the Middle Ages.[47] This is why my conclusions will say nothing on this matter, but instead be directed towards the question of how a book like this one can contribute to broader discussions.

The question of the meaning of childhood is an excellent case study for one of the most difficult and controversial topics in European medieval studies, namely the "Europeanization" (or "Christianization") of Central, Northern, and Eastern Europe. Piotr Górecki has written extensively on how the effort to place Poland and East Central Europe generally into the European "Christian" framework, made popular by Robert Bartlett, Nora Berend, and Jerzy Kłoczwoski, has produced many different models of how to approach the problem.[48] Górecki collated and categorized all of these approaches into three major paradigms. The first is based on time, and in it Eastern Europe is a "younger" version of western Europe, where progress in envisioned linearly and the east is constantly backwards and struggling to catch up. The second paradigm is based on the concept of diffusion, which uses the concept of core-periphery to explain the gradual spread of ideas, practices, and institutions from the well-developed core in the post-Carolingian realms to the frontiers of the east. The third approach attempts to identify similarity, difference, or co-existence in higher-level aspects of culture, religions, or society in east and west. Górecki himself suggests a more nuanced approach that focuses more specifically on a local regions and supplies rich detail about each to compare the "interplay, timing, dynamics, and incidence" of various features.[49] Górecki's work has focused on everything from lordship and hierarchy, law, rural economy to the formation of ecclesiastical institutions. This book, combines rich detail in the contexts of specific texts or archaeological contexts featuring children, along with more general, higher level comparisons with various contexts across Europe in terms of childhood.

---

47   Louis Haas and Joel Rosenthal, "Historiographical Reflections and the Revolt of Medievalists," in *Essays on Medieval Childhood: Responses to Recent Debates*, ed. Joel Rosenthal (Donington: Shaun Tyas Press, 2007), 12–23.

48   Piotr Górecki, "Medieval Poland in its world, then and today," in *East Central Europe in European History. Themes and Debates*, ed. Jerzy Kłoczowski and Hubert Łaszkiewicz (Lublin: Wydawnictwo Instytuta Europy Środkowo-Wschodniej, 2009), 157–92. Piotr Górecki, "Ambiguous beginnings: East Central Europe in the making, 950–1200," in *European Transformations. The Long Twelfth Century*, ed. Thomas F.X. Noble and John van Engen (Notre Dame: University of Notre Dame Press, 2012), 194–228.

49   Górecki, "Medieval Poland," 169.

My book shows that, at least in the broadest of terms, the concept and portrayal of childhood in Piast Poland from 1000 to 1300 are strongly within the contours of what one might expect to find in the rest of Europe. While the details may differ, the structure and relationships are similar. Tropes from the west, such as *puer senex* appear in the earliest texts from Poland, namely Gallus Anonymus and appear everywhere afterwards. The expected bad behavior of youth and childhood, namely rashness, unwise choices, sexual proclivity, and general stupidity, along with the stylized behavior of heroic children, is remarkably similar. Likewise, the use of language related to children to establish a place within a dynasty and to define the process to masculinity has parallels in both monastic contexts as well as in the *chanson de geste*. Despite the insistence that prominent children are born great, with adorning inborn qualities, they also evidently need to achieve greatness through a process of education, whether martial or ecclesiastical, which is also the case for western children in similar circumstances. Underlying all of this is the assumption in all places of medieval Europe that children deserved care, and this manifested itself in rules for guardianship of orphaned children. Parental, familial, and even societal emotional care and attachment to children was assumed.

All of this begs the question of whether these characteristics were endemic to Poland in pre-Christian times, when Poland stood at the margins of Europe prior to the late tenth century, or whether they were imported to Poland by clergy, knights, settlers, and merchants from the west. The fact that all the written sources produced in Poland from this period were either written by foreigners from the west or from Polish-born scholars who were educated in the west, raises the question of the depth of the penetration of the ideas of the Christianized elite into the general population. Indeed, the existence of the Henryków Book itself is a testament to the fact that there was still considerable resistance to western concepts of landholding and the role of children within the family social hierarchy and inheritance patterns in rural Poland. The argument in favor of western influence trickling down to the general population, however, is bolstered by a consideration of the archaeological evidence. The transition from cremation to row grave to churchyard cemeteries, and the special treatment of children within the row grave and churchyard cemeteries, from special grave provisions to multiple burials to children's quarters, is demonstrably similar to what is seen throughout European and Europeanizing societies from this era. At least the stylized communities of the dead in Poland were shifting to adapt western constructions and conceptions of the children.

Despite the many highlighted instances of apparent western influence, there are numerous examples from earliest Christian times in Poland that some features of Polish conceptions of childhood were unique. The obvious archaeological examples of regionally specific grave goods, such as eggs, large quantities of beads, bells, and animal teeth as amulets are cases in point. Gallus Anonymus' use of three childhood initiation rituals to underpin the transition to a new dynasty and Christianity, is unparalleled, not only in the contemporary texts of the Czech lands or Hungary, but also in the west. Gallus' extensive focus on the heroic exploits and childhood growth of Bolesław III is also particularly well-developed in comparison to relevant parallels. Gallus was a foreigner in Poland, but he claims to be drawing his stories from prominent Polish sources, and the distinctiveness of children in his story could be one example of the consequences of this. Both Gallus and Vincent were particularly insistent on using age-related language to establish the value of men. Vincent, in stories such of that of Wanda the maiden warlord, and in constant rhetorical flourishes against weak men, defined true masculinity not against the feminine, but against the follies of youth and old age. While this is not by any means unique to Vincent, his consistent use of these metaphors is not typical and age features heavily in his worldview. This is similar to the Henryków Book, where children of all ages appear in all sorts of contexts, from threats to future monastic holdings, to foolish wastrels at all social levels, to salacious tales of dancing girls, to even pleasant memories of boyhood leading to a successful business deal. While the cartularies of England bear resemblance to the second half of the Henryków Book, the colorful stories of the first book and the interweaving of children and childhoods within stand in marked contrast to the rather dry references to posterity in the second half of the Henryków book and in England. This discussion would not be complete without a nod to the four major female saints of thirteenth century Poland. Of these four, Hedwig, Salomea, Kinga, and Anna, three have significant references to the childhood of the saint (Hedwig, Salomea, and Kinga). Female saints are rare enough from this period, and three female saints with developed childhood discussions is a remarkable instance.[50] The role of children in the organization of the *miracula* and their high levels of incidence within them is also unparalleled in contemporary European sources. Children and childhood, at least as far as the material surveyed in this book suggest, had a unique place in the minds of the early medieval inhabitants of the Piast realm.

---

50   It should be noted that the royal princess was not a particularly Polish phenomenon, but a central European one, and that the thirteenth century generally had a higher rate of canonization for women than other centuries. For this see: Gábor Klaniczay, *Holy Rulers and Blessed Princesses: Dynastic Cults in Medieval Central Europe* (Cambridge: Cambridge University Press, 2007), 196–199.

Appendix

A   Multiple Burials

TABLE 1   Multiple burials in selected Polish cemeteries

Cemetery	Region	Grave	Occupants	Notes
Brześć Kujawski	Kujawski-Pomorania	64, 65	Young boy and young girl	Knife with boy, the girl provisioned with fifty beads, finger ring of glass, two temple rings of bronze
Brześć Kujawski	Kujawski-Pomorania	84, 91	Adult male, adult male	Remnants of a bucket and at foot of grave and knives for each male
Brześć Kujawski	Kujawski-Pomorania	161–162	Adult male and boy	Boy buried near remnants of buckets, man buried with knife and sheath
Brześć Kujawski	Kujawski-Pomorania	172	Boy and small child	Remnants of a knife
Czekanów	Mazovia	15, 16	Woman and child of 3–4 years	
Czekanów	Mazovia	21, 24	Woman and 2–3 year old	Child buried with egg
Czekanów	Mazovia	20, 22, 25	Woman and 9–12 month old, also a 12–18 month old	9–12 month old has bronze finger ring
Czekanów	Mazovia	29, 30	Child of 8–9 years and youth	
Czekanów	Mazovia	32, 33	Child of 10 years and woman	
Czekanów	Mazovia	45, 46	Fetus/Newborn and two year old	Two year old has 38 beads

TABLE 1   Multiple burials in selected Polish cemeteries (*cont.*)

Cemetery	Region	Grave	Occupants	Notes
Czekanów	Mazovia	64, 66	9 month old and child between 1 and 2	
Czekanów	Mazovia	63, 67	Woman and 2–4 month old	
Czekanów	Mazovia	70, 71	2–3 year old and 0–12 month old	2–3 year old received an amulet of dog teeth, and over 50 beads, 0–12 month old received 4 beads
Czekanów	Mazovia	84, 87	3 year old and 6–9 month old	6–9 month old received egg
Czekanów	Mazovia	99, 100	Two children between 1 and 2 years old	One child received a necklace with 32 beads
Czekanów	Mazovia	107, 109	Man and 6 month old	
Masłowice	Mazovia	19, 20	Adult female and 2 year old child	Adult woman with 7 temple rings, one finger ring, and a knife
Masłowice	Mazovia	Unstated	Adult male and female	
Radom	Kujavia-Pomorania	9	Infans I (5–6 years old), adult man, adult female	Knife and iron object associated with the adult
Radom	Kujavia-Pomorania	34	Infans II/J and adult female	2 bronze finger rings and 1 glass ring associated with adult
Radom	Kujavia-Pomorania	82	Infans I (fetus or newborn), adult female	3 temple rings, earrings, finger ring, pottery fragments associated with adult

TABLE 1   Multiple burials in selected Polish cemeteries (*cont.*)

Cemetery	Region	Grave	Occupants	Notes
Kałdus	Łodz	13A, 13B	Adult male and female	Male buried with knife and fittings and pottery, female buried with earrings, 21 beads, clasp, kaptorga, and pottery
Kałdus	Łodz	194A, 194B	Infans II and mature adult	Infans II received iron tool
Kałdus	Łodz	221A, 221B	Female adult and Infans I	Female received knife, one temple ring, and four beads
Kałdus	Łodz	256A, 256B	Male and female mature adults	
Kałdus	Łodz	261A, 261B	Two adult men	
Kałdus	Łodz	356A, 356B	Adult female and Infans I	Female received 3 temple rings
Poddębice	Łodz	11A, 11B	Adult female and child	Pottery and two temple rings in female grave
Pyzdry	Greater Poland	9A, 9B	Juvenis of 15 years and Infans I (0–3 months)	Juvenis received knife, finger ring, and pottery, infant on breast
Pyzdry	Greater Poland	14A, 14B	Infans II (12–14) and Maturus (35)	Adult received 7 temple rings and pottery, the Infans II received 8 temple rings
Pyzdry	Greater Poland	16A, 16 B	Two adults	One adult received a knife, a bucket, and pottery
Stary Zamek	Silesia	48	Adult female and newborn	Stone coffin, woman buried with silver and bronze temple rings

TABLE 1   Multiple burials in selected Polish cemeteries (cont.)

Cemetery	Region	Grave	Occupants	Notes
Stary Zamek	Silesia	76, 77	Adult man and woman	Stacked grave, unclear if intentional
Stary Zamek	Silesia	103, 104	Maturus and Infans II	Adult grave on top of child grave, unclear if intentional
Stary Zamek	Silesia	107	Maturus and unidentified	Badly damaged grave

SOURCES: Eleonora and Zdzisław Kaszewscy, "Wczesnośredniowieczne cmentarzysko w Brześciu Kujawskim, pow Włocławek," in *Materiały Starożytne i Wczesnośredniowieczne, Volume 1* (Warsaw: Zakład Narodowy Imienia Ossolińskich, 1971), 427–432. Barbara Zawadzka-Antosik, "Z problematyki pochówków dziecięcych odkrytych na cmentarzysku w Czekanowie, Woj. Siedleckie," *Wiadomości Archeologiczne* 47 (1982): 25, 33. Bogusław Abramek, "Wczesnośredniowieczne cmentarzysko szkieletowe w Masłowicach, wow Sieradz," *Sprawozdania Archeologiczne* 32 (1980): 232–233. Agnieszka Kozdęba, Tomasz Kurasiński and Kalina Skóra "Catalog Gróbow" and "Tablice 170," in *Przestrzeń Osadnicza Wczesnośredniowiecznego Radomia, Tom 1: Cmentarzysko w Radomiu, Stanowisko 4*, ed. Tadeusz Baranowksi (Łodz: Wydawnictwo Instytutu Archeologii i Etnologii, PAN, 2016), 133–136. Wojciech Chudziak, *Wczesnośredniowieczne cmentarzysko szkieletowe w Kałdusie* (Toruń: Wydawn. Uniwersytetu Mikołaja Kopernika, 2010), 95–103. Table 5. Henryk Wiklak, "Cmentarzysko z XII i XIII w. w Poddębicach," in *Prace i materiały muzeum archeologicznego i etnograficznego w Łodzi Seria Archeologiczna* 5 (1960). Ilona Jagielska, "Wczesnośredniowieczne cmentarzysko na stanowisku Pyzdry 11," *Studia Lednickie* 10 (2010): 129–150. Krzysztof Wachowski and Grzegorz Domański, *Wczesnopolskie cmentarzysko w Starym Zamku* (Wrocław: Uniwersytet Wrocławski, 1992), 61–62.

B   Correspondence Analysis Data

All information for units and types were taken from the tables attached to their respective archaeological reports. The data was further winnowed according to the following rules:
1. Units were arranged according to sex for adults and according to age for children. All skeletons of indeterminate or sex (in the case of adults) by osteological means were eliminated from consideration. In cemeteries with adequate preservation, child age categories are broken down into standard anthropological age categories (Infans I, Infans II, etc.), but in other instances are simply grouped together in one category.

APPENDIX

2. To avoid the confusion caused by assigning grave goods to a particular individual in double or triple burials, all multiple burials were eliminated from consideration.
3. To avoid skewing the data from outliers caused by overabundance of types, often the result of one or two unusual burials, the data has been recorded as presence/absence.
4. To avoid extremes due to outliers in types, for an artifact type to be included in the analysis it had to appear at least two times in cemeteries of less than 100 burials and at least three times in cemeteries of over 100 burials.
5. In cases were the age of a skeleton was determined to be at the margins of age categories, I rounded to the higher age.

TABLE 2 Graves and incidences at Kałdus

	Infans I	Infans II/J	Male	Female
Beads	7	6	3	19
Bell	3	1	0	0
Belt	0	0	3	0
Bucket	0	0	2	1
Ceramic	1	1	3	1
Earring	0	0	0	2
Finger Ring	2	5	0	13
Knife	4	17	20	33
Money	1	6	5	6
Pot	0	0	2	1
Spindle Whorl	0	0	1	3
Temple Ring	6	14	1	36
Tool	1	2	0	7
Weapon	0	1	2	0
Whetstone	2	1	1	0

SOURCE: WOJCIECH CHUDZIAK, *WCZESNOŚREDNIOWIECZNE CMENTARZYSKO SZKIELETOWE W KAŁDUSIE* (TORUŃ: WYDAWN. UNIWERSYTETU MIKOŁAJA KOPERNIKA, 2010), 95–103. TABLE 5.

TABLE 3 Graves and incidences at Radom

	Male	Female	Children
Beads	0	5	0
Buckle	2	1	0
Bucket	1	1	0
Coin	3	3	1
Finger Ring	0	6	0
Flint	1	2	0
Knife	6	10	1
Pottery	6	13	3
Temple Ring	0	12	2
Weapon	2	0	0

SOURCE: AGNIESZKA KOZDĘBA, TOMASZ KURASIŃSKI AND KALINA SKÓRA "CATALOG GRÓBOW" AND "TABLICE 170," IN *PRZESTRZEŃ OSADNICZA WCZESNOŚREDNIOWIECZNEGO RADOMIA, TOM 1: CMENTARZYSKO W RADOMIU, STANOWISKO 4*, ED. TADEUSZ BARANOWKSI (ŁODZ: WYDAWNICTWO INSTYTUTU ARCHEOLOGII I ETNOLOGII, PAN, 2016), 133–136.

TABLE 4 Graves and incidences at Masłowice

	Male	Female	Children
Beads	0	11	3
Bucket	1	1	0
Coin	2	1	1
Finger Ring	0	15	2
Flint	10	0	0
Knife	20	14	6
Pottery	5	7	5
Temple Ring	0	22	4
Weapon	2	0	0
Whetstone	2	0	1

SOURCE: BOGUSŁAW ABRAMEK, "WCZESNOŚREDNIOWIECZNE CMENTARZYSKO SZKIELETOWE W MASŁOWICACH, WOW SIERADZ," *SPRAWOZDANIA ARCHEOLOGICZNE* 32 (1980): 232–233.

APPENDIX

TABLE 5   Graves and incidences at Cedynia

	Infans I	Infans II	Juvenis	Male	Female
Beads	3	5	0	2	4
Button	1	1	1	0	2
Belt Fitting	1	0	0	8	1
Buckle	2	2	2	9	4
Coin	1	5	3	16	19
Finger Ring	0	2	4	22	21
Knife	0	1	0	6	6
Necklace	0	4	0	0	4
Temple Ring	0	3	2	2	16
Spindle Whorl	1	0	0	2	1

SOURCE: HELENA MALINOWSKA-ŁAZARCZYK, *CMENTARZYSKO ŚREDNIOWIECZNE W CEDYNI* (SZCZECIN, MUZEUM NARODOWE, 1982), 171–212.

TABLE 6   Graves and incidences at Czersk

	Men	Women	Children
Arrow Head	8	0	1
Amulets	1	2	4
Beads	8	24	15
Keys	0	3	1
Finger Ring	4	11	5
Flint	2	1	0
Needle	0	1	2
Knife	11	13	2
Knife Sheath	2	3	0
Iron Nail	6	9	4
Pendant	1	4	4
Temple Rings	4	37	6
Spindle Whorl	0	3	2
Unknown Iron	19	9	4

SOURCE: JADWIGA BRONICKA-RAUHUT, *CMENTARZYSKO WCZESNOŚREDNIOWIECZNE W CZERSKU* (WARSAW, POLISH ACADEMY OF SCIENCES, 1998), 51–116.

Bibliography

Primary Sources

Anonymus, Gallus. *The Deeds of the Princes of the Poles*. Translated by Karol Maleczyński and edited by Paul W. Knoll and Frank Schaer. Budapest/New York: Central University Press, 2003.

Kadłubek, Vincent. *Chronicle of the Poles*. Translated by Eduard Mühle and edited by Marian Plezia. Darmstadt: Wissenschaftliche Buchgesellschaft, 2014.

Peter, Anonymous. *The Text and the World: The Henryków Book, Its Authors, and Their Region 1160–1310*. Translated and edited by Piotr Górecki. Oxford: Oxford University Press, 2015.

Prague, Cosmas. *The Chronicle of the Czechs*. Translated by Lisa Wolverton. Washington: Catholic University of America Press, 2012.

"De sancto Adalberto episcopo" and "Miracula sancti Adalberti." Edited by Wojciech Kętrzyński. *Monumenta Poloniae Historica* (= MPH), T. 4. Lwów: Lwowska Komisya Historycznej Akademii Umiejętności, 1884, 206–238.

"Vita et Miracula sanctae Kyngae ducissae Cracoviensis." Edited by Wojciech Kętrzyński. *Monumenta Poloniae Historica*, T. 4. Lwów: Lwowska Komisya Historycznej Akademii Umiejętności, 1884, 662–744.

"Vita sanctae Salomeae reginae Haliciensis." Edited by Wojciech Kętrzyński. *Monumenta Poloniae Historica*, T. 4. Lwów: Lwowska Komisya Historycznej Akademii Umiejętności, 1884, 770–796.

"Vita sancti Stanislai Cracoviensis episcopi (vita major)." Edited by Wojciech Kętrzyński. *Monumenta Poloniae Historica*, T. 4. Lwów: Lwowska Komisya Historycznej Akademii Umiejętności, 1884, 319–438.

"Vita sancti Stanislai episcopi Cracoviensis, vita minor" and "Miracula sancti Stanislai." Edited by Wojciech Kętrzyński. *Monumenta Poloniae Historica*, T. 4. Lwów: Lwowska Komisya Historycznej Akademii Umiejętności, 1884, 238–285.

"Vita santae Kyngae ducissae Cracoviensis." Edited by Aleksander Semkowicz. *Monumenta Poloniae Historica*, T. 4. Lwów: Lwowska Komisya Historycznej Akademii Umiejętności, 1884, 501–655.

Secondary Sources

Abramek, Bogusław. "Wczesnośredniowieczne cmentarzysko szkieletowe w Masłowicach, Woj, Sieradz." *Sprawozdania Archeologiczne* 22 (1980): 227–246.

Adamska, Anna. "Founding a monastery over dinner: the case of Henryków in Silesia (1222–1228)." In *Medieval Legal Process: Physical, Spoken and Written Performance in the Middle Ages*, edited by Marco Mostert and Paul S. Barnwell, 211–231. Turnhout: Brepols, 2011.

Adamska, Anna. "The Study of Medieval Literacy: Old Sources, New Ideas." In *The Development of Literate Mentalities in East Central Europe*, ed. Anna Adamska and M. Mostert, 13–47. Turnhout: Brepols, 2004.

Alexandere-Bidon, Daniele, and Didier Lett. *Children in the Middle Ages: Fifth–Fifteenth Centuries*. Notre Dame: University of Notre Dame Press, 1999.

Ariès, Philippe. *Centuries of Childhood: A Social History of Family Life*. New York: Vintage Books, 1965.

Banaszkiewicz, Jacek. *Polskie dzieje bajeczne mistrza Wincentego Kadłubka*. Wrocław: Leopoldinum, 1998.

Baranowksi, Tadeusz, editor. *Przestrzeń Osadnicza Wczesnośredniowiecznego Radomia, Tom 1: Cmentarzysko w Radomiu, Stanowisko 4*. Łodz: Wydawnictwo Instytutu Archeologii i Etnologii, PAN, 2016.

Bartlett, Robert. *The Making of Europe: Conquest, Colonization and Cultural Change 950–1350*. Princeton: Princeton University Press.

Baxter, Jane Eva. "The archaeology of childhood." *Annual Review of Anthropology* 37 (2008): 159–175.

Berend, Nora, Felipe Fernandez-Armesto, and James Muldoon. *The Expansion of Central Europe in the Middle Ages*. Florence: Taylor and Francis, 2013.

Bisson, Thomas. *The Crisis of the Twelfth Century: Power, Lordship, and the Origins of European Government*. Princeton: Princeton University Press, 2009.

Brown, Warren. "Charters as weapons. On the role played by early medieval dispute records in the disputes they record." *Journal of Medieval History* 28 (2002): 227–248.

Buko, Andrzej, editor. *Kleczanów: Badania Rozpoznawcze 1989–1992*. Warsaw: Instytut Archeologii i Etnologii Polskiej Akademii Nauk, 1997.

Buliński, Tadeusz, "Średniowieczny obraz dziecka." *Studia Edukacyjne* 4 (1998): 89–103.

Carpenter, Jennifer. "Juette of Huy, Recluse and Mother (1158–1228): Children and Mothering in the Saintly Life." In *Power of the Weak: Studies on Medieval Women*, edited by Jennifer Carpenter and Sally-Beth MacLean, 57–93. Chicago: University of Illinois Press, 1995.

Carruthers, Mary. *The Book of Memory: A Study of Memory in Medieval Culture, Second Edition*. Cambridge: Cambridge University Press, 2008.

Čechura, Martin. "Christian, Non-Christian, or Pagan? Newborns as the Source to Understanding of Medieval and Post-Medieval Mentality." In *Kim Jestes Człowieku?*, edited by Wojciech Dzieduszycki and Jacek Wrzesinski, 289–297. Poznan: Stowarzyszenie Naukowe Archeologow Polskich, 2011.

Cetwiński, Marek. "Bog, Szatan, i człowiek w księdze Henrykowskiej." *Nasza Przeszłość* 83 (1994): 81–87.
Cetwiński, Marek. "Formularz dokumentów a opis rzeczywistośći w 'Księdze henrykowskiej.'" In *Formuła, archetyp, konwencja w źródle historycznym: materiały IX Sympozjum Nauk Dających Poznawać Żródła Historyczne, Kazimierz Dolny, 14–15 gr 2000 r.*, edited by Artur Górak and Krzysztof Skupieński, 78–81. Radzyń Podlaski: Radzyńskie Stowarzyszenie Inicjatyw Lokalnych, Instytut Badawczy "Libra," 2006.
Chołodowska, Małgorzata. "Matka—opiekunka małoletnich dzieci w Polsce wcesnośredniowiecznej na podstawie opisów cudow św. Jadwigi i św. Stanisława." In *Partnerka, matka, opiekunka: status kobiety w starożytności i średniowieczu*, edited by Julia Jundziłł, 260–69. Bydgoszcz: Wydadnictwo Uczelniane Wyższej Szkoły Pedagogicznej, 1999.
Chudziak, Wojciech. *Wczesnośredniowieczne cmentarzysko szkieletowe w Kałdusie*. Toruń: Wydawn. Uniwersytetu Mikołaja Kopernika, 2010.
Cinthio, Maria. *De första stadsborna. Medeltida gravar och människor i Lund*. Stockholm/Stehag: Brutus Östlings Bokförlag Symposion, 2002.
Clanchy, Michael. *From Memory to Written Record*. Chichester, West Sussex: Blackwell, 2013.
Clark, Elizabeth. "Thinking with Women: The Uses of the Appeal to 'Woman' in the pre-Nicene Christian Propaganda literature." In *The Spread of Christianity in the First Four Centuries: Essays in Explanation*, edited by William V. Harris, 44–51. Leiden: Brill, 2005.
Classen, Albrecht. *Childhood in the Middle Ages and the Renaissance: The Results of a Paradigm Shift in the History of Mentality*. Berlin: Walter de Gruyter, 2005.
Cochelin, Isabelle, and Karen Elaine Smyth. *Medieval Life Cycles: Continuity and Change*. Turnhout: Brepols, 2013.
Crawford, Sally, and Gillian Shepherd. *Children, Childhood and Society*. Oxford: Archaeopress, 2007.
Crawford, Sally. *Childhood in Anglo-Saxon England*. Gloucester: Sutton Publishing, 1999.
Curta, Florin, and Matthew Koval. "Children in Eleventh- and Twelfth-Century Poland and Hungary: An Archaeological Comparison." In *The Medieval Networks in East Central Europe Commerce, Contacts, Communication*, edited by Balázs Nagy, Felicitas Schmieder, and András Vadas, 87–122. London: Routledge Press, 2019.
Curta, Florin. *East Central & Eastern Europe in the Early Middle Ages*. Ann Arbor: Univ. of Michigan Press, 2007.
Cushing, Kathleen. "*Pueri, iuvenes, and viri*: Age and utility in the Gregorian Reform." *The Catholic Historical Review* 94 (2008): 435–449.
Dąbrowska, Maria, and Andrzej Klonder, editors. *Od narodzin do wieku dojrzałego: dzieci i młodzież w Polsce, V/1. Od średniowiecza do wieku XVIII*. Warsaw: Instytut Archeologii i Etnologii Polskiej Akademii Nauk, 2002.

Dalewski, Zbigniew. "A new chosen people? Gallus Anonymus's narrative about Poland and its rulers." In *Historical Narratives and Christian Identity on a European Periphery. Early History Writing in Northern, East-Central, and Eastern Europe* (c. 1070–1200), edited by Ildar H. Garipzanov, 145–166. Turnhout: Brepols, 2011.

Delimata, Małgorzata. *Dziecko w Polsce średniowiecznej*. Poznań: Wydawnictwo Poznańskie, 2004.

Duby, Georges. *The Chivalrous Society*. Translated by Cynthia Postan. London: Arnold Press, 1977.

Dygo, Marian. "Czy istniał feudalizm w Europie środkowo-wschodniej wśredniowieczu?" *Kwartalnik historyczny* 120 (2013): 667–717.

Dymmel, Piotr. "Traces of oral tradition in the oldest Polish historiography: Gallus Anonymus and Wincenty Kadłubek" In *The Development of Literate Mentalities in East Central Europe*, edited by Anna Adamska, 343–363. Turnhout: Brepols, 2004.

Dzieduszycki, Wojciech, and Jacek Wrzesiński. *Dusza maluczka, a strata ogromna*, Funeralia Lednickie spotkanie 6. Poznań: Oddział w Poznaniu, 2004.

Finucane, Ronald. *The Rescue of the Innocents. Endangered Children in Medieval Miracles*. New York: St. Martin's Press, 2000.

Gaffney, Phyllis. *Constructions of Childhood and Youth in Old French Narrative*. Burlington: Ashgate, 2011.

Garas, Monika. "Pochówki Atypowe na cmentarzyskach zachodniopomorskich w dobie Chrzystianizacji." *Acta Archeologica Lodziensia* 56 (2010): 51–64.

Gardeła, Leszek, and Kamil Kajkowski. "Groby podwójne w Polsce wczesnośredniowiecznej. Próba rewaluacji." *Acta Archaeologica Lodziensia* 60 (2014): 103–120.

Garver, Valerie. "The Influence of Monastic Ideals upon the Carolingian Conceptions of Childhood." In *Childhood in the Middle Ages and the Renaissance: The Results of a Paradigm Shift in the History of Mentality*, edited by Albrecht Classen, 67–85. Berlin: Walter de Gruyter, 2005.

Gaunt, Simon. *Gender and Genre in Medieval French Literature*. Cambridge: Cambridge University Press, 1995.

Gawlas, Sławomir. "Die Probleme des Lehnswesens und des Feudalismus aus polnischer Sicht." In *Das europäische Mittelalter im Spannungsbogen des Vergleichs. Zwanzig internationale Beiträge zu Praxis, Problemen und Perspektiven*, edited by Michael Borgolte, 97–123. Berlin: Akademie-Verlag, 2001.

Geary, Patrick. *Phantoms of Remembrance. Memory and Oblivion at the End of the First Millennium*. Princeton: Princeton University Press, 1994.

Glaser, Manfred. *Lübecker Kolloquium zur Stadtarchäologie im Hanseraum VIII: Kindheit und Jugend, Ausbildung und Freizeit*. Lübeck: Schmidt-Römhild, 2012.

Goodich, Michael. "Childhood and adolescence among the thirteenth century saints." In *Lives and Miracles of the Saints: Studies in Medieval Latin Hagiography*. Burlington: Ashgate, 2004.

Goodich, Michael. *Lives and Miracles of the Saints: Studies in Medieval Latin Hagiography*. Burlington: Ashgate, 2004.

Goodich, Michael. *Vita Perfecta: The Ideal of Sainthood in the Thirteenth Century*. Stuttgart: Anton Hiersemann, 1982.

Górecki, Janusz. "Nekropola tzw. II kościoła na Ostrowie Lednickim." *Studia Lednickie* 4 (1996): 137–156.

Górecki, Piotr. "Ius ducale revisited: twelfth-century narratives of Piast power." In *Gallus Anonymus and His Chronicle in the Context of Twelfth-Century Historiography from the Perspective of the Latest Research*, edited by Krzysztof Stopka, 35–44. Kraków: Polska Akademia Umiejętności, 2010.

Górecki, Piotr. "Words, concepts, and phenomena: knighthood, lordship and the early Polish nobility (c. 1050–1150)." In *Nobles and Nobility in Medieval Europe. Concepts, Origins, Transformations*, edited by Anne J. Duggan, 115–55 Woodbridge/Rochester: Boydell Press, 2000.

Górecki, Piotr. *Economy, Society and Lordship in Medieval Poland: 1100–1250*. New York: Holmes & Meier, 1992.

Górecki, Piotr. *The Text and the World: The Henryków Book, Its Authors, and Their Region 1160–1310*. Oxford: Oxford University Press, 2015.

Gręzak, Anna, and Beata Kurach. "Konsumpcja mięsa w średniowieczu oraz w czasach nowożytnych na terenie obecnych ziem Polski w świetle danych archeologicznych." *Archeologia Polski* 41 (1996): 139–167.

Grodecki, Roman. "Mistrz Wincenty Kadłubek, biskup krakowski." *Rocznik Krakowski Vol. XIX*, edited by Jozef Muczkowski. Kraków: Wydawnictwo Towarzystwo Miłośników Historii i Zabytków Krakowa, 1923.

Grzesik, Ryszard. "The study of the Middle Ages in Poland." *Annual of Medieval Studies at CEU* 15 (2009): 265–277.

Güttner-Sporzyński, Darius von, editor. *Writing History in Medieval Poland. Bishop Vincentius of Cracow and the Chronica Polonorum*. Turnhout: Brepols, 2017.

Haas, Louis, and Joel Rosenthal. "Historiographical Reflections and the Revolt of Medievalists." In *Essays on Medieval Childhood: Responses to Recent Debates*, edited by Joel Rosenthal, 12–23. Donington: Shaun Tyas Press, 2007.

Hadley, Dawn. *Masculinity in Medieval Europe*. London: Routledge Press, 1999.

Halborg, John, Gordon Whatley. *Sainted Women of the Dark Ages*. Durham and London: Duke University Press, 1992.

Halsall, Guy. *Settlement and Social Organization: the Merovingian region of Metz*. Cambridge: Cambridge University Press, 1995.

Hanawalt, Barbara. *Growing Up in Medieval London: The Experience of Childhood in History*. Oxford: Oxford University Press, 1993.

Houts, Elizabeth von. *Memory and Gender in Medieval Europe, 900–1200*. London: Macmillan Press, 1999.

Hudson, John. *Land, Law, and Lordship in Anglo-Norman England*. Clarendon Press, 1994.

Jagielska, Ilona. "Wczesnośredniowieczne cmentarzysko na stanowisku Pyzdry 11." *Studia Lednickie* 10 (2010): 129–150.

Jaritz, Gerhard, and Katalin Szende. *Medieval East Central Europe in a Comparative Perspective From Frontier Zones to Lands in Focus*. London: Routledge, 2016.

Jasiński, Tomasz. "*Cursus velox cum consillabicatione* w Kronice polskiej Galla Anonima i w Translacji św. Mikołaja Mnicha z Lido." In *Memoria viva. Studia historyczne poświęcone pamięci Izabeli Skierskiej (1967–2014)*, edited by Grażyna Rutkowska and Antoni Gąsiorowski, 114–31. Warsaw/Poznań: Instytut Historii Polskiej Akademii Nauk, 2015.

Jasiński, Tomasz. "Rozwój średniowiecznej prozy rytmicznej a pochodzenie i wykształcenie Galla Anonima." In *Cognitioni gestorum. Studia z dziejów średniowiecza dedykowane Profesorowi Jerzemu Strzelczykowi*, edited by Dariusz Adam Sikorski and Andrzej Marek Wyrwa, 185–93. Poznań/Warsaw: DiG, 2006.

Jasiński, Tomasz. "Czy Gall Anonim to Monachus Littorensis?" *Kwartalnik historyczny* 112 (2005): 69–89.

Jażdżewski, Konrad. "Cmentarzysko wczesnośredniowieczne w lutomiersku pod łodzią świetle badan Z.R. 1949." In *Materiały Wczesnośredniowieczne, Volume 1: 1949*, 92–191. Warsaw: Muzeum Archeologicznego w Warszawie, 1951.

Justus, Hedy. "Initial Demographic Observations of the Giecz Collection: Sex and Age-at-Death Assesment of Skeletal Remains Excavated at GZ4 between 1999 and 2003." *Studia Lednickie* 8 (2005): 197–206.

Karras, Ruth Mazo. "Aquinas's Chastity Belt: Clerical Masculinity in Medieval Europe." In *Gender and Christianity in Medieval Europe: New Perspectives*, edited by Lisa Bitel and Felice Lifshitz, 52–67. Philadelphia: University of Pennsylvania Press, 2008.

Kaszewscy, Eleonora and Zdzisław. "Wczesnośredniowieczne cmentarzysko w Brześciu Kujawskim, pow Włocławek." In *Materiały Starożytne i Wczesnośredniowieczne, Volume 1*, 365–434. Warsaw: Zakład Narodowy Imienia Ossolińskich, 1971.

Kemp, Kathryn. "Where Have All the Children Gone?: The Archaeology of Childhood." *Journal of Archaeological Method and Theory* 8 (2001): 1–34.

Klaniczay, Gábor. "The Cinderella Effect: Late Medieval Female Sainthood in Central Europe and in Italy." *East Central Europe* 20–23 (1993–1996): 51–68.

Klaniczay, Gabor. *Holy Rulers and Blessed Princesses: Dynastic Cults in Medieval Central Europe*. Cambridge: Cambridge University Press, 2002.

Kłoczowski, Jerzy. *History of Polish Christianity*. Cambridge: Cambridge University Press, 2000.

Kowalczyk, Elżbieta. "Chrześcijańskie miłosierdzie. Rzecz o pochówkach dzieci nie ochrzczonych (na przykładzie północnego Mazowsza)." In *Dusza maluczka, a strata ogromna*, Funeralia Lednickie spotkanie 6, edited by Jacek Wrzesiński and

Wojciech Dzieduszycki, 103–113. Poznań: Stowarzyszenie Naukowe Archeologów Polskich, Oddział w Poznaniu, 2004.

Kozak, Jerzy, and Robert Dąbrowski. "Wczesnośredniowieczne cmentarzysko w Daniszewie, pow. Kolski, woj. Wielkopolskie—analiza antropologiczna." *Slavia Antiqua* 49 (2008): 213.

Krawiec, Adam. *Król bez korony: Władysław I Herman, książę polski.* Warsaw: Wydawnictwo Naukowe PWN, 2014.

Krzyżaniak, Lech. *Wczesnośredniowieczne cmentarzyska szkieletowe w Lądzie, woj Konin.* Poznań: Muzeum Archeologiczne w Poznaniu, 1986.

Kufel-Dzierzgowska, Anna. "Wczesnośredniowieczne cmentarzysko w Brzegu, Województwo Sieradzkie," *Seria Archeologiczna* 30 (1983): 309–322.

Kurasiński, Thomas. "Dziecko i strzała. Z problematyki wyposażania grobów w militaria na terenie Polski wczesnopiastowskiej (XI–XII wiek)." In *Dusza maluczka, a strata ogromna,* Funeralia Lednickie spotkanie 6, edited by Jacek Wrzesiński and Wojciech Dzieduszycki, 131–138. Poznań: Stowarzyszenie Naukowe Archeologów Polskich, Oddział w Poznaniu, 2004.

Kurasiński, Tomasz, and Kalina Skóra. "Children's burials from the early medieval inhumation cemetery in Radom, site 4." *Fasciculi Archaeologiae Historicae* 28 (2015), 41–52.

Kurasiński, Tomasz, and Kalina Skóra. *Cmentarzysko w Radomiu, Stanowisko 4.* Łodz: Wydawnictwo Instytutu Archeologii i Etnologii PAN, 2016.

Lett, Didier. *L'enfant des miracles. Enfance et société au Moyen Âge (XII–XIII siècle).* Paris: Aubier, 1997.

Lewis-Simpson, Shannon. *Youth and Age in the Medieval North.* Leiden: Brill, 2008.

Lillehammer, Grete. "A child is born: the child's world in an archaeological perspective." *Norwegian Archaeological Review* 22 (1989): 89–105.

Malinowska-Łazarczyk, Helena. *Cmentarzysko średniowieczne w Cedyni.* Szczecin: Muzeum Narodowe, 1982.

Marciniak, Joze. "Cmentarzysko szkieletowe z okresu wczesnośredniowiecznego w Strzemieszycach Wielkich pow. Będzin." In *Materiały Wczesnośredniowieczne V*, 141–186. Warsaw: Panstwowe Muzeum Archeologiczne, 1960.

McNamara, Jo Ann. "Women and Power through the Family Revisited." In *Gendering the Master Narrative: Woman and Power in the Middle Ages,* edited by Mary Erler and Maryanne Kowaleski, 17–30. Ithaca: Cornell University Press, 2003.

Melicharova, Petra. "Crown, veil, halo: confronting ideas of royal female sanctity in the West and in the Byzantine East in the Late Middle Ages (13th–14th Century)." *Byzantion* 77 (2007): 315–344.

Michalski, Maciej. *Kobiety i świętość w żywotach trzynastowieczynch księżnych polskich.* Poznań: Poznańska Durkarnia Naukowa, 2004.

Mitchell, Linda. *Family Life in the Middle Ages*. Westport: Greenwood Press, 2007.
Modzelewski, Karol. "The system of the ius ducale and the idea of feudalism." *Quaestiones Medii Aevi* 1 (1977): 71–99.
Moreland, John. *Archaeology and Text*. London: Duckworth, 2007.
Mühle, Eduard. "Cronicae et gesta ducum sive principum Polonorum. Neue Forschungen zum so genannten Gallus Anonymus." *Deutsches Archiv für Erforschung des Mittelalters* 66 (2009): 459–96.
Müller, Miriam. *Childhood, Orphans, and Underage Heirs in Medieval England*. Cham: Palgrave Macmillan, 2019.
Murray, Jacqueline. "Flesh, Two Sexes, Three Genders?" In *Gender and Christianity in Medieval Europe: New Perspectives*. Edited by Lisa Bitel and Felice Lifshitz, 24–51. Philadelphia: University of Pennsylvania Press, 2008.
Murray, Jaqueline. "Thinking about Gender: The Diversity of Medieval Perspectives." In *Power of the Weak: Studies on Medieval Women*, edited by Jennifer Carpenter and Sally-Beth MacLean, 1–15. Chicago: University of Illinois Press, 1995.
Musin, Aleksandr. "Czy król Zygmunt III Waza był w dzieciństwie poganinem? Między pogaństwem a chrześcijaństwem, o fenomenie amuletów z zębów i kości zwierząt." In *Od Bachórza do Światowida ze Zbrucza. Tworzenie się słowiańskiej Europy w ujęciu źródłoznawczym. Księga jubileuszowa Profesora Michała Parczewskiego*, edited by Barbara Chudzińska, Michał Wojenka and Marcin Wołoszyn, 421–40. Kraków/Rzeszów: Wydawnictwo Uniwersytetu Rzeszowskiego, 2016.
Myśliwski, Grzegorz. "Feudalizm—'rewolucja feudalna'—kryzys władzy w Polsce XI–początku XII w. Punkt widzenia mediewistyki anglosaskiej." *Przegląd historyczny* 93 (2002): 73–102.
Nikodem, Jarosław. "*Parens tanti pueri*: Władysław Herman w Gallowej wizji dziejów dynastii." *Kwartalnik historyczny* 117 (2010): 5–22.
Noble, Thomas, and John H. Van Engen. *European Transformations: The Long Twelfth Century. European Transformations*. Notre Dame, Ind: University of Notre Dame Press, 2013.
Nowak, Andrzej. "Badania archeologiczne na Ostrowie Lednickim, pow. Gniezno, w roku 1963." *Sprawozdania Archeologiczne* 18 (1966): 179–189.
Orme, Nicholas. *Medieval Children*. New Haven: Yale University Press, 2001.
Ortman, Scott. "Conceptual Metaphor in the Archaeological Record: Methods and an Example from the American Southwest." *American Antiquity* 65 (2000): 613–645.
Plezia, Marian. *Kronika Galla na tle historiografii XII w.* Kraków: Nakład Polskiej Akademii Umiejętnośći, 1947.
Pukuta, Zbigniew, and Leszek Wojda. "Wczesnośredniowieczne cmentarzysko we wsi Dębina, Woj. Sieradzkie." *Prace i materiały muzeum archeologicznego i etnograficznego w Łodzi Seria Archeologiczna* 26 (1979): 89–142.

Quéret-Podesta, Adrien. "Travaux philologiques, recherches textuelles et identifications des auteurs anonymes dans la médiévistique du XIXe siècle: l'exemple du Gallus Anonymus." In *La naissance de la médiévistique. Les historiens et leurs sources en Europe (XIXe–début du XXe siècle). Actes du colloque de Nancy, 8–10 novembre 2012*, edited by Isabelle Guyot-Bachy and Jean-Marie Moeglin, 269–284. Geneva: Droz, 2015.

Romanowicz, Paulina. *Child and Childhood in the Light of Archaeology: Studies*. Wrocław: Wydawnictwo "Chronicon," 2013.

Rosik, Stanisław. "The World of Paganism in Gallus' Narrative." In *Gallus Anonymous and His Chronicle in the Context of Twelfth-Century Historiography From the Perspective of the Latest Research*, edited by Sztopka, Krzystof, 92–102. Kraków: Polish Academy of Arts and Sciences, 2010.

Rossignol, Sébastien. "The authority and charter usage of female rulers in medieval Silesia, c.1200–c.1330." *Journal of Medieval History* 40 (2014): 82–84.

Rubin, Miri. *Medieval Christianity in Practice*. Oxford: Princeton University Press, 2009.

Ryan, Patrick Joseph. *Master-Servant Childhood: A History of the Idea of Childhood in Medieval English Culture*. New York: Palgrave Macmillan, 2013.

Schultz, James. *The Knowledge of Childhood in the German Middle Ages, 1100–1350*. Philadelphia: University of Pennsylvania Press, 1995.

Sedlar, Jean. *East Central Europe in the Middle Ages, 1000–1500*. Seattle: University of Washington Press, 1994.

Shahar, Shulamith. *Childhood in the Middle Ages*. London and New York: Routledge, 1990.

Skorzewska, Joanna. "'Sveinn einn ungr fell i syruker.' Medieval Icelandic Children in Vernacular Miracle Stories." In *Youth and Age in the Medieval North*, edited by Shannon Lewis-Simpson, 103–126. Leiden: Brill, 2008.

Spiegel, Gabrielle. *New Directions in Historical Writing After the Linguistic Turn*. New York, NY: Routledge, 2005.

Stefaniak, Lech, Ewa Andrzejczyk, Krzysztof Gorczyca, Katarzyna Schellner. *Cmentarzysko Wczesnośredniowieczne w Bilczewie, Pow. Konin*. Konin: Muzeum Okręgowe w Konie, 2012.

Stoodley, Nick. "Multiple Burials, Multiple Meanings? Interpreting the Anglo-Saxon Multiple Interment." In *Burial in early medieval England and Wales*, edited by Sam Lucy and Andrew Reynolds, 103–121. Society for Medieval Archaeology Monograph 17. London: Routledge, 2002.

Trawkowski, Stanisław. "Spory o feudalizm w polskiej historiografii." *Roczniki Dziejów Społecznych i Gospodarczych* 58 (1998): 91–100.

Třeštík, Dušan. *Kosmova Kronika. Studie k počátkům českého dějepisectví a politického myšlení*. Prague: Academia, 1968.

Vida, Tivadar. "Heidnische und christliche Elemente der awarenzeitlichen Glaubenswelt. Amulette in der Awarenzeit." *Zalai Múzeum* 11 (2002): 179–209.

Wachowski, Krzysztof, and Grzegorz Domański. *Wczesnopolskie cmentarzysko w Starym Zamku*. Wrocław: Uniwersytet Wrocławski, 1992.

Wawrzeniuk, Joanna. "Symbolika jajka w grobie dziecka w okresie wczesnośredniowiecznym." In *Dusza maluczka, a strata ogromna*, edited by Wojciech Dzieduszycki and Jacek Wrzesiński, 143–54. Poznań: Stowarzyszenie Naukowe Archeologów Polskich, Oddział w Poznaniu, 2004.

Weinstein, Donald, and Rudolph Bell. *Saints & Society: The Two Worlds of Western Christendom, 1000–1700*. Chicago: University of Chicago Press, 1982.

Wenta, Jarosław. *Kronika tzw. Galla Anonima. Historyczne (monastyczne i genealogiczne) oraz geograficzne konteksty powastania*. Toruń: Wydawnictwo Naukowe Uniwersytetu Mikołaja Kopernika, 2011.

Westholm, Gun. "Infancy and Adolescence, Education and Recreation from the Medieval Period to the 17th century." In *Lübecker Kolloquium zur Stadtarchäologie im Hanseraum VIII: Kindheit und Jugend, Ausbildung und Freizeit*, edited by Manfred Glaser, 478–479. Lübeck: Schmidt-Römhild, 2012.

Wiszewski, Przemysław. *Domus Bolezlai. Values and Social Identity in Dynastic Traditions of Medieval Poland (c. 966–1138)*. Leiden/Boston: Brill, 2010.

Witkowska, Aleksandra. "The thirteenth-century Miracula of St. Stanisław, Bishop of Cracow." In *Procès de canonisation au Moyen Age. Aspects juridiques et religieux*, edited by Gábor Klaniczay, 149–163. Rome: Ecole Française de Rome, 2004.

Wojciechowska, Beata. "Dziecko w kulturze średniowiecznej." *Kieleckie Studia Historyczne* 9 (1991): 5–21.

Wojcieszak, Magdalena, and Krzysztof Wachoski. "Średniowieczne cmentarzysko przy kościele Św. Wojciecha we Wrocławiu." In *Średniowieczne i nowożytne nekropole Wrocławia, cz. 1*, edited by Krzysztof Wachowski, 60–65. Wrocław: Uniwersytet Wrocławski Instytut Archeologii, 2010.

Wrzesińska, Anna, and Jacek Wrzesiński. "Pochówki dzieci we wczesnym średniowieczu na przykładzie cmentarzyska w Dziekanowicach." *Studia Lednickie* 6 (2000): 141–160.

Wrzesiński, Jacek. "The Dziekanowice Cemetery—Christian Cultivating Venerable Traditions." In *Rome, Constantinople and Newly-Converted Europe. Archaeological and Historical Evidence*. Edited by Maciej Salamon, Marcin Wołoszyn, Aleksander Musin, and Perica Spechar, 535–552. Warsaw: Instytut Archeologii i Etnologii PAN, 2012.

Wyczółkowski, Dariusz. "Pochówki dziecięce związane z najstarszą fazą cmentarzyska przy kościele św. Maurycego w Zawichoście." In *Dusza maluczka, a strata ogromna*, Funeralia Lednickie spotkanie 6, eds. Jacek Wrzesiński and Wojciech Dzieduszycki (Poznań: Stowarzyszenie Naukowe Archeologów Polskich, Oddział w Poznaniu, 2004), 161–165.

Zawadzka-Antosik, Barbara. "Z problematyki pochówków dziecięcych odkrytych na cmentarzysku w Czekanowie, Woj. Siedleckie." *Wiadomości Archeologiczne* 47 (1982): 25–57.

Zawadzka-Antonsik, Beata. "Pochówki dzieci w naczyniach glinianach." *Wiadomości Archeologiczne* 38 (1973): 165–171.

Żoładż-Strzelczyk, Dorota. *Dziecko w dawnej Polsce*. Poznań: Wydawnictwo Poznańskie, 2002.

Zoll-Adamikowa, Helena. "Frühmittelalterliche Bestattungen der Würdenträger in Polen (Mitte des 10. bis Mitte des 12. Jahrhundert)," *Przeglad archeologiczny* 38 (1991): 109–134.

Index of Modern Authors

Abramek, Bogusław   78n, 81n
Adamska, Anna   78n, 81n
Ariès, Philippe   7, 66, 173, 189n, 198

Banaszkiewicz, Jacek   16n, 27, 28n, 29n, 67
Bartlett, Robert   9n, 75, 199
Buko, Andrzej   139, 140n, 145n, 146n
Buliński, Tadeusz   136

Carruthers, Mary   77, 179
Cetwiński, Marek   84, 97n
Chudziak, Wojciech   148n, 155n
Clanchy, Michael   78, 97, 98n
Clark, Elizabeth   195
Classen, Albrecht   6, 188n, 189
Curta, Florin   2n, 150n, 153n, 167n, 185n
Cushing, Kathleen   37, 182, 183, 196n

Dalewski, Zbigniew   10, 18n–19n, 20–21, 22n, 32–33, 66n
Delimata, Małgorzata   10, 17n, 26–27, 79, 104n, 130–131, 141
Duby, Georges   183

Gaffney, Phyllis   2, 5, 12, 104, 180, 194
Gardeła, Leszek   153n
Goodich, Michael   102, 109, 122n, 178, 190, 192n
Górecki, Piotr   47, 73–101, 187n, 199
Grodecki, Roman   48–72

Hanawalt, Barbara   5

Jagielska, Ilona   156n
Jasiński, Tomasz   18, 19n, 22n
Jażdżewski, Konrad   142n

Kaszewscy, Eleonora and Zdzisław   151n, 156n

Klaniczay, Gábor   77n, 103n, 127n, 193, 201n
Kozak, Jerzy   144n
Krawiec, Adam   25, 39n, 42n, 43n
Krzyżaniak, Lech   142n, 158n
Kufel-Dzierzgowska, Anna   160n
Kurasiński, Tomasz   119, 149n–150n, 152–154n, 159n, 166n–167n, 170n

Lett, Didier   94n, 120n, 124n, 126n, 136, 188
Lewis-Simpson, Shannon   7

Malinowska-Łazarczyk, Helena   168n
Michalski, Maciej   102n, 104n

Noble, Thomas   12n, 199n
Nowak, Andrzej   148n, 162n

Orme, Nicholas   4, 7

Ryan, Patrick Joseph   6

Schultz, James   2, 5, 104n, 115n
Skora, Kalina   119, 149n–150n, 152n–153, 159n, 166–167, 170n
Stefaniak, Lech   153n

Wachowski, Krzysztof   146n, 148n, 152n, 156n
Wiszewsky, Przemysław   10, 13, 17n–21n, 23n, 27, 49n
Wojciechowska, Beata   10
Wrzesiński, Jacek   11, 112n, 120n, 139n, 152n, 160n, 165n, 167
Wyczółkowski, Dariusz   157n, 163n–164n

Zawadzka-Antosik, Barbara   147n, 151n, 154n
Żołądź-Strzelczyk, Dorota   11, 79n

Index of Subjects

Age Relations
    Infant   56, 58, 65, 69, 103, 107–108, 116, 118, 119–127, 132–133, 139–173
    Old Age   52, 40–42, 52, 56–57, 65, 89, 123, 130, 153, 157
    Youth   23, 25–27, 31, 35–36, 45, 52, 56–59, 67–69, 73–74, 86–95, 167, 172, 183

Childhood (mis)behavior   23, 56–59, 63–67, 89–94, 101, 192–195
    Nurture/education   37–43, 98–100, 112–119, 185–188
    Prophecy and Foreshadowing   21–34, 67–69, 127–135, 177–178
    Rhetorical use of age   69–71, 94–98, 127–130, 135–137, 195–198

Comparisons
    Czechia   43–45, 163, 198
    England   77–79, 97–98, 119, 141, 157–158, 166, 187, 191, 197, 198
    France   74, 94, 166, 180–181, 183, 194–195
    Germany   189, 193, 198
    Scandinavia   143, 158, 166, 185–186, 191, 198
    Spain   178

Gender
    Femininity   42–43, 51, 112–119, 183–184, 193, 201
    Masculinity   36, 40, 45, 52, 56, 58, 64, 153, 201

Puer senex   27, 30, 52–53, 56, 69, 104–112, 112–113, 127, 178, 189–192, 194, 200

Tropes
    Dynasty and Inheritance   34–37, 80–89
    Emotional associations   40, 57–59, 119–127